MODERN HUMANITIES RESEARCH ASSOCIATION
TEXTS AND DISSERTATIONS
VOLUME 99

THE MAKING OF JORGE LUIS BORGES AS AN
ARGENTINE CULTURAL ICON

MODERN HUMANITIES RESEARCH ASSOCIATION
TEXTS AND DISSERTATIONS

Established in 1970, the series promotes important work by younger scholars by making the most accomplished doctoral research available to a wider readership. Titles are selected and edited by a Board of distinguished experts from across the modern Humanities.

Editorial Board

English: Professor Catherine Maxwell, Queen Mary, University of London
French: Professor William Brooks, University of Bath
Germanic: Professor Ritchie Robertson, University of Oxford
Hispanic: Professor Derek Flitter, University of Exeter
Italian: Professor Brian Richardson, University of Leeds
Latin American: Professor Catherine Davies, University of Nottingham
Portuguese: Professor Thomas Earle, University of Oxford
Slavonic: Professor David Gillespie, University of Bath

The Making of Jorge Luis Borges as an Argentine Cultural Icon

by
Mariana Casale O'Ryan

Modern Humanities Research Association
2014

Published by

The Modern Humanities Research Association,
1 Carlton House Terrace
London SW1Y 5AF
United Kingdom

© *The Modern Humanities Research Association, 2014*

Mariana Casale O'Ryan has asserted her right under the Copyright, Designs and Patents Act 1988 to be identified as the author of this work. Parts of this work may be reproduced as permitted under legal provisions for fair dealing (or fair use) for the purposes of research, private study, criticism, or review, or when a relevant collective licensing agreement is in place. All other reproduction requires the written permission of the copyright holder who may be contacted at rights@mhra.org.uk.

First published 2014

ISBN 978-1-78188-077-7 (hardback)
ISBN 978-78188-078-4 (paperback)
ISSN (MHRA Texts and Dissertations) 0957-0322

www.texts.mhra.org.uk

CONTENTS

List of Illustrations	x
List of Abbreviations	xii
Abstract	xiii
Acknowledgements	xiv
Dedication	xvi

Introduction — 1
- A Textual Approach to Cultural Analysis — 4
- Constructing the Icon — 7
- Branding Argentina, Branding Borges — 8
- A Historical Approach — 10
- Critical Perspective — 13
- *Borges en todas partes*: Narrowing down the Scope — 16
- Outline of the Chapters — 18

1. Weaving through the Threshold: Literary Biographies of Borges — 24
- Introduction — 24
- Literary Biography: 'Something Betwixt and Between' — 27
- The Imminence of a Revelation: Borges Off-centre — 31
- Weaving Through the Threshold: Embroidering Images of Borges — 35
  - (i) Alicia Jurado's *Genio y figura de Jorge Luis Borges* (1964) — 36
  - (ii) Emir Rodríguez Monegal's *Borges: Una biografía literaria* (1987) — 39
  - (iii) Estela Canto's *Borges a contraluz* (1989) — 47
  - (iv) María Esther Vázquez's *Borges. Esplendor y derrota* (1996) — 53
  - (v) Edwin Williamson's *Borges: A Life* (2004) — 56
- Conclusion — 61

2. Portrait of the Artist as an Old Man: Images of Borges — 63
- Introduction — 63
- Portraiture: Representation, 'Realism' and Subjectivity — 66
- From Image to Icon: Borges as *chora* — 68
- '*Vi interminables ojos inmediatos escrutándose en mí como en un espejo*': Image and Identity in Borges — 71

Constructing Borges in the Post-Perón Years	77
Photographs of Borges on the Covers of Books	79
'*El nuevo Borges*': Borges's Centenary and Retrograde Innovation	87
'*El anciano gurú*': Borges in the Argentine Press	94
The 1970s and Early 1980s and Venerable Borges	98
Borges's Reception in the USA and the Irreverence of American Photographers	106
Conclusion	110

3. Borges para sobrevivientes: Culture, Politics and Comic Strips of the 1980s — 112

Introduction	112
'Pictureness', 'Verbalness' and Comic-strip Conventions	113
Cartoons, Politics and Borges	115
'*Entre la alta cultura y las ilustraciones populares*'	122
Argentine 'New Generations' and Borges: From Patricide to Restoration	125
'*Ochenta y dos disfrazados*': Borges's Relationship with the Videla Regime	130
The Beginning of the Restoration	132
'*Historietas para sobrevivientes*'	134
'*Cruce y condensación*': 'Historia del guerrero y de la cautiva' in *La Argentina en pedazos*	137
Perramus: 'Borges' guerrillero	141
The Beginning of Closure: 'El fin'	149
Conclusion	150

4. El desaforado caminador: Buenos Aires's 'Borgesian Spaces' — 152

Introduction	152
Spatialities and Identity Formation	157
Buenos Aires siglo XX: From Homogenizing Project to Fractured Reality	160
Buenos Aires Today	163
Buenos Aires '*marca literaria*': Recorrido Jorge Luis Borges	165
Borges's Singular Mode of *Flânerie*	168
Crossing Borders: 'La inútil discusión de Boedo y Florida'	172
'Yo leo en el bar': 'Cafés porteños' as Borgesian Spaces	176
'Ghostly' Borgesian Spaces	179

From 'correcta interpretación' to Posthumous Possession	183
Conclusion	187
Conclusion	**188**
Bibliography	**192**
Newspaper and Magazine Articles	200
Articles and Audiovisual Material Accessed Online	200
Miscellaneous Websites	204
Index	**205**

LIST OF ILLUSTRATIONS

Figure 1.	Emir Rodríguez Monegal, *Borges: Una biografía literaria*	43
Figure 2.	Estela Canto, *Borges a contraluz*	49
Figure 3.	Alicia Jurado, *Genio y Figura de Jorge Luis Borges*	54
Figure 4.	Edwin Williamson, *Borges: A Life*	58
Figure 5.	'Si Borges lo dice', *Revista Somos*	64
Figure 6.	A selection of covers of books by and about Borges	81
Figure 7.	Borges by Grete Stern	83
Figure 8.	Julio Cortázar at age 53	85
Figure 9.	'Borges en la Biblioteca Nacional' by Ronald Shakespear	86
Figure 10.	Martín Lafforgue, *Antiborges*	88
Figure 11.	Adolfo Bioy Casares, *Borges*	89
Figure 12.	Cover of one of the books published by Emecé between 1997 and 1999	91
Figure 13.	Cover of one of the books published by Emecé between 1997 and 1999	92
Figure 14.	Cover of one of the books published by Emecé between 1997 and 1999	93
Figure 15.	*Diario Popular*, 2 November 1980	99
Figure 16.	*Clarín*, 8 August 1984	100
Figure 17.	*Tiempo Argentino*, 28 June 1985	101
Figure 18.	*Clarín*, 25 August 1979	103
Figure 19.	Borges by Hermenegildo Sábat, Commemorative stamp, 2000	117
Figure 20.	Borges by Sábat, *La Opinión*, 1973	117
Figure 21.	Sábat, *Georgie Dear*, text for 8th drawing	118
Figure 22.	Sábat, *Georgie Dear*, 8th drawing	119
Figure 23.	Sábat, *Georgie Dear*	119
Figure 24.	Sábat, *Georgie Dear*, 2nd drawing	120
Figure 25.	Sábat, *Georgie Dear*, 21st drawing	121
Figure 26.	Breccia and Sasturain, *Perramus. Diente por diente*	145
Figure 27.	Breccia and Sasturain, 'La sonrisa perdida', *Perramus. Diente por diente*	147
Figure 28.	Breccia and Sasturain, 'Epílogo', *Perramus. Diente por diente*	148
Figure 29.	Recorrido biográfico 'Jorge Luis Borges'	154

Figure 30.	Recorrido biográfico 'Jorge Luis Borges' (detail)	155
Figure 31.	Café Tortoni, sculpture	178
Figure 32.	Borges's house on calle Serrano	181
Figure 33.	Calle Jorge Luis Borges	181

LIST OF ABBREVIATIONS

The complete works of Jorge Luis Borges have been abbreviated throughout the book as follows:

OCI   *Obras completas*, 3rd edn, vol. 1 (Barcelona: Emecé, 1996)
OCII   *Obras completas*, 2nd edn, vol. 2 (Barcelona: Emecé, 1999)
OCIII   *Obras completas*, vol. 3 (Barcelona: Emecé, 1997)
OCIV   *Obras completas*, vol. 4 (Barcelona: Emecé, 1996)
OCEC   *Obras completas en colaboración*, 5th edn (Buenos Aires: Emecé, 1997)

ABSTRACT

Jorge Luis Borges, a literary figure intimately linked to Argentina's sense of cultural identity, has evoked both veneration and vilification among the country's intellectuals and the general public. Despite the vast amount of work written about his life and work in Argentina and abroad, no comprehensive examination of the construction of the author as an Argentine cultural icon has been produced so far. The present study focuses on Borges as cultural signifier and it examines the often conflicting facets of the construction of Borges as icon. It argues that the ideas, hopes, fears and demands that Argentine people have placed upon the author — thus constructing the icon — are also those that allow them to define their cultural identity. Thus, the study sheds light on the mechanisms of the ongoing construction of Argentine identity and exposes the complexity of the process by drawing from critical, political and media discourses.

The main images and conceptions of Borges examined and contested in the present work include his perceived social, political and intellectual elitism; his perceived positioning as a writer detached from Argentina's socio-political reality; the interpretation of his admiration for English literature as a way of disregarding Argentine culture; and finally the image of the author as a perpetual old blind sage with no links to popular culture. The examination of these images and conceptions is elaborated through the analysis of biographies, photographs, comic strips and the promotion of so-called 'Borgesian' spaces in the city of Buenos Aires. These are studied in relation to the socio-political, historical and cultural contexts in which they were produced.

This study is based on the view that the intertwined processes of the construction of the icon and of identity formation are fluid and in constant development. In this way, it does not seek to reveal an essence of Borges; it aims to uncover the complexity of the operations that constitute the definition of Argentine cultural identity through Borges, focusing on the process rather than on an end result.

ACKNOWLEDGEMENTS

In 1985, during a talk which took place in my hometown of San Fernando, only a few hundred metres away from the house where, at the time, I was busy being a teenager, Borges said: 'A mí se me hace cuento que empezó Buenos Aires, la considero tan eterna como el agua y el aire, y mis versos, unos logrados y otros no tanto, no hubiesen sido posibles sin ese aire y esa agua.'[1] This thesis would not have been possible without the air, the river or the people of San Fernando, my family and friends.

I was able to embark on this thanks to funding from the School of Languages, Linguistics and Cultures of the University of Manchester. Travel to Buenos Aires to carry out research was enabled by a Postgraduate Travel Grant from the Society for Latin American Studies. I am indebted to my parents, Zully and Eduardo Casale, for their infinite generosity, particularly in covering my childcare costs in the last six months of my writing-up period. My husband Rory supported our family financially during the last year of my PhD, when other sources of funding had run out.

I am very grateful for the guidance and support that I received from my supervising team at the Department of Spanish, Portuguese and Latin American Studies, particularly Fernanda Peñaloza and Chris Perriam, who believed in the project and supported it from the start. Edwin Williamson made my viva an enjoyable, stimulating and unforgettable experience.

In Buenos Aires, I am indebted to Agustín Maurín for his friendship and help with advice and material, particularly from the archive of *Clarín*. Hermenegildo Sábat generously shared his experience of the 70s and his love of Borges with me. Mario Mattarucco kindly allowed me access to the video archive of television station *Canal 13* and patiently sat with me as I trawled through hours of footage. Alejandra Correa gave me plenty of help and advice at the *Audiovideoteca de Escritores* at the Centro Cultural Recoleta. Mary Godward, from the British Council, provided me with interesting material. Pablo Sirvén at *La Nación* gave me valuable information and also shared with me accounts of his experience of Borges and the 'progre' generation. I am particularly grateful to Luisa Granato and Santiago Grasso for their generous hospitality.

Ciaran Cosgrove at Trinity College, Dublin, guided me through my first steps and kept reminding me of the inexhaustible pleasure of the Borgesian texts. I had

---

[1] Darío L. Luciano, *Borges en San Fernando: Jorge Luis Borges en el Ateneo Popular Esteban Echeverría* (Victoria, Pcia. Bs. As: Ediciones Ocruxaves, 1996), p. 86.

the fortune of sharing this journey with my fellow Borgesian scholars and friends, Eamon McCarthy, Ricki O'Rawe, Sarah Roger, Sarah Puello Alfonso and Eoin Barrett, with whom I shared many fascinating conversations and exchanged many wonderful ideas. James Scorer and Jordana Blejmar were a source of stimulating conversation, advice and friendship. Cristina Banfi told me, a long time ago, that this journey was possible, and I believed her.

Helen Böhme agreed to let me 'talk through' this project: without our conversations, this journey, which we narrated together, would not have been possible. My mother, Zully, was an unwavering source of support and inspiration: she found the old issues of *Sur* and the comic books in Buenos Aires, she looked after me and my family. My sister, Araceli, was a sister and a friend throughout, she was extremely generous with her time, proofreading each chapter as it was written and, finally, the entire book with me: I will never be able to repay her her kindness and generosity. Rory agreed to this project in full awareness that it would mean a shared effort: he gave me support, love and companionship.

DEDICATION

> Dejo a los varios porvenires (no a todos) mi jardín de senderos que se bifurcan.
>
> J.L. Borges, 'El jardín de senderos que se bifurcan'

This book is dedicated to the memory of Don Tito Anselmi, my grandfather, who didn't read books but told me the stories that have largely made me who I am. And also to the memory of Dr Michael O'Ryan, who was proud of my 'pursuit of wisdom'.

I experienced the uncertainties, anxieties and unimaginable pains and joys of labour, birth and parenting whilst working on an exploration of the discourses that construct my country's — my own — cultural identity. This would not have been possible otherwise: the richness and uniqueness of this book is due to — and not in spite of — the fact that I am a woman, an Argentine émigré and a mother. It is for my son, Santiago and for my daughter, Fianna, to whom the future belongs, a future that I hope will be filled with infinite possible paths and hours of pleasurable reading.

INTRODUCTION

> Buscar en Jorge Luis Borges el *factor Borges*, esa propiedad, ese elemento singular, esa molécula que hace que Borges sea Borges y que […] desde hace más o menos cuarenta años vienen encarnizándose con Borges y con su obra, hace también que el mundo sea cada día un poco más borgeano. […] No hay, por supuesto, *un* elemento Borges sino muchos, y todos son históricos, acotados como están por la ceguera fatal del horizonte mismo que los establece.[1]
>
> Alan Pauls, *El factor Borges* (2000)

The search of the 'Borges factor' has been intense: vast amounts of critical work and biographical accounts have been written as part of it. Surprisingly little, however, has been written about the mechanisms of this ongoing quest itself. This study focuses on that 'fatal blindness of the horizons' which constructs the variety of historical 'Borges elements' that Pauls mentions. It seeks to demonstrate the fluid quality of the process and the illusory nature of its aim. Crucially, it intends to uncover the intimate links between the processes of construction of Borges and of formation of an Argentine cultural identity.[2] The latter comprises a culture's history but also its mythology, a sense of the present and anxieties and expectations about the future. The study investigates the role of the figure of Borges in the mythical universe which encompasses the collective dreams of Argentines.[3] There are many other figures, notably Carlos Gardel, Diego Maradona and Eva Perón, who also play a part in this complex reality which penetrates the various aspects of what constitutes the culture, memory and identity of Argentina: ranging from the quotidian to the sacred, they include politics, economics, religion, art and literature. Thus, the role of Borges within the Argentine mythical universe, which, 'se re-mitifica todos los días,'[4] is regarded as the locus where some of the voids and lacks of its culture are articulated.

---

[1] Alan Pauls, 'Prólogo', *El factor Borges: Nueve ensayos ilustrados* (Buenos Aires: Fondo de Cultura Económica, 2000), pp. 7–8, italics in the original.
[2] In a discussion on Argentina's quest for a definition of its national 'essence', Gabriela Nouzeilles and Graciela Montaldo note that 'in his essays and fictional works, the writer Jorge Luis Borges contended that Argentine identity was an elusive and mobile frontier between conflicting cultural worlds,' in Gabriela Nouzeilles and Graciela Montaldo (eds.), *The Argentina Reader. History, Culture, Politics* (Durham and London: Duke University Press, 2002), p. 9.
[3] See María Cristina Pons and Claudia Soria (eds.), *Delirios de grandeza. Los mitos argentinos: memoria, identidad, cultura* (Rosario: Beatriz Viterbo, 2005).
[4] Pons, *Delirios de grandeza*, p. 11.

Borges was born in 1899 in Buenos Aires, where he spent most of his life and wrote most of his work. His greatest ambition was to be a poet: he wrote various collections of poems and essays, but he is best known for his short 'fictions', which are considered to have been crucial in the later development of what is commonly known as the Latin American literary 'boom'. It was also for his short stories that Borges became well-known abroad. He gained international fame in the 1960s, after his work had been translated into French, Italian and English. For much of the last twenty years of his life, he travelled extensively, giving lectures and receiving awards, particularly from highly regarded foreign universities. He received, amongst many other honours and awards, the International Publishers' Prize in 1961; honorary doctorates from Oxford and Columbia Universities in 1971, a gold medal from the Académie Française in 1979, and the Premio Cervantes in 1980, to name but a few. Consequent media exposure, which placed him in the spotlight for the rest of his life, made Borges a very public figure, whose presence in Argentine cultural life was strongly felt, and whose every word was closely scrutinized. He died in Switzerland in 1986.

'Vende patria' and 'Maestro' are among the most common names used in Argentina to refer to Borges. These terms represent two extreme but crucial constructions of the writer by fellow Argentines over the last six decades. How do they compare? What do they say about Borges? What does their use say about Argentina's conceptions of the writer? And how does this shed light on Argentina's relationship with its own sense of cultural identity? It is the aim of this book to respond to these questions.

'Vende patria' is a phrase loaded with impassioned denunciation typical of the 1960s and 1970s, when it was most widely used. It is an accusation of treason and has strong links with two other facets of the figure of Borges: that of a writer in an ivory tower detached from the socio-political reality of his country; and his perceived preference for foreign cultures, particularly British culture. In turn, the assumption that Borges was an elite writer and therefore concerned exclusively with the production and consumption of high culture is based on the combination of these two factors. As early as 1957, Juan José Hernández Arregui wrote: 'El rasgo definitorio de la obra de este escritor es su desdén por lo argentino.'[5] Reactions such as this would gain increasing strength throughout the 1960s and 1970s. In 1969, for example, Blas Matamoro complained, referring to Borges: 'mal puede representar a la cultura nacional un cipayo incorregible como él.'[6]

---

[5] Juan José Hernández Arregui, 'La imagen colonizada de la Argentina: Borges y el *Martín Fierro*', *Imperialismo y cultura (La política de la inteligencia argentina)* (Buenos Aires: Editorial Amerindia, 1957), in *Antiborges*, ed. by Martín Lafforgue (Buenos Aires: Vergara, 1999), pp. 147–66 (p. 147).
[6] Blas Matamoro, 'Detrás de la penumbra está Inglaterra', *Borges o el juego trascendente* (Buenos Aires: Peña Lillo, 1971), in *Antiborges*, pp. 193–250 (p. 249). 'Cipayo' is another word for traitor.

These reactions constitute a demand for the writer to engage in national culture and their strength of feeling responds to a seemingly inevitable need to define cultural identity in terms of Borges, whose central position as cultural role model cannot be escaped, as this book will demonstrate.

Borges is nowadays often referred to — and indeed, addressed, apostrophically — as 'maestro'. 'Ya entendimos, maestro,' wrote Juan Sasturain in 2006, to conclude a reflection on Borges's 1933 article 'Modos de G.K. Chesterton'.[7] Here, Borges said about his greatly admired Chesterton, who had recently died: 'Quedan las caras de su fama, quedan sus proyecciones inmortales,' a phrase which later applied to Borges himself.[8] Arguably, the more positive trend represented by the use of 'maestro' is characteristic of recent years, although it has by no means replaced the old 'vende patria': both have existed side by side, together with other more nuanced perceptions of the writer. The constructions of Borges as cultural role model and as a writer in an ivory tower are related. The image of a Borges in old age is a case in point: the construction of the writer as a perpetually old man — an image reinforced by his blindness — is, at the same time, a way of accentuating his conservatism and a depiction of a venerable tribal elder. These constructions of the writer tend to intersect, as this study will demonstrate. The figure of the labyrinth is used, for example, to associate Borges with an almost mythological, higher intellectual plane, where he is detached from the world of mere mortals. If used in conjunction with political accusations of elitism or Euro-centrism, this yields a writer in an ivory tower whose work can only appeal to the learned elite. It has, however, been used positively, to refer to Borges as a godlike figure whose eternal old age is a sign of wisdom.

What these constructions of the writer have in common is that they are based on Borges's perceived position as Argentine cultural signifier: a central figure that has been instrumental in the quest for a definition of the country's cultural identity. The study seeks to prove that this position, reinforced by the emergence of the 'Parricida' generation of intellectuals of the 1960s (whose aim was to kill the 'father' Borges), is still strong today.[9] This is evidenced in the words of Josefina

---

[7] Juan Sasturain, 'Los modos de J.L.B.', *Página/12*, 14 June 2006, online at www.pagina12.com.ar/diario/suplementos/espectaculos/subnotas/2826-1021-2006-06-14.html [last accessed 27 September 2013].

[8] Jorge Luis Borges, 'Modos de G.K. Chsterton', *Sur*, 22 (1933), in *Borges en Sur. 1931–1980*, ed. by Sara Luisa del Carril and Mercedes Rubio de Socchi (Buenos Aires: Emecé, 1999), pp. 18–23 (p. 18). Most recently, Alan Pauls also refers to Borges as 'maestro' in an article that assesses the impact of the Borgesian tradition on contemporary Argentine writers in 'La herencia Borges', *Variaciones Borges*, 29 (2010), 177–88 (p. 177).

[9] See Hernández Arregui and Matamoro in *Antiborges*. See also Emir Rodríguez Monegal, *El juicio de los parricidas: la nueva generación argentina y sus maestros* (Buenos Aires: Deucalión, 1956).

Ludmer who, in 1999, wondered: '¿Cómo salir de Borges?'[10] and came to the conclusion that the starting points for 'otra posición de lectura que me permita salir de Borges están en Borges' (p. 297). This was in the context of an attempt to think of Argentine literature from a different perspective, one in which Borges is not necessarily the pivotal point. Seven years later, Noé Jitrik referred to the writer as a national success story and reflected that Borges 'sigue estando en todas partes [...] su figura se extiende como un manto.'[11] The evolution of this relationship of Argentine thinkers with the figure of Borges was traced and analysed by Martín Lafforgue in *Antiborges* (1999), a collection of critical texts dating from as early as 1926 to 1997. This study goes beyond this by incorporating the general public's construction of the Borges image.

When the reflections on Borges's canonical status within the Argentine literary tradition are considered alongside the reception of his life and work outside of intellectual circles, it becomes evident that, to borrow Ludmer's words, Argentina is not ready to define itself culturally without reference to Borges. This responds to the points of contact between the iconicity of Borges and the formation of Argentine cultural identity, which the present work explores. The intersections between the milieus of intellectual activity, the media and politics where the construction of the writer emerges are here explored through an in-depth analysis of cultural products such as biographies, photographs and comic strips; and of the promotion of what I call 'Borgesian' urban spaces. This is the first substantial piece of research to analyse the figure of Borges by bringing together this variety of discourses.

A Textual Approach to Cultural Analysis

Although brief analyses of some Borgesian texts are provided, this study does not pivot around literary analysis per se. Even though a large number of critical texts are used, this research considers cultural practices other than written text as forms of text. Thus, my analysis mainly inscribes itself within the conceptual and methodological discourse of Cultural Studies. The largely Poststructuralist approach underlying this study is reflected in my reading of a variety of cultural products as text, which is based on Derrida's famous words: '*Il n'y a pas de hors-texte*.'[12] Thus, Derrida warns us against attempting to look behind texts in the

---

[10] Josefina Ludmer, '¿Cómo salir de Borges?', in *Jorge Luis Borges. Intervenciones sobre pensamiento y literatura*, ed. by William Rowe, Claudio Canaparo and Annick Louis (Buenos Aires: Paidós, 2000), pp. 289–300 (p. 297).

[11] Noé Jitrik, 'Apuntes sobre el manto borgeano', *Página/12*, 14 June 2006, online at www.pagina12.com.ar/diario/suplementos/espectaculos/subnotas/2826-1022-2006-06-14.html [last accessed 27 September 2013].

[12] Jacques Derrida, *Of Grammatology*, trans. by Gayatri Chakravorty Spivak (Baltimore: John Hopkins University Press, 1976), p. 158.

hope of finding an ultimate truth which exists independently of '*other* texts, other horizons, other socio-historico-linguistico-political presuppositions.'[13]

In this context, the study echoes the Barthesian demystification of cultural practices by showing that they are based on historical constructions, teasing out the conventions that underlie them.[14] Following Umberto Eco, these 'discursos cotidianos' are approached with permanent suspicion, as 'no se trata de que haya que descubrir las cosas bajo los discursos, a lo sumo, discursos bajo las cosas.'[15] The work thus proceeds by deconstructing certain oppositions surrounding the figure of Borges in order to expose the ways in which dichotomous notions such as popular/high culture; centre/periphery (or nationalism/Euro-centrism) are played out in the construction of certain images of the author. In this context, it would be unrealistic to claim that I am able to position myself completely outside of the discourses that underlie the construction of Borges, as doing so would go against my claim that studies like this one contribute to such construction. It would also presuppose a de-contextualization that would contradict the basic tenets of the thesis, that is, it would imply the existence of absolute truths or essentialisms. Thus, this book itself constitutes yet another construct, that is another chapter in the transformation of Borges into a cultural icon.

This study particularly considers the notion of authorial decentring and the pre-eminence of the reader (a reader constructed in the text) in its analysis of five biographies of Borges in Chapter 1. How do biographers relate to the premise, advanced by poststructuralist thought, that the author is not a guarantor of absolute truth, but, rather, that, separate from the historical person, it is a function of the text which is 'historically and structurally variable according to the cultural assumptions of specific systems of discursive arrangement'?[16] Here, bearing in mind the complex and eclectic nature of biographical activity, the objective is to expose the possible other discourses that have gone into the biographers' own construction of the author. The use of the term 'discourses' is based on the basic foucauldian notion that categories that we take for granted are not based on inalterable truths, but, rather, they have been constructed historically and are imbued with power and knowledge, as Umberto Eco explains in a discussion of Foucault: 'el poder no solo es represión e interdicción, sino también incitación al discurso y producción de saber.'[17] My approach focuses on the concept of

---

[13] Jacques Derrida, *Deconstruction in a Nutshell. A Conversation with Jacques Derrida*, ed. by John D. Caputo (New York: Fordham University Press, 2004), p. 80.
[14] Consider, for example, Roland Barthes's analysis of everyday activities in *Mythologies* (1957).
[15] Umberto Eco, *La estrategia de la ilusión*, trans. by Edgardo Oviedo (Buenos Aires: Lumen, 1992), pp. 9–10.
[16] Seán Burke, 'Ideologies and Authorship', in *Authorship: From Plato to the Postmodern. A Reader* (Edinburgh: Edinburgh University Press, 1995), pp. 215–21 (p. 217).
[17] Umberto Eco, 'La lengua, el poder, la fuerza', in *La estrategia de la ilusión*, pp. 336–54 (p. 339).

projection taken in its widest sense. One of the main premises of psychoanalysis, the notion of projection is picked up by Foucault as the main mechanism for the textual construction of the author-function mentioned above. The foucauldian view claims that the projections that are involved in this process are based on certain motivations and anxieties which a reader brings to texts. I extend this notion to a variety of media, including the photographic and the audiovisual in order to disentangle a particular set of discourses that contribute to the construction of the author and the definition of a cultural identity.

Most of the ideas that can be identified in this study as poststructuralist are drawn primarily from Borgesian thought. Thus, it follows Uruguayan critic and Borges biographer Emir Rodríguez Monegal, who had difficulty understanding why Derrida had taken so long 'en llegar a las luminosas perspectivas que Borges había abierto hacía ya tantos años.'[18] Deconstruction, he claims 'la había practicado en Borges *avant la lettre*' (para. 1). Among the most relevant of these concepts, Borges had shifted the focus of the aesthetic experience away from the attainment of an end result and emphasized the richness of the process itself in his article 'La muralla y los libros' in 1950.[19] A year later he explored notions of decentring in 'La esfera de Pascal', where he also wrote: 'Quizá la historia universal es la historia de la diversa entonación de algunas metáforas,'[20] a sentence which Derrida later quoted in his famous *L'écriture et la différence*, as Monegal points out.[21] In an article which considers the influence of Borgesian thought on thinkers such as Derrida and Foucault, among others, Alfonso de Toro summarizes these tenets:

> Borges aclara que no hay mimesis, y con esto no hay origen, sino una infinidad de trazas. Cada libro, cada texto [...] se disuelve en otro [...] socava la autoría y la autoridad de la palabra y de su productor, socava *la verdad*, para construir una escritura [...] diseminante, para establecer la *búsqueda* como último y único sentido.[22]

---

[18] Emir Rodríguez Monegal, 'Borges y Derrida: Boticarios', *Maldoror. Revista de la ciudad de Montevideo*, 21 (1985), 125–32, online at http://www.archivodeprensa.edu.uy/biblioteca/emir_rodriguez_monegal/bibliografia/criticas/crit_06.htm [last accessed 27 September 2013], para. 1, I.
[19] Jorge Luis Borges, 'La muralla y los libros', *La Nación*, 22 October 1950, later published in *Otras Inquisiciones*, OCII, p. 13.
[20] Jorge Luis Borges, 'La esfera de Pascal', in *Otras Inquisiciones*, OCII, p. 16.
[21] Rodríguez Monegal, 'Borges y Derrida', para 1, III.
[22] Alfonso de Toro, 'Borges/Derrida/Foucault: *Pharmakeus*, heterotopia o más allá de la literatura ('hors-littérature'): escritura, fantasmas, simulacros, máscaras, carnaval y … Atlön/Tlön, Ykva/Uqbar, Hlaer/Jangr, Hrön (N)/Hrönir, Ur y otras cifras', in *Jorge Luis Borges: Pensamiento y saber en el siglo XX*, ed. by Fernando de Toro and Alfonso de Toro (Madrid: Iberoamericana, 1999), online at www.uni-leipzig.de/~detoro/sonstiges/Pharmakeus_spanisch.pdf [last accessed 27 September 2013], p. 149, italics in the original.

Reference is made throughout this work to these basic concepts in the work of Borges, which are either examined in his essays or illustrated by his 'ficciones' or poems.

The next section explains my approach to the question of the cultural icon. In this way, Borges's importance within the context of contemporary Argentina, and the delineation of the methodology of the study — which follow — can be seen in the light of how the icon is defined here, particularly in terms of its complexity.

Constructing the Icon

The ways in which Borges's positioning in relation to the intellectual and political arenas was perceived and judged by fellow Argentines throughout his life (and indeed posthumously) has determined the ways in which this salient figure was constructed as an Argentine cultural icon. In this sense, I understand a cultural icon to be an empty vessel into which a culture pours its anxieties and questions about identity. As an image which in its quasi-religious dimension invokes the presence of what we may call a 'cultural divinity', the icon is revered. Chapter 2 explores this, focusing particularly on the photographic image of Borges. However, our relationship with the icon is more complex than one of worship as it becomes, at the same time, the object of our demands. The icon must fulfil our expectations because we think that it is given to it to do so. Failure to deliver results in our disappointment and sometimes, condemnation, as Chapter 3 demonstrates. In this sense, this book departs from studies such as Nicola Miller's 'Contesting the Cleric: The Intellectual as Icon in Modern Spanish America' (2003), which examines the making of six Latin American intellectuals, including José Martí and Gabriela Mistral, as cultural icons.[23] Miller's analysis works by linking positive traits present in each of these personalities which are consistent with certain utopias related to the various struggles that are generally perceived as being characteristic of the region. Each figure is identified with a religious phrase which in turn further elevates their consecrated position. Miller's analysis is straight-forwardly positive and touches on the idealistic construction of icons as god-like figures worthy of reverence. She recognizes that this is simplifying the issue:

> There are, of course, problems that arise from making icons out of intellectuals, not least that their ideas tend to be reduced to one-dimensional form. Icons are touchstones to what Erwin Panofsky called 'intrinsic meaning': they are telling about the cultural concerns of any particular

---

[23] Nicola Miller, 'Contesting the Cleric: The Intellectual as Icon in Modern Spanish America', in *Contemporary Latin American Cultural Studies*, ed. by Stephen Hart and Richard Young (London: Arnold, 2003), pp. 62–75 (p. 74).

moment of history, but they do not allow for tension, conflict or debate about these concerns. (Miller, p. 75)

The evolution of the iconization of Borges examined in this study proves that Miller's simplification does not necessarily follow, as the notion of worship is only one of the many, often contradictory, facets of the construction of Borges's iconicity.

The next section introduces the role of the figure of Borges in the branding of Argentina as a global product for export, in order to emphasize the importance of the icon within the delineation of an Argentine identity outside of the field of intellectual activity and into the arena of cultural consumption by the general public.

Branding Argentina, Branding Borges

En estos tiempos Borges se compra más "para tener" que con fines de lectura.[24]

Marcelo Abadi, 1999

The central role of the image of Borges in the construction of the image of Argentina can be clearly seen in 'Estrategia de Marca País' (EMP), a set of plans and targets aimed at the creation of a brand profile for the country. The project, launched in 2004, led by the national government's 'Secretaría de Medios de Comunicación', aimed to publicize Argentina abroad with a view to its insertion in foreign markets, thus benefiting from revenue generated from, among others, the tourist, cultural and educational industries. The strategy pivoted on the desired qualities of inalterability and perpetuity of a cohesive image for Argentina, and was expected to stand above the ideology and political agendas of successive governments. The result, in the shape of a concrete 'brand' for Argentina, would be presented officially to coincide with the bicentennial celebrations of the revolution that opened the way to Argentina's independence in May 2010.[25]

As part of the plans to identify the basic components of an Argentine identity which could be marketed abroad, the public opinion consultancy firm 'CEOP' (Centro de Estudios de Opinión Pública) carried out a survey in early 2005 in which 1,211 members of the public and 1,144 'líderes de opinión' took part.[26] The survey identified the figure of Jorge Luis Borges as one of the 'personajes históricos más representativos de la Argentina.' Interestingly, opinion leaders

---

[24] Marcelo Abadi, 'Siete noches y un error', *Variaciones Borges*, 8 (1999), p. 134–37 (p. 134).
[25] The outcome of this project can be seen at http://www.marcapaisargentina.org/index.php [last accessed 27 September 2013].
[26] 'Líderes de opinión' refers to leading personalities who have the power to influence public opinion because of their position as business directors, politicians or media personalities.

also identified Borges as Argentina's fifth most representative *current* personality.[27] This speaks of the writer as a figure who threads through high, dominant, popular or mass and emerging sectors of Argentine culture.

However, a similar study which was carried out in 2006 to assess the general reading habits of Argentines, found that 'desde el punto de vista cuantitativo, y según lo manifiestan los entrevistados, no aparecen títulos ni autores emblemáticos. Desde lo cualitativo, solo se puede mencionar [...] la recuperación de algunos pocos títulos de autor nacional'.[28] Borges does not appear among the very few Argentine authors mentioned in this study. So what makes this internationally acclaimed and influential writer whose books are not widely read by the 'average' twenty-first-century Argentine so emblematic of 'Argentineness'? What does the choice of the writer as representative figure shown in the first survey say about the 'average' Argentine's own perception of their own cultural identity?

This study does not, of course, assume the existence of an 'average' Argentine. However, it does identify certain more or less consistent historical and cultural trends which inform a notion of Argentine identity, which, in turn, can be recognized as motivations for the construction of Borges as a cultural icon. Among these, the development of Argentina's relationship with Europe, particularly France and Britain, throughout the twentieth century is perhaps the most relevant. The tensions within this complex relationship lie at the core of the Argentine anxiety regarding cultural identity: Europe as cultural model oscillated between veneration and rejection, where the definition of an Argentine culture was supposed to lie in the measure of the distance between the two. Thus, for the elite, the success of the definition lay in how well foreign models were imitated; and for the nationalist populists, in how effectively these models were repudiated. This dominates most of the twentieth century and it can be clearly seen as an important contributing factor in the construction of Borges's love of all things British, for example, as cultural elitism and disdain of Argentine culture. The politicisation of these binaries fuelled, particularly throughout the 1960s and 1970s, the construction of Borges as 'enemy' in the eyes of the more politically engaged intellectuals of the left, who believed that writers should focus on the national and have a commitment to the struggle for a better, fairer world. An

---

[27] Carlos Galván, 'San Martín y Maradona, los que mejor representan al país', *Clarín*, 31 March 2005, online at www.clarin.com/diario/2005/03/31/sociedad/s-03015.htm [last accessed 27 September 2013].

[28] The study was carried out by a specialized research team of 'Sistema de Consumos Culturales (Secretaría de Medios de Comunicación, Presidencia de la Nación)', led by the Secretary of Media, Enrique R. Albistur. Renowned sociologist Roberto Bacman was among the chief investigators. All social strata are represented in the study. 'Consumos culturales 2006', online at http://industriasdecontenido.files.wordpress.com/2010/08/ic-arg-sistema-nacional-de-consumos-culturales-3-20061.pdf [last accessed 27 September 2013].

analysis of this politicisation — which occurred at a crucial time of great political and social unrest — shows the important role played by the discursive practices dominant at different historical moments of the twentieth century in Argentina in this particular construction of Borges.

A Historical Approach

With the celebration of Argentina's bicentenary, the year 2010 offered a suitable time to reflect on what it meant to be Argentine. As the national government took the opportunity to exploit this occasion, not only by organizing a variety of celebratory events, but also by creating 'Argentina' as a brand, the choice of Borges as one of the figures which best represent a sense of 'Argentineness' is highly significant.

As a national cultural referent, Borges condenses certain anxieties and expectations regarding Argentine cultural identity. These anxieties, I argue, rest largely on Argentina's complex relationship with 'foreignness', which has been perceived either as something valuable or as a threat. The accompanying expectations are related to a perceived need for national cultural cohesion. This need for cohesion — as chapter 2 will argue in relation to the construction of Borges as national cultural treasure — can be traced back to a homogenizing approach to nation-wide, state education in response to the perceived threat of lawlessness ('barbarism') in the shape of, among others, mass immigration, particularly during the first half of the twentieth century. In this period, the impact of 'foreignness' on Argentina's developing sense of identity was twofold. On the one hand, this notion referred to powerful nations from where refinement and high culture were imported: the Argentine elite were traditionally educated following French or British models. A different — undesirable — perception of 'foreignness' was that associated with the immigrants that arrived from impoverished nations, particularly Italy and Spain.

In an analysis of the context in which the Radical Party developed in Argentina during the first three decades of the twentieth century, Torcuato S. di Tella refers to the impact of mass immigration on the country in the context of this two-fold approach to foreignness: 'Local elites, even if they certainly distrusted the massive waves of new entrants [...] had no qualms about the incorporation of the more successful immigrants, who had made it into the bourgeoisie.'[29] As far as the immigrants themselves were concerned, di Tella points out that, instead of the situation in other countries, of the 'native discriminating against the foreigner [...] it was the foreigners who discriminated against the natives' (p. 34). This

---

[29] Torcuato S. di Tella, *History of Political Parties in Twentieth-Century Latin America* (New Brunswick and London: Transaction, 2004), p. 34.

attitude made a lasting impact on the way future Argentine-born generations would relate to their own native land, as, in effect, their immigrant parents and grandparents 'discriminated what in time became the country of their own children, and their children inherited those attitudes' (p. 34). This binding of foreignness and class (where poor Spaniards or Italians were seen as undesirable, whilst the British and the French were admired and emulated, for example), and a consequent perception of Argentina as inferior, is crucial to the quest for a national identity throughout the twentieth century. Di Tella reflects that, 'most probably, this is the source of [Argentina's] large literature of uprootedness and lack of identity which has been dominant for decades' (p. 34), and he describes the situation as a 'Borges nightmare' (p. 34). This indicates that these important issues are as inherent to the writer as they are to the nation.

Di Tella's so-called 'Borges nightmare' consists in the repetition of the trope that lies at the core of a national literature built upon what Ricardo Piglia identified as 'el intento de representar el mundo del enemigo, del distinto, del otro (se llame bárbaro, gaucho, indio o inmigrante).'[30] Thus, the perceived need for national cohesion which motivated much of the nationalistic agendas of the twentieth century can be traced back to the nineteenth-century discourse of 'civilization and barbarism', which, as Di Tella rightly points out, lies at the core of Argentina's earliest and most influential literary manifestations. Edwin Williamson observed in relation to Spanish American societies towards the mid-nineteenth century:

> There was a general awareness among educated creoles that lawlessness threatened to become endemic and might frustrate the creation of the free and prosperous nations envisaged by the Liberators. It was fear of this 'barbarism', this appalling breakdown of social and political order, that informed much of the literature that would be produced in the nineteenth century and beyond.[31]

This was the case, notably, of Argentine works such as Domingo Faustino Sarmiento's *Facundo o la civilización y la barbarie* (1845), Esteban Echeverría's *El matadero* (written in 1840 and published posthumously in 1871), and José Hernández's *El gaucho Martín Fierro* (1872). Piglia traces the origin of the repeated narration of a basic violent scene to Sarmiento and Echeverría; and he claims that this confrontation 'ha sido narrada de distinto modo a lo largo de nuestra literatura por lo menos hasta Borges.'[32] This study explores this

---

[30] Ricardo Piglia, 'Echeverría y el lugar de la ficción', in *La Argentina en pedazos* (Buenos Aires: Ediciones de la Urraca, 1993), pp. 8–10 (p. 9).
[31] Edwin Williamson, "Civilization and Barbarism': Literary and Cultural Developments I', in *The Penguin History of Latin America* (Revised Edition) (London: Penguin, 2009), pp. 285–310 (p. 285).
[32] Piglia, *La Argentina en pedazos*, p. 8.

fundamental nineteenth-century narrative which persisted in the twentieth century and its role in the definition of a national identity, as it unravels its articulation with the construction of Borges as national cultural icon.

The relevance of a historical approach to the study of the construction of Borges the icon responds to a need to disentangle 'the ways in which narratives of the past [...] have been iconized as images of identity that have been incorporated into notions of nationality and statehood.'[33] Several historical moments in twentieth-century Argentina are particularly relevant here, as the prevalent political and ideological discourses determined the reception of the author and his work and thus were crucial to the construction of the icon. It was the singular intertwining of Borges's personal history and the historical development of the country, that made this author amongst all others, a cultural icon.

Argentine public opinion has traditionally seen politics in terms of opposition and rivalry.[34] This way of approaching politics, which is still prevalent, implies a simplification of the terms of the political equation, as a complex set of differences and determinations is replaced by a stark dichotomy (Laclau).[35] In contrast, this study positions itself away from such dichotomies by treating relevant historical moments as transitions, focusing on the tensions that characterize them in order to expose the complexity of discourses prevalent at the time and which contributed to the various constructions of Borges. The analysis of these issues is, of necessity, general, as the in-depth exploration of their complexity exceeds the scope of the present study.

The first historical moment of the twentieth century that is of particular interest and relevance to this analysis is the struggle of the middle classes (largely represented by Yrigoyenist Radicalism with which a young Borges identified) to maintain power in the transition between the end of exclusive rule by the oligarchy in 1912 and the rise of nationalist populist Peronism in the 1940s. David Rock identifies the strained relationship between the traditional elites and the urban middle-classes as the defining characteristic of the political situation of this period.[36] At the same time, the transition was mirrored in the change in the demographic configuration of Argentina, and particularly of its capital city, as

---

[33] Stephen Hart and Richard Young (eds.), *Contemporary Latin American Cultural Studies* (London: Arnold, 2003), p. 8.
[34] Noé Jitrik, for example, exhorts Argentines to move beyond such antagonistic views: 'conservar esos 'sí' y esos 'no' como si no pudieran disolverse en un 'acaso' supone la aniquilación de unos y la esclavitud de los otros' in Noé Jitrik, 'Exquisitos y justos', *Página/12*, 3 April 2007, online at http://www.pagina12.com.ar/diario/contratapa/13-82698-2007-04-03.html [last accessed 27 September 2013].
[35] Ernesto Laclau, *On Populist Reason* (London and New York: Verso, 2005), p. 18.
[36] David Rock, *Argentina 1516–1982* (London: Tauris, 1986), p. 215.

the dominance of the 'criollo' elite was gradually replaced by a more multicultural population given the mass immigration between the 1870s and the 1930s.[37]

The influence of the oligarchic governments and their close ties with Britain and France is particularly relevant to the definition of the city of Buenos Aires being essentially European, as Chapter 4 explores. After World War II, Argentina failed to replace its declining connection with Europe with an alignment with the United States, which was reflected by the collapse of the conservatives in 1940–1943, paving the way for nationalism, eventually leading to the rise of Perón.[38] Peronism brought with it an unprecedented political protagonism for the working class, forcing another change in the configuration of the political arena which would determine the history of the rest of the century.[39]

Another fundamental aspect of recent Argentine history is the intermittent succession of de facto governments, both civil and military, culminating in the brutally repressive, extreme-right military dictatorship of 1976–1983.[40] Borges's mature years and his rise to international fame coincide with this period of intermittence, particularly after Perón was toppled by the Revolución Libertadora of 1955. The writer's public reactions to de facto governments in general largely determined popular perceptions of him as a supporter of oppressive regimes, which, coupled with his construction as a writer in an ivory tower on the part of 'progresista' intellectuals, fuelled his vilification in the 1960s and 1970s. The transition to democracy after 1983 is the period in which this construction is re-evaluated. Borges died in this crucial period of political change.

Critical Perspective

This study is informed by the most relevant debates in Latin American cultural criticism, particularly the work of Argentine writer and academic Beatriz Sarlo. Sarlo's singular position, both as protagonist and cultural critic of the turbulent 1970s, allows for a valuable 'Argentine' perspective on these debates. Thus, the figure of Borges is examined in terms of the tension between popular culture and high culture and the place of the intellectual in his/her Latin American and national context. These debates, in particular as regards the figure of the

---

[37] See, for example John Lynch, Roberto Cortés Conde, Juan Carlos Torre and Liliana de Riz, *Historia de la Argentina* (Barcelona: Crítica, 2001), pp. 68–69.
[38] Rock, *Argentina*, p. 261.
[39] Di Tella briefly discusses the early configuration of the Peronist party in *History of Political Parties in Twentieth-Century Latin America*, where he underlines the fact that 'what started as an attempt at class harmony, ended up arousing the most intense experience of class confrontation in Argentina's history.' p. 73.
[40] David Rock provides an account of the impact of authoritarian factions in Argentina in *Authoritarian Argentina. The Nationalist Movement, its History and its Impact* (Berkeley, Los Angeles and London: University of California Press, 1995).

intellectual, began in earnest in the late 1950s, when the Southern Cone saw the rise of a generation of left-wing intellectuals such as those grouped around *Contorno* magazine in Buenos Aires and *Marcha* in Montevideo. Strongly guided by dependency theory and national populist views which largely characterized the seminal work of Ángel Rama, these debates subsequently developed throughout the 1960s and 1970s.[41] They coincide, chronologically, with Borges's mature years and international renown. Their impact is evident, firstly, in the particular constructions of the author as elitist and foreign-loving during the period; and secondly, in the subsequent analyses of his work up until the 1990s.

In 1985, Beatriz Sarlo manifested her impatience with the Argentine left-wing intelligentsia, whose attitude could be summarized by the idea, 'proclaimed in the name of the Revolution, that it is futile, if not a covert treason, to change the political positions maintained during the last two decades; as a result, ideological and theoretical immobility is thus vindicated as merit.'[42] Her position, especially in relation to Rama's pioneering critical stance, was that the reductionist approach to Latin American criticism predominant in the 1960s and 1970s represented a methodological flaw that prevented the field from moving forward.[43] Most importantly, Sarlo's re-evaluation of the term 'periphery' interrogates the dichotomy between Argentina as peripheral and Europe as central, and proposes an acknowledgement that its peripheral position enables an intertextual relationship which does not occur in a socio-cultural vaccum (p. 197). Sarlo proposes a break from the close ties between politics and cultural criticism in order to achieve a wider view of the complexity of cultural production and critical activity.

I follow Sarlo's style of criticism, which is less restricted by outmoded political views, and her problematization of the notion of national identity as a homogenizing project.[44] Instead of focusing on a logic of binaries, which inevitably leads to a sense of exclusion, Sarlo questions the hierarchical validity of cultural production in terms of centre and periphery and, also, in terms of high and popular culture.[45] I have focused on what I consider to be a new wave of

---

[41] Patricia D'Allemand, 'Hacia una crítica literaria latinoamericana: Nacionalismo y cultura en el discurso de Beatriz Sarlo', in *Mapas culturales para América Latina: culturas híbridas, no simultaneidad, modernidad periférica*, ed. by Sarah de Mojica (Bogotá: CEJA, 2001), pp. 189–200 (p. 190).

[42] Beatriz Sarlo, 'Intellectuals: Scission or Mimesis?', in *The Latin American Cultural Studies Reader*, ed. by Ana del Sarto, Alicia Ríos and Abril Trigo (Durham and London: Duke University Press, 2004), pp. 250–61 (p. 250). First published in Spanish in *Punto de Vista*, 25 (1985).

[43] D'Allemand, 'Hacia una crítica literaria latinoamericana', p. 193.

[44] Beatriz Sarlo, 'La izquierda ante la cultura: del dogmatismo al populismo', *Punto de vista*, 20 (1984), 22–25 (pp. 24–5), quoted in D'Allemand, 'Hacia una crítica literaria latinoamericana', p. 195, emphasis in the original.

[45] D'Allemand, 'Hacia una crítica literaria latinoamericana', p. 197.

Borgesian criticism whose emergence is closely linked to the publication of Sarlo's influential *Borges, a Writer on the Edge* (1993), which was later translated and revised as *Borges, un escritor en las orillas* (1995). This new way of conceiving the works of Borges entailed a repositioning of his work 'on the edge', both in terms of his narrative technique and of the context of their production. This is in contrast with traditional Borgesian criticism based upon notions of universality which saw him as the creator of cosmogonies, stripped of all regionalisms.[46] Instead, it looks at Borges's 'Argentineness', but only by situating the writer 'en los límites (entre géneros literarios, entre lenguas, entre culturas) [...] un marginal en el centro, un cosmopolita en los márgenes.'[47] From this perspective, this work goes beyond Sarlo's singular take on the 'peripheral' nature of Borges's positioning and, following Sylvia Molloy,[48] re-positions the writer 'in-between' rather than 'on the edge'. Sarlo's idea of 'filo de dos orillas'[49] is thus replaced by a kind of liminality, an 'irresolvable, ever fruitful in-between,'[50] where the boundary is blurred and the two edges merge into one.

In this sense, the study also differs from the approach chosen by Borges's latest biographer, Edwin Williamson, who sees the writer's life in terms of a struggle between opposing forces. Williamson considers that this is mirrored in the trope of the duel in Borges's 'ficciones':[51] the writer's life, he suggests, was punctuated by a 'yearning to assert identity by eliminating a rival,' even when 'Borges often liked to show how the victor might in the end be no more than a mirror image of his victim' (p. ix). I prefer to use the tactic of seeing Borges the man as a complexity, taking care to note and embrace the contradictory nature and the tensions that go into the construction of an identity, and the fact that it is a process rather than an end result. The Borgesian oeuvre does not reveal core truths and, by the same token, Borges the man did not try to delineate a personal or a national identity that might be in any way simplified. Instead, I believe that it is his complexity and embracing of contradictions which pervade his work. It is the crossing of boundaries that positions Borges in the in-between, rather than in the centre or the periphery, as has been claimed.

---

[46] In 1996, a conference was held in London where this new positioning was evidenced in the contributions of various academics writing about Borges at the time. These were collected in *Borges and Europe Revisited* (London: Institute of Latin American Studies, 1998).
[47] Beatriz Sarlo, *Borges, un escritor en las orillas* (Madrid: Siglo XXI, 2007), p. 9.
[48] Sylvia Molloy, 'Lost in Translation: Borges, the Western Tradition and Fictions of Latin America', in *Borges and Europe Revisited*, ed. by Evelyn Fishburn (London: Institute of Latin American Studies, 1998), pp. 8–20.
[49] Sarlo, *Borges*, p. 6.
[50] Molloy, 'Lost in translation', p. 20.
[51] Edwin Williamson cites many instances of this trope throughout his biography, such as 'El puñal' (1953), 'El desafío' (1952), 'El duelo' (1970), 'El sur' (1952) and 'Guayaquil' (1970) amongst others in Edwin Williamson, *Borges: A Life* (London: Viking, 2004).

Borges en todas partes: Narrowing down the Scope

> Como objeto, se lo consagra y consume: se suceden homenajes y conferencias, se 'reedita' su 'arqueología literaria', se redescubren 'nuevos inéditos', pululan biografías y aparecen con llamativa frecuencia otras tantas recopilaciones de entrevistas, diálogos y anécdotas ingeniosas. Se anuncian películas. Hay remeras, llaveros, posters y almanaques con su efigie; muestras fotográficas y concursos literarios se escudan tras su nombre. Las agencias gubernamentales se lo disputan. La opinión pública lo reverencia. La Legislatura porteña avanza un poco más y consagra, con el peso de la ley, el año borgeano. Borges, en fin, está en todas partes.
>
> Martín Lafforgue, 'Introducción', *Antiborges*

The life and works of Jorge Luis Borges have been the subject of a wealth of critical work and media coverage. The beginnings of this vast production can be traced back to the publication of the first book entirely devoted to Borgesian criticism, Adolfo Prieto's *Borges y la nueva generación* (1954).[52] Later, the first biography, Alicia Jurado's *Genio y Figura de Jorge Luis Borges* (1964), has been followed by more than a dozen others written in Spanish and in English.[53] The panorama described by Martín Lafforgue therefore justifies my metacritical study: rather than inscribing itself within the long tradition of Borgesian criticism, it examines the relationship between Borges and his work as the subject of criticism and consumption, and the production of portrayals of the man and analysis of his work. This would be a Herculean task if it were not that I chose to focus on a limited number of areas of appropriation of Borges. Instead of attempting a more or less comprehensive survey of a vast field, I have narrowed the scope of my sources by carefully selecting the material that appeared most representative, in order to provide a well-documented assessment of both the consumption and study of Borges. As far as possible, wherever a book or article or image is referred to, acknowledgement of the existence of further evidence is provided, generally in footnotes, as the availability of a variety of such products lies at the core of the circulation of a certain image of the writer.

The names of certain experts in the field stand out and this is also reflected in the study. Most are academics whose work has been published immediately before or during the period of research leading up to the completion of this study. Thus, I refer to the work of contemporaries of Beatriz Sarlo, many of whom

---

[52] María Luisa Bastos examines the earliest critiques of Borges dating back to 1923 and she points out the significance of the publication of Prieto's book in *Borges ante la crítica argentina 1923–1960* (Buenos Aires: Hispamérica, 1974), p. 75.

[53] Williamson cites ten other than his own and Jurado's in *Borges*, pp. 544–45, but these do not include, for example, Alejandro Vaccaro's two later publications: *El señor Borges* (2004, with Epifanía Robledo de Uveda) and *Borges: Vida y literatura* (2006); or Jason Wilson's *Jorge Luis Borges* (2006).

publish regularly in the journal *Variaciones Borges*. *Variaciones Borges* has been published biannually since 1996, in Spanish, English and French by the Borges Centre at the University of Pittsburgh; its editor is writer and academic Daniel Balderston.

Apart from specialized books and articles in literary journals, I have also examined press coverage in the three main national newspapers: *La Nación*, *Clarín* and *Página/12*, normally accessed online. I have aimed for a balanced use of these publications as a means of reflecting the main ideological views and political positions prevalent in Argentina, given that *Clarín* is positioned in the centre of the political spectrum, with a generally liberal tendency; *Página/12*'s position is towards the left with a clearly 'progresista' outlook, and *La Nación* is perceived to be a conservative newspaper with close ties to the Catholic Church, even though it publishes material from a variety of ideologies. Of the three, *Clarín*'s circulation and readership are the widest, and it is read across all socio-economic levels.[54] *La Nación* also has wide circulation. Although its readership is smaller than that of the other two, *Página/12*'s relevance lies in that it represents the views of important sectors of the intelligentsia. A selection of articles about Borges's appearance in the media between 1971 and 1980 was obtained from the archive of *Clarín* newspaper, which includes tabloid newspapers such as *La Razón*, *La Prensa* and *Diario Popular*.

Audiovisual material was accessed through a variety of archives: material broadcast on Argentine national television and in cinemas was viewed at Buenos Aires-based television channel *Canal 13*, the *Archivo General de la Nación* and the *Audiovideoteca de Escritores*, run by the government of the City of Buenos Aires. These include documentaries, interviews and news reports. Commercially available documentaries on VHS or DVD, as well as those available online, were also consulted.

There are still numerous cultural products on Borges whose analysis exceeds the scope of this study. It is worth mentioning, in this context, the attribution of Borges's authorship to the poem best known as 'Instantes' and the phenomenon it has given rise to, that is, its reproduction in several media, such as book marks and as accompaniment to images in video montages circulated widely, particularly on the Internet. This, which Iván Almeida approaches as a mystery worthy of detective fiction,[55] could also be interpreted as a projection of the lacks and voids in the sense of Argentina's cultural identity that such appropriation fills. Almeida hints: 'Tal vez el fenómeno resida en una íntima voluntad de ser

---

[54] Hernán Fernández, '¿Quién lee cuál?', *Infobrand Digital*, 6 February 2007, online at www.infobrand.com.ar/notas/8556-%BFQui%E9n-lee-cu%E1l%3F [last accessed 27 September 2013].
[55] Iván Almeida, 'Jorge Luis Borges, autor del poema 'Instantes'', *Variaciones Borges*, 10 (2000), 227–46.

engañados cuando el mundo no llega a acomodarse a los propios sueños' (p. 246). The attribution of this poem to Borges is perhaps linked to a need for a widely accessible style of writing, one which 'ordinary' Argentines can read and enjoy, and which will bring them closer to the icon. Among the manifestations of a wish to recuperate Borges as a cultural role model for the younger generations which are not studied here, are those expressed through the musical milieu and the Internet. As an example of the first, we have the case of the Argentine band *Cuentos Borgeanos*, whose songs revolve around Borgesian tropes such as the labyrinth and infinite time.[56] A study of the context of the band's emergence, as well as a comparative analysis of some of their lyrics and videos in relation both to Borgesian images and elements of Argentine identity, would yield very interesting conclusions which would complement and reinforce those arrived at in this study. With regards to the Internet, the popular broadcasting website *YouTube* contains a variety of video postings ranging from televised interviews with the writer, computer-generated animations of Borges's stories, to personal accounts of favourite Borges poems set to music from all over the world.[57] Reference is made in this research to the various Borges fan groups on the social network *Facebook*. However, an in-depth study of the contexts of the creation of these web phenomena and the wide range of discourses associated with them exceeds the scope of this research.

The specific sources analysed at each stage of the study are discussed in the following section.

Outline of the Chapters

This study comprises four chapters, each of which centres on the analysis of the construction of Borges, either through the use of urban space (Chapter 4) or in one type of cultural product: biographies (Chapter 1), portrait photography (Chapter 2), and comic strips (Chapter 3). Each chapter starts with an appraisal of the fundamental characteristics and specific issues relating to the medium, which are laid out in order to provide a general framework against which each of the products is analysed. An overview of the historical context of production and consumption has been provided in every case, taking into account the socio-political configuration of Argentina during each of the periods considered.

---

[56] See, for example, Guillermo Zaccagnini, 'Cuentos borgeanos: Nada de "rock literario"', *Clarín*, 3 January 2008, online at www.clarin.com/diario/2008/01/03/espectaculos/c-157 6361.htm [last accessed 27 September 2013].
[57] See, for example, www.youtube.com/watch?v=aBVpq6oolLw; www.youtube.com/watch?v=coc3Wtqn6I8; http://www.youtube.com/watch?v=mLovc5jYaqY or http://www.youtube.com/watch?v=W-agdfS1yvo [last accessed 27 September 2013] amongst many others.

A brief examination of a small selection of Borges's work follows, in order to establish how Borges's view of the genre or medium or space may have influenced the way in which the figure of the author has been appropriated in each. Reference is made to the poetry, essays and stories collected in the 1996 version of *Obras Completas* published by Emecé; and to a variety of articles published in popular magazines which are not included in it. I have tried to refer to work written at different stages of Borges's life, although a linear chronology is neither my concern nor recuperable from the multiple and retroactive readings that will be analysed here.

Wherever available, the production of Argentine thinkers, scholars, journalists and artists has been either analysed as primary sources, or generally brought to bear on the critique of the making of the figure of the writer. However, international images of the writer are also taken into account in order to emphasize, sometimes by contrast, the modes of construction that are considered Argentine. Irreverent portraits of Borges taken by American photographers, for example, are in strong opposition to those produced by their Argentine counterparts, whose work was inscribed in a discourse that created the author as a revered figure. Some instances of foreign reception and critical analysis of the Borgesian oeuvre, as well as the construction of the figure of the author abroad, are themselves examined. This is done in relation to the value of this international exposure in Argentine public opinion and its evaluation as confirmation of greatness. The international milieus taken into consideration are mainly the English- and Spanish-language United States and European markets.

The core of each chapter is devoted to an in-depth analysis of representations and appropriations of Borges: Chapter 1 deals with the 'genre' of literary biography, which is arguably closest, both formally and critically, to the author's literary works. The origins and influence of differing images of Borges are examined through an analysis of five literary biographies considered in order of publication. These are: Alicia Jurado's, which was the only one available for many years;[58] Emir Rodríguez Monegal's *Borges: Una biografía literaria* (1987), arguably, the most widely cited; María Esther Vázquez's *Borges: Esplendor y derrota* (1996) and Estela Cantos's *Borges a contraluz* (1989), which offer invaluable insiders' views; and Edwin Williamson's *Borges: A Life* (2004), which is the most recent work of length written in English and it provides valuable contrast to the other four.

The ways in which these biographies respond to the expectations, agendas and contexts in which they have been written are brought to bear on their construction of the author. Here, Gerard Genette's concept of the paratext as an

---

[58] Rodríguez Monegal's *Borges: a Literary Biography* was published fourteen years later, in 1978, and it was not translated into Spanish until 1987.

interstitial space where meaning is produced is applied to the biographies. Thus, they are seen as fundamental mediators of the consumption of the Borgesian oeuvre.[59] The peripheral elements of the biographical texts, such as titles, chapter headings, illustrations and cover design, are analysed, highlighting their significance as providing a unique in-between space where meaning is created. A link is also established between these and the significance of interstitial spaces in Borges's narratives: footnotes, epigraphs and general marginalia. This, together with the writer's preference for a marginal positioning in terms of literary theory, general politics and philosophy, is highlighted throughout the book, which thus aligns itself with the latest general trend within Borgesian literary analysis.

The biographical information present throughout the study should be approached in the light of the conclusions arrived at in the first chapter, which demonstrates that even when rigorously documented, historical facts are constructs in so far as they are subjective narrations of details of the author's life. (This is partly the reason why my analysis of the role of biography in the making of the figure of the author is developed in the first chapter.) The next three chapters proceed to an examination of the images of Borges first considered in relation to these biographies but as presented through other discursive and visual practices.

In chapter 2, the recurrent image of the author as elderly is examined in portraits that have circulated in a variety of settings, including magazine and newspaper articles, but particularly on book covers. This chapter argues that the image of Borges as an old blind sage is partly achieved through the wide circulation of portraits which accentuate the features of old age and blindness. The visual dimension of the writer's iconic status is emphasized by examining the construction of the writer as a figure of veneration, a 'national treasure' whose most salient characteristic is the wisdom of his old age. The chapter focuses on the impact of Borges's rise to international fame in the 1960s and Argentina's reaction to it. It is in this chapter that representations of the writer in the media are looked at in detail, through an analysis of the images that accompany newspaper articles particularly in the 1970s and early 1980s. International reception of Borges is brought to bear on this analysis of local press coverage, and images taken by Argentine photographers are compared to those by American photographers. Reference is also made to Borges's appearance in televised interviews. The appropriation of the image of the writer as a legitimising figure on the part of the last military dictatorship is examined through reference to the censorship of a popular television programme of the time, 'Operación Ja Ja'.

---

[59] Gerard Genette, *Paratext: Thresholds of Interpretation*, trans. by Jane E. Lewin, (Cambridge: Cambridge University Press, 1997) was first published under the title *Seuils* in French in 1987.

Portraits of the writer which appeared on a variety of book covers are also examined and compared in Chapter 2, in order to demonstrate the consistency of the depiction of the writer as elderly. Among the publications which appeal to the general public, pictorial collections such as Argentine photographer Sara Facio's *Jorge Luis Borges en Buenos Aires* (2005) contain some of the most circulated portraits of the writer. Other image-based books referred to here are Miguel de Torre Borges's *Borges: Fotografías y manuscritos* (1987), Alan Pauls's *El factor Borges* (2000) and *Borges: 1001 imágenes* (2003), where portraits of Borges and his family are accompanied by images of book covers, manuscripts and other documents. As an example of the circulation of the Borges image in the Argentine popular press of the 1970s, I have referred to Editorial Atlántida's 'Todo Borges' (1977). This special issue magazine contains portraits of the writer, copies of press clippings and other items of memorabilia that contributed to the image of the writer in that particular historical context.

The exploration of the all important visual component of the construction of Borges as icon continues in the following chapter, as the analysis moves from the photographic image to cartoon depictions of the writer. Chapter 3 focuses on the changing relationship of the 'progre' generation with Borges as a cultural role model, which is traced through an analysis of depictions of the author in comic strips of the mid-1980s. Cartoons of Borges produced in the 1970s, particularly Hermenegildo Sábat's, are also analysed. In relation to these comics I trace an ideological arc from rejection to celebration which takes place due to critics' strong historical and political motivations from the 1960s to the dictatorship and the post-dictatorship years. This arc is best represented through the changes in depictions of Borges in comics. In particular I examine the case of *Fierro* magazine.

By linking the comic strips with Borges's early work for popular magazines, the chapter achieves an interrogation of Borges's perceived position in the debate between high and popular culture. For this purpose, two comic strip adaptations of stories by Borges are analysed: Alfredo Flores and Norberto Buscaglia's 'Historia del guerrero y de la cautiva' and Alberto Breccia and Juan Sasturain's 'El fin'. The figure of Borges drawn as a subversive character is studied in relation to Breccia and Sasturain's comic strip series *Perramus*. Both the latter and Flores and Buscaglia's strip appeared in the mid-1980s in *Fierro*. In the aftermath of the tragic defeat of Argentina's left in the 1970s and early 1980s,[60] the appropriation of the figure of Borges as a revolutionary in comic strips signals, not only a change in the way the intelligentsia related to him, but also the hope for a future reconstruction of an Argentine cultural identity.

---

[60] D'Allemand, 'Hacia una crítica literaria latinoamericana', p. 194.

Chapter 4 evaluates the impact of the main traits of the construction of Borges as perpetuated in the creation of what I call 'Borgesian' spaces in the city of Buenos Aires in recent years. It demonstrates that these traits serve the purposes of urban politics in the delineation of a particular image for the city as a cultural product for export, which is consistent with the objectives of the 'Estrategia Marca País'. Some of these Borgesian spaces are included in a walking tour promoted by the city's department of tourism; these spaces are analysed alongside other private 'Borgesian spaces' within the city. The fact that the city's current administration does not belong to the same political party as the national government leads to a greater need for Argentina's international legitimisation; it also points to the city's tension with populist nationalist ideals. In this context, the relevance of the role of the city in the construction of a national identity lies in the virtual impossibility of discussing Argentine culture without reference to Buenos Aires.[61]

Borges's friend Ulyses Petit de Murat wrote in 1980 that 'Georgie era un desaforado caminador. Batía todos los rumbos de la ciudad.'[62] Many of his friends would later corroborate this as they narrated the seemingly endless wanderings on which the author liked to take them. Importantly, however, this love of roaming the city was always felt by his friends and companions to relate to an individual, intimate experience of Buenos Aires.[63] In all likelihood, and given his renowned love of etymology, Borges would have approved of Petit de Murat's use of the adjective 'desaforado'. A word describing a breaking away from the centre, literally and figuratively, straying away from the norm; a 'desaforado' Borges is one who strays away from the centre of the city and ventures into the marginal areas of the 'arrabal', zigzagging his way across the boundaries of an urbanized Buenos Aires, inhabiting a topological and a literary in-between. 'Desaforado' also talks of an ardent lack of restraint, describing a young and passionate Borges experiencing the city on his own terms, regardless of tradition and etiquette. The role of the polemic surrounding Borges's final resting place, which is played out in the porteño context, results in the ultimate objectification of the writer and brings the chapter to a close.

The analysis of urban spaces in the last chapter is arguably the furthest detached from the medium of the book and the one that covers events in very recent history. However, in Chapter 4 I examine how urban spaces are read as texts that

---

[61] Cf. David William Foster, *Buenos Aires: Perspectives on the City and Cultural Production* (Gainesville: University Press of Florida, 1998), p. 6.
[62] Ulyses Petit de Murat, *Borges — Buenos Aires* (Buenos Aires: Municipalidad de Buenos Aires, 1980), cited in *El Buenos Aires de Borges*, by Carlos Alberto Zito (Buenos Aires: Aguilar, 1999), p. 32. 'Georgie' was the nickname that Borges's family and closest friends liked to use to refer to the writer.
[63] Cf. María Esther Vázquez, *Borges: esplendor y derrota* (Barcelona: Tusquets, 1996), pp. 73–74.

are constantly being written and rewritten following Henri Lefebvre, Michel de Certeau and Andreas Huyssen. It is hoped that this final analysis will refer the reader back to the beginning of the book, as it brings together elements of the writer discussed in Borges's biographies and those which have been perpetuated through the circulation of his visual image, providing a coherent sense of the evolution of the construction of the icon. Chapters have been organised in this way to enable a clear understanding of how the historico-political discourses have contributed to the constructions of Borges as a key signifier of Argentine identity.

CHAPTER 1

∼

Weaving through the Threshold: Literary Biographies of Borges

Introduction

> Hay muchos Borges. Somos muchos [...] Decir que uno es muchos es un modo jactancioso de decir que no se es nadie, que uno es nadie.
>
> J.L. Borges, 1982[1]

This chapter explores the construction of a multiplicity of Borgeses in a selection of literary biographies written between 1964 and 2004 in Argentina and abroad. These are Alicia Jurado's *Genio y figura de Jorge Luis Borges* (1964); Emir Rodríguez Monegal's *Borges: Una biografía literaria* (1987, first published in 1978); Estela Canto's *Borges a contraluz* (1989); María Esther Vázquez's *Borges: Esplendor y derrota* (1996); and Edwin Williamson's *Borges: A Life* (2004). Many other biographical accounts of the author have been written in Spanish and English.[2] Among these is, notably, Adolfo Bioy Casares's *Borges* (2006), which provides valuable insight into both Borges and Bioy; crucially, it sheds light on four decades of Argentine literature as seen through their fruitful friendship. However, it is not examined here due to its form: it is a selection of extracts from Bioy's diary and is not directly comparable to the biographies studied here. Moreover, its relatively recent publication date does not allow for a comparable analysis of its reception.

I argue, following Foucault, that it is not possible to have one sole construction of an identity or one unique idea of author because constructions are the product

---

[1] From a radio interview, in Antonio Carrizo, *Borges el memorioso: Conversaciones de Jorge Luis Borges con Antonio Carrizo* (Mexico and Buenos Aires: Fondo de Cultura Económica, 1982), cited in *Borges Verbal*, by Pilar Bravo and Mario Paoletti (Buenos Aires: Emecé, 1999), p. 50.

[2] Consider, for example, Argentines Roberto Alifano's *Borges: biografía verbal* (1988) and Horacio Salas's *Borges: una biografía* (1994), British James Woodall's *The Man in the Mirror of the Book* (1996) or Chilean Volodia Titelboim's *Los dos Borges: vida, sueños, enigmas* (1996).

of a combination of individual projections.³ By identifying certain recurrent projections within a culture and by perpetuating the old idea of the power and authority of the writer, a series of more or less consistent fantasy-images of Borges have been historically circulated and commercialised, thus turning the author into a commodity. The shift from author to reader that Barthes discussed in the 1970s led him to explain that 'a text's unity lies not in its origin but in its destination,' and that 'the reader is simply that *someone* who holds together in a single field' the 'traces by which the written text is constituted.'⁴ The reader as a consumer satisfies a need to create an origin by constructing an author for the work.

The publishing market, which taps into the anxieties and expectations that make up the readers' projections, has been successful in constructing an author-commodity. As Borges himself suggested on many occasions (consider, for example, 'Borges y yo' or 'El otro'), there are multiple Borgeses and Borges the commodity is a construction who is neither the author, nor the fictional character, nor the historical man who lived between 1899 and 1986. He is, rather, an amalgam of all those, inasmuch as they each constitute a discourse. As such, it varies as each culture transforms its mode of 'circulation, valorisation, attribution, and appropriation'.⁵ So there is the separation between Borges the man and the creator of fictions described by a third Borges who wrote this in 'Borges y yo' (*OCII*, p. 186) in 1957, plus the other Borges on the covers of books, whose image seems endlessly reproduced on the promotional posters and carrier bags of bookshops and book fairs. But as Borges also pointed out, to say that there is a multiplicity of Borgeses is to say that there is no Borges. This may be interpreted as Borges's response to the quest for a fundamental, unique Borges who may lurk behind the texts, holding the key to their mysteries. This chapter takes up Foucault's invitation to 'locate the space left empty by the author's disappearance, follow the distribution of gaps and breaches, and watch for the openings that this disappearance uncovers' (p. 177). Therefore, consistent with Borges's own positioning and narrative technique, it shifts the focus away from the quest for any real, core, original Borges.

Consistent with the traditionally-held belief that the author can provide the basis for explaining the characteristics of his work, and therefore reinforcing the idea of the author as a sacred, originating force which precedes the text, literary biography attempts a reconstruction of the man through analysis and interpretation of his life and his work. By looking at biographical texts from a

---

³ Michel Foucault, 'What is an author?', in *Modern Criticism and Theory: A Reader*, by David Lodge and Nigel Wood, 2ⁿᵈ edition (New York: Pearson Education, 2000), pp. 174–87 (p. 180).
⁴ Roland Barthes, 'The Death of the Author', in *Image, Music, Text*, trans. by Stephen Heath (London: Fontana, 1977), pp. 142–48 (p. 148), italics in the original.
⁵ Foucault, 'What is an Author?', p. 185.

poststructuralist perspective, considering that 'every text is eternally written *here and now*,'[6] I will argue that the construction of the author emerges from depictions created through narrative technique, that the revelation of the truths generally promised by biographers can only be a set of constructs and that the information or interpretations that are put forward as revelations are not sacred or unalterable. I shall discuss how each of the images of Borges constructed in the biographies selected responds to the expectations, agendas and contexts in which they were written.

Literary biographies are powerful mediations of our approach to, perception and understanding of literary texts. I will therefore refer to this 'genre' using Gerard Genette's concept of the paratext: 'a threshold, a zone between text and off-text, not only of transition but also of transaction,'[7] a space that allows for the production of further meaning which the reader will then take to his/her experience of the fictional text. I shall begin by providing a brief theoretical review of the 'genre' of literary biography and its role as paratext.[8] I will then give an overview of Borges's narrative technique and his position as a forerunner of Post-Structuralism in order to emphasise how these render problematical some of the claims of literary biography. In this context, it becomes necessary to clarify that 'Borgesian' here refers to the qualities of the text, even though these qualities are anchored through a reference to the name of the person who wrote them. The paradox remains, with the inevitable references to Borges as a historical subject-creator resulting in the creation of a fictive version of my own.

Finally, I shall explore the images of Jorge Luis Borges constructed in the five biographies mentioned above and how these have impacted on the public imaginary in order to create and perpetuate certain myths and prejudices that make up Borges as a cultural icon. I shall offer a brief survey of their reception by general readers, academics and intellectuals and I will also look at their dissemination in the mass media as a means of secondary projection to a general public. An assessment of their reception in Argentina and, where relevant, in the English-speaking world, will follow.

---

[6] Barthes, 'The Death of the Author', p. 145, italics in the original.
[7] Gerard Genette, *Paratext: Thresholds of Interpretation*, trans. by Jane E. Lewin, (Cambridge: Cambridge University Press, 1997), p. 2.
[8] The word 'paratext' is used throughout the chapter in a wider sense to refer to biographies as paratextual to the works of Borges. The word is also used, more specifically, to refer to paratextual elements such as titles, covers, indexes within the biographies themselves.

Literary Biography: 'Something Betwixt and Between'[9]

The practice of biography can be traced back to ancient civilizations, as Nigel Hamilton suggests in his *Biography: A Brief History* (2007).[10] Hamilton refers, particularly, to the Scandinavian sagas: ancient oral accounts of the lives of heroes. Throughout the centuries, biographies continued to serve a pedagogical purpose, as the lives of the great and the good constituted noble examples for ordinary people to follow. Perhaps the best known early biographer is the Roman essayist Plutarch in the first century AD, who wrote, amongst others, the *Lives of Alexandre the Great and Julius Caesar*. This writing of exemplary lives continued throughout the Middle Ages with the practice of hagiography.[11] Dr Samuel Johnson is considered to have inaugurated modern literary biography with the publication of *Lives of the English Poets* in 1781. Johnson's innovation lay in his 'depictions that included elements both "beautiful and base", embracing "vice and virtue", rather than relying on the "sober sages of the schools".'[12] His own biographer, James Boswell, author of perhaps the most famous biography in history, *Life of Samuel Johnson* (1791), was only one of the many contemporaries upon whom Johnson's 'valuation of biography would have a powerful impact' (p. 91). Indeed, according to Hamilton, Johnson's 'opinions would provide a vision of the modern *purpose* of biography that has lasted to this day' (p. 85).

Literary biography differs from biography in general in that the biographer is at the same time historian and literary critic, and his or her fundamental challenge lies in keeping the delicate balance between 'reading the life in the works or reading the works through the life' of his or her biographee.[13] David Ellis warns: anyone embarking on a systematic study which would cover the entire field of literary biography 'would go mad, or die before their task was done.'[14] The difficulty of this task lies, primarily, in the resistance of literary biography to classification, as it is, by nature, a bewilderingly diverse and heterogeneous form (Ellis). Instead, as Michael Benton suggests, 'the diversity is best served by viewing literary biography from a range of perspectives — historical, comparative, referential auto/biographical and so on.'[15] Suffice to say, then, that the examination of biographies of Borges in this chapter is based on Michael Benton's

---

[9] Virginia Woolf, 'The Art of Biography', in *Collected Essays*, vol. 4 (London: Hogarth Press, 1967), p. 227, cited in 'Literary Biography: The Cinderella of Literary Studies', by Michael Benton, *The Journal of Aesthetic Education*, 39.3 (2005), 44–57 (p. 55).
[10] Nigel Hamilton, *Biography: A Brief History* (Cambridge: Harvard University Press, 2007).
[11] For a discussion of the writing of the lives of saints, see Hamilton, *Biography*, pp. 33–59.
[12] Hamilton, *Biography*, pp. 87–8.
[13] Michael Benton, *Literary Biography: An Introduction* (Oxford: Wiley-Blackwell, 2009), p. xv.
[14] David Ellis, *Literary Lives: Biography and the Search for Understanding* (New York: Routledge, 2002), p. viii.
[15] Michael Benton, *Literary Biography*, p. xv.

treatment of this particular form of life-writing as hybrid, and assessed from a historical and comparative perspective. Indeed, the different biographies considered here are testimony to the diversity of the form, even though they all contain an element of chronology and, as Benton explains, 'the principles that underpin each representation are sufficiently similar to be recognizably biographical.'[16]

The 'genre' of literary biography is based on the assumption that there is an author, that this author exists prior to his work, that this author has a certain intention and motive in the production of his work, and also that there is a meaning in the author's work which constitutes the key to a certain truth about a real person responsible for the production of the work. This seems to suggest a hermeneutic model of literary biography as a series of layers, which the biographer can penetrate in order to reveal certain truths about the author and his/her works. Literary biography's piecing together of the life of a writer from his/her literary yield creates the illusion that the reader may get to know him/her by reading his/her work. A phenomenon that arises as a consequence of this is the possibility that the public, although not necessarily the reading public, appropriate the writer's life through literary biography, completely bypassing the writer's work, as the biographer has done the reading for them. This is part of the reason why this activity has been treated with suspicion by literary theorists in recent decades.[17]

Michael Benton refers to literary biography as 'Cinderella' because of its renowned shunning by British academia, who have considered it, throughout the twentieth century, incapable of establishing 'any theoretical foundation upon which to build.'[18] This is a particular consequence of the dominance of post-structuralist thought and literary biography's clear resistance to its modes of enquiry, nor even to engage 'with the practical questions of selection, organization or presentation.' (p. 45). Yet, as Benton highlights, literary biography enjoys immense popularity, which is only partly due to commercial success. The fact that a considerable number of biographies of one same author have been written, and new ones continue to appear — Borges is a case in point — speaks, according to Benton, of the uniqueness of an activity with infinite possible variations.[19]

---

[16] Michael Benton, 'Literary Biography: The Cinderella of Literary Studies', *The Journal of Aesthetic Education*, 39.3 (2005), pp. 44–57, p. 46.
[17] Ellis considers biography one of the few remaining points of interaction between the academic world and the rest of society, as he investigates the reasons for the notorious lack of theorization surrounding the subject, in 'Lives Without Theory', *Literary Lives*, pp. 1–19.
[18] Benton, 'Literary Biography', p. 45.
[19] I use the word 'activity' advisedly, to draw attention to the unease with which literary biography sits next to literary genres. I shall therefore use the word 'genre' to refer to literary biography — for want of a better one — between inverted commas, in order to indicate the resistance of this activity to classification, as a form which lies in between history and fiction.

The main generic element of literary biography that Benton identifies is 'its concern to document facts' and he approaches its study 'in the light of its narrative impulse.'[20] Thus, Benton highlights the hybridity of this form, which constitutes a nexus where history and fiction cross. A further aspect of the task of the literary biographer consists in allowing his or her work to 'tell its story through the dynamic biographer/biographee relationship unique to every biography' (p. 46). In this way, the allure of the intertwined activities of writing and consuming literary biography lies in its power to enable us to study ourselves by writing/reading about the lives of others. This is particularly relevant to the study of the construction of Borges, as by their very nature, his biographies construct, not only the author, but also the biographer and the various historical, political and literary discourses underlying their work.

It is the great number of possible combinations of this kind that allows for the production of a potentially endless number of biographies of the same author which in essence should tell the same story, but which use a unique combination of narrative approaches and devices. Under the guise of pure fact, information about the life of the historical figure is mixed with interpretations of his work, to narrate the author-man. Selection of facts, style and rhetoric, the choice to follow or ignore a teleological approach to events and chronology, are all narrative techniques which serve the purpose of holding a text together cohesively, providing the unity required for the life of a writer to make sense, and resulting 'in a provisional construct created from that mixture of elements' (p. 49).

Even though the biographer may intend to hide behind them, his/her choice of narrative devices and the way in which they are combined represent a projection of his/her own particular expectations and desires upon the text, which result in a fictional construction of their subject. In the words of Paul de Man, 'in the end there is only writing:'[21] a biography's efforts to 'conceal its own fictionalisation' (p. 13), paradoxically results in naming it. Thus, when reading a biography, the reader is confronted by the construction of the biographer in all its cultural complexity. Precisely because biographies are modes of narrative, the voice of the narrator is unavoidable, and in literary biography in particular, in interpreting the work of an author and making choices concerning the narration of their life, literary biographers end up achieving a double construction: that of themselves and of their subject. This poses the question of the biographer as an author: his or her claims to legitimacy in the shape of, for example, a personal relationship with the subject would suggest that the truth of the text lies with its author. In this sense, this same text may not necessarily

---

[20] Benton, 'Literary Biography', p. 46.
[21] Anderson refers to de Man's 'Autobiography as De-Facement' (1979) in *Autobiography*, by Linda Anderson (London & New York: Routledge, 2001), p. 13.

have been true had it not been written by a figure of such authority. Both the author-biographer and the author-biographed are vehemently put forward as legitimizing forces of origin. In this sense, it could be argued that the hegemonic model of certain illuminated minds embarking in the conveyance of certain truths is thus perpetuated by literary biography, its historical development and, most relevantly, its consumption. Although, as Benton cautions, of course 'the idea that there is some essential personality to be revealed is an illusion [...] Instead there is a representation to be created in all its complexities and contradictions.'[22]

Images created by the narration of an author's life in literary biography have the power of influencing the way we read the author's work. This type of space of production of meaning or 'paratext' is 'a *threshold*, or — a word Borges used apropos of a preface — a "vestibule",'[23] the space surrounding the text, but which is in interaction with it and mediates our experience of the text itself. The titles of sections or chapters within a book are a specific example of paratext, which Genette admits 'is a relay' which may '— if the author is too heavy-handed — impede and ultimately block the text's reception' (p. 94). We shall see how the choice of chapter headings and other paratextual elements can indicate the over eagerness of a biographer to push a point too far, revealing their fictionalizing intentions and motivations.

Within the category of the paratextual, Genette identifies something he calls the public epitext, that is, something which is not materially attached to the text but circulates in the social sphere and is directed at the general public. The public epitext is constituted by a variety of media, as is the case of published conversations with Borges, for example.[24] In general terms, the publicity apparatus put in motion by any given publishing house is a key element of the public epitext of an author's work. Together with general iconography, information that appears in the various media, and academic discourses (as this study will subsequently explore), literary biography is epitextual to the Borgesian oeuvre, its influence over the reading of the literary works, virtually unavoidable.[25] Similarly, epitextual elements represent a liminal space for the production of meanings associated with the persona of the author.

---

[22] Benton, 'Literary Biography', p. 52.
[23] Genette, *Paratexts*, p. 344.
[24] Cf. Genette, *Paratexts*, pp. 358–59.
[25] Cf. Genette, *Paratexts*, p. 344.

The Imminence of a Revelation: Borges Off-centre

> Sacamos los pesados revólveres (de pronto hubo revólveres en el sueño) y alegremente dimos muerte a los Dioses.
>
> J.L. Borges, 'Ragnarök'(1959)

The last line of Borges's 'Ragnarök', which constitutes its last paragraph, thus reinforcing its importance, is a fitting metaphor for the death of the author occurring within discourse: the author-god is killed by guns which are themselves generated within the narrative that the dream represents.[26] A brief overview of Borges's off-centre narrative stance suffices to illustrate its direct opposition to the idea of the author as origin and genesis underlying literary biography. In his introduction to his reading of 'Fundación Mítica de Buenos Aires', in the recording *Jorge Luis Borges por él mismo. Sus poemas y su voz* (1967), Borges's famous voice can be heard saying: 'Es un poema escrito hace tanto tiempo que lo veo como ajeno [...] Lo releo y me parece escrito por otra persona. Por una persona que no me es antipática, pero que ciertamente no es el Borges que está hablando ahora.'[27] This dissociation between Borges the writer and the Borges whose voice is recognisable in the recording, constitutes a warning against any kind of epiphany occurring as a consequence of hearing what might be generally perceived as the man himself reading his own work. The particular intention behind these statements does not concern us directly, but it might be argued that, perhaps aware of the theoretical discussions going on at the time, they are based on Borges's own developing notion of authorship, as someone who exists solely for the creation of a certain work: 'yo vivo, yo me dejo vivir, para que Borges pueda tramar su literatura,' says the narrative voice of 'Borges y yo' (*OCII*, p. 86), and then evaporates forever, irretrievably: 'yo estoy destinado a perderme, definitivamente [...] mi vida es una fuga' (p. 86). This particular parable, in which 'the mysterious commerce between the proper name and its bearer'[28] is enacted but not resolved, as Seán Burke points out, is perhaps the most faithful expression

---

[26] Williamson provides a very convincing political interpretation of the anger and violence in 'Ragnarök' in *Borges: A Life*, pp. 339–40.
[27] Héctor Yánover (dir.), 'Fundación Mítica de Buenos Aires', *Jorge Luis Borges por él mismo: Sus poemas y su voz* (Buenos Aires: AMB Discográfica, 1967).This vinyl record, containing recordings of Borges reading and sometimes commenting on some of his poems, is held in *The Borges Collection* at the University of Notre Dame, U.S.A. Available online at http://rarebooks.library.nd.edu/collections/latin_american/south_american/southern_cone_lit/borges-audio.shtml [last accessed 27 September 2013]. It was also digitalized on CD and published together with the poems in book format by Visor in 1999. The original recording was then re-released on CD in 2002.
[28] Seán Burke, 'Writing the Self', in Seán Burke (ed.), *Authorship: From Plato to the Postmodern. A Reader* (Edinburgh: Edinburgh University Press, 1995), pp. 301–39 (308).

of Borges's in-betweenness. That is, a certain reluctance to define unequivocally a definite place for the author, who is neither at the centre nor outside of the text.

Further metaliterary evidence of Borges's conception of the author can be found in a conversation recorded by his partner in writing and good friend, Adolfo Bioy Casares, as early as 1949, who remembers Borges reflecting that in *Martín Fierro* there is 'una nobleza estoica' which has created the character, and that 'las circunstancias de su biografía — o las intenciones del autor — se dejan de lado o se olvidan.'[29] The writer's assertion that characters are a product of style of speech, rather than of stable pre-existent notions, points to a conviction that characters do not represent underlying persons, but that they emerge from discourse. This view of literature goes against the notion that literary biography can uncover the writer underneath the characters in his/her books.

These ideas pervade the Borgesian oeuvre: the refutation of the author as origin; musings on the notion of a higher force — perhaps a muse, god or spirit — as source of inspiration, as described in his poem 'El otro' (*OCII*, p. 268); the breaches opened up in the articulation of what has traditionally been perceived as Borges, the name as signifier, and Borges, the man as signified. Of these, the best known, and perhaps most analyzed instance, is the story 'Borges y yo' (*OCII*, p. 186), which provides a succinct parable of the dissociation of Borges the fictional character from Borges the writer, as mentioned above.[30] Or, in a further dissociation, the image created in the story of a Borges writing the story by a Borges whose image we consume as readers. Other stories such as 'Funes el memorioso', 'El Sur' and 'El Aleph' also explore this issue in their self-referentiality.[31] In the intersection between fiction and criticism, 'Examen de la obra de Herbert Quain' and 'Pierre Menard, autor del Quijote' also embark on the fictional problematization of traditional categories for the study of literature, in particular the notion of authorship, through the creation of a fictional author.[32] Thus, the fact that it is possible to create a new author for an already existing work of literature illustrates the point that the author function emanates from discourse.

---

[29] Adolfo Bioy Casares, '1949', *Borges*, ed. by Daniel Martino (Barcelona: Destino, 2006), p. 37. The conversation concerned their work on the Bustos Domecq detective stories.
[30] See Seán Burke, *The Death and Return of the Author: Criticism and Subjectivity in Barthes, Foucault and Derrida* (Edinburgh: Edinburgh University Press, 2004), p. 53 for a discussion of this dissociation.
[31] Lorena Amaro Castro explores the opposition between referentialism and textualism and reflects on autobiography as fiction, invention and construction of the self in writing in *Autobiografía y nombre propio en los textos de Jorge Luis Borges* (unpublished doctoral thesis, Universidad Complutense de Madrid, 2003) and in her article 'La imposible autobiografía de Jorge Luis Borges', *Variaciones Borges*, 17 (2004), 229–52.
[32] María del Carmen Marengo, 'El autor ficticio en la obra de Jorge Luis Borges: Crítica y renovación de la literatura argentina', *Variaciones Borges*, 10 (2000), 167–83.

This off-centre positioning that Borges assumes is explored in Beatriz Sarlo's *Jorge Luis Borges: A Writer on the Edge*.³³ First published in 1993, it is the fruit of a significant shift in Borgesian criticism in the 1990s: from the focus on the universalizing notion of Borges and of Borgesian cosmogonies as self-contained totalities, to a more 'angular and splintered mode of truth.'³⁴ Sarlo rethinks the author's stance in relation to Argentine cultural identity and contemporary views of the literary canon, repositioning him 'on the edge': Borges, she claims, 'hace del margen una estética. [...] La máquina literaria borgeana ficcionaliza estas cuestiones, y produce una puesta en forma de problemas teóricos y filosóficos.'³⁵ Sarlo locates Borges's writing on the periphery, giving prominence to the space of the scission: 'un juego en el filo de dos orillas' (p. 2), moving away from the notion of a central truth which defines the 'genre' of literary biography.

Sylvia Molloy has a more productive view of this space, which is reminiscent of the space where Foucault locates the operation of the author-function: 'a space into which the writing space constantly disappears,'³⁶ which she prefers to see as an 'ever fruitful in-between.'³⁷ Borges, she claims, prefers the 'dispersion and not the moment of resolution' (p. 13). Similarly, in a much quoted passage from the 1950 essay 'La muralla y los libros', Borges defines aesthetic experience as the imminence of a revelation that never occurs:

> La música, los estados de felicidad, la mitología, las caras trabajadas por el tiempo, ciertos crepúsculos y ciertos lugares, quieren decirnos algo, o algo dijeron que no hubiéramos debido perder, o están por decir algo; esta inminencia de una revelación, que no se produce, es, quizá, el hecho estético.³⁸

Borges's narrative technique is perhaps where this shifting of the focus away from the centre is most noticeable. By associating the quest for absolute reason, knowledge and perception with madness and horror (consider Funes's plight in 'Funes el memorioso', for example), Borges's fictions tend to focus on the approximation to, rather than the reaching of, any kind of core truth (impeccably

---

³³ Later translated and published as *Borges, un escritor en las orillas* in 1995. Subsequent citations throughout are from Beatriz Sarlo, *Borges, un escritor en las orillas* (Madrid: Siglo XXI, 2007).

³⁴ As early as 1930, Borges quotes Thomas De Quincey in his epigraph to *Evaristo Carriego*: 'A mode of truth, not of truth coherent and central, but angular and splintered.' *OCI*.

³⁵ Sarlo, *Borges*, p. 8.

³⁶ Foucault, 'What is an Author?', p. 175.

³⁷ Sylvia Molloy, 'Lost in Translation: Borges, the Western Tradition and Fictions of Latin America', in Evelyn Fishburn (ed.), *Borges and Europe Revisited* (London: Institute of Latin American Studies, 1998), pp. 8–20 (p. 20). See also S. Molloy, 'Placer y desconcierto: la desarticulación del hiato', *Las letras de Borges y otros ensayos* (Rosario: Beatriz Viterbo, 1999), pp. 141–64.

³⁸ J.L. Borges, 1950. 'La muralla y los libros', in *Otras Inquisiciones*, *OCII*, p. 13. (First published in *La Nación*, Buenos Aires, 22 October 1950).

explored in Arnett's nephew's road to discovery in 'There Are More Things', for example). The narrative is usually approached from the periphery, rather than a centre that the characters do not — and are not able to — know, hinting at the idea of a core truth as an illusory and elusive myth.[39] Futile quests for totalities, of knowledge in 'La Biblioteca de Babel', of perception in 'El Aleph', of memory in 'La memoria de Shakespeare', to give a few of the best-known examples, appear to lead to a certain centre or resolution, end or revelation, whereas in fact, they are generally an exploration of the quest itself, a lingering on the road, rather than an arrival anywhere. The prevalent image in Borges is the paradox, and the juxtaposition of seemingly contradictory concepts and settings, which opens an in-between space which is neither and both at the same time. 'El Sur' is perhaps the classic example: Dahlmann's train journey could be said to represent a liminal space, which is, in turn, a metaphor for a state of consciousness which is not possible to define as wakefulness, dream or delirium. At the same time, this story makes the roaming across the geographical and cultural boundaries of the city of Buenos Aires, whilst in a non-defined state of consciousness, a wandering across the boundaries of personal identity. This promises to find its resolution as the story seems to approach the limits of a narrative which, by virtue of its lack of an ending, gives value to the journey over its destination. This is reinforced in Spanish by the fact that destiny and destination are one and the same word: 'destino'.

Borges's famous prologues are also a good example of the aesthetic of the in-between, but it is in his own experiments in biography (*Historia Universal de la Infamia*, 'Biografías sintéticas', and *Evaristo Carriego*) where his views regarding authorship and his aesthetics of the in-between coalesce with his views on the impossibility of the 'genre'. Annick Louis points out that Borges's life has motivated writings which are based on devices that he himself had condemned in his incursions into the 'genre': the narrative strategies used in life writing as an exercise in fiction writing; the logical falsity of any claim to factuality; and the inevitable autobiographical inscription of the biographer,[40] as we shall see next.

Evaristo Carriego begins by incorporating elements of authenticity and factuality through very detailed references to documents: 'La vindicación de la antigüedad de Palermo [...] la registran los *Anales de la Biblioteca*, en una nota de la página 360 del tomo cuarto; las pruebas [...] fueron publicadas mucho después en el número 242 de *Nosotros*'(*OCI*, p. 105). Only to turn, a few lines

---

[39] Consider, for example, 'El fin', where the events are narrated from the point of view of an outsider, Recabarren, who is physically unable to stand centre stage. The main event of the story is approached peripherally, at an angle. This is particularly apparent if considered in contrast with its precursor, José Hernandez's *Martin Fierro*, where the story is not only centrally narrated but acted out by its protagonists.

[40] Annick Louis, 'La biografía o las formas del yo', *Variaciones Borges*, 3, (1997), 207–13 (p. 1).

further on, to the realm of fiction: 'el entreverado estilo de la realidad, con su puntuación de ironías, de sorpresas, de previsiones extrañas como las sorpresas, sólo es recuperable por la novela' (p. 105). Borges does not hesitate to point out that biographers are writers of fiction, boldly uncovering the characteristics of the 'genre', which is what might have led some critics to treat *Evaristo Carriego* as an unorthodox or failed biography.[41] Sylvia Molloy calls it an 'edgy text',[42] and Beatriz Sarlo prefers to see it as the simulation of a biography which is, in fact, both a mythology of Buenos Aires and a literary manifesto.[43] Borges reflects that it is not possible to stay within the boundaries of factuality; and that his omissions would only include what he knows, and not, as many biographers promise on the covers of their books, the whole unadulterated universal truth (*OCI*, p. 107). By deconstructing the 'genre', he exposes what he considers the obvious fact that it is just not possible to engender in others memories that do not belong to them (p. 113), in other words, this amounts to writing fiction. He justifies the attempt, though, claiming that a certain naivety is involved in the process: 'Ejecutar esa paradoja, es la inocente voluntad de toda biografía' (p. 113), where the rather clever use of 'ejecutar' brings to mind both 'to realize' and 'to sacrifice, or destroy in the name of justice'. Perhaps Borges feels that biographers rather arrogantly expect to be able to ignore such evident characteristics of the process. In this context, 'inocente' becomes ironic, as factuality dissolves into fiction as the narrative progresses.

Weaving Through the Threshold: Embroidering Images of Borges

The five biographies of Jorge Luis Borges considered here (out of the great deal of material of biographical interest such as memoirs, testimonies and interviews that have been published) have been chosen for the extent of their impact, as measured in references to them in other biographies and academic publications, and their reception in the media. The influence of these biographies on the consumption of Borges as a cultural icon will be demonstrated by comparing and contrasting the images of the writer that each of them constructs.[44] This will be approached in terms of the perceived position of each of the biographers in terms of an author's creative work as evidence for his/her own life narrative; their

---

[41] See for example Daniel Balderston, 'Beatriz Viterbo *c'est moi*. Visión angular en *Borges a contraluz* de Estela Canto', in *Borges: realidades y simulacros* (Buenos Aires: Biblos, 2000), pp. 109–15 (p. 110).
[42] Sylvia Molloy, *Signs of Borges*, translated and adapted by Oscar Montero (Durham: Duke University Press, 1994), p. 11.
[43] Sarlo, *Borges*, p. 44.
[44] Cf. Rodrigo Fresán, 'Una guía de las biografías de Borges escritas en la Argentina', *Página/12*, 16 January 2005, online at www.pagina12.com.ar/diario/suplementos/radar/9-1953-2005-01-16.html [last accessed 27 September 2013].

constructions of the notion of authorship, and the biographers' autobiographical inscriptions. As stated in the introduction I will proceed in order of date of publication.

(i) Alicia Jurado's Genio y figura de Jorge Luis Borges (1964)

Argentine writer, biographer, and translator Alicia Jurado was around twenty years younger than Borges and a good friend of his, a position that she hastens to define in the introduction to her biography, where she points out the challenge of 'aventurarme al retrato de un amigo querido, cuyas debilidades sin duda atenuaré por lealtad.'[45] Subsequent biographers refer to her as intelligent, loyal and generous. Edwin Williamson, for example, includes her in the category of female friends of Borges 'whom he respected for their literary or intellectual work.'[46] Highly educated and a member of the traditional 'criollo' elite, Jurado's obvious affection for the writer coexists in her biography with a strong personal conservatism which is not only evident in her literary analyses but which she also projects on to her subject. In her defence of Borges against the critics of the time, who appeared to perceive him as cold, unfeeling and removed from the political realities of 1960s Argentina, she is careful to separate the sphere of the private man from that of his works:

> Si pasamos al campo de sus opiniones políticas, que apenas figuran en sus libros pero de las que no falta constancia en diarios y revistas y son tema permanente de su conversación, es difícil imaginar hombre más apasionado que Borges [...] No le pidamos pasión a los cuentos de Borges, porque no la tienen y porque es posible que si la tuviesen [...] fueran menos admirables.[47]

She does, however, admit that the poems of his youth contain his 'emociones más intensas,' although she clearly prefers a more mature Borges, as she repeatedly points out throughout (p. 118). Jurado complains that Borges is admired for an esoteric quality that his work does not actually possess, and she claims that 'Borges confirmó mi sospecha de que sus cuentos no son alegóricos ni encierran significados ocultos' (pp. 59–60) so she refrains from making explicit political or psychological analyses of Borges's work.

On a personal level, the Borges depicted by Jurado is friendly, warm-hearted and fun-loving. Used as we are now to an image of Borges as an old man lost in thought, it is a pleasant surprise to discover that most of the photographs reproduced in Jurado's book show a smiling Borges, usually enjoying a conversation with friends. However, this image has been overshadowed by that

---

[45] Alicia Jurado, *Genio y Figura de Jorge Luis Borges* (Buenos Aires: EUDEBA, 1964), p. 5.
[46] Williamson, *Borges: A Life*, p. 301.
[47] Jurado, *Genio y figura*, pp. 66–68.

of a conservative Borges, in terms of his views of both literature and politics, which the biographer puts forward: 'Intelectualmente, es demasiado argentino para ser nacionalista y no ha hecho sino heredar la vieja tradición criolla de mirar hacia Europa; reprocharle esta preferencia es ignorar el pensamiento de las generaciones ilustradas que nos precedieron' (p. 115). Jurado's notion of 'Argentineness' seems rather narrow, and her reference to past enlightened generations points to a cultural elitism that must have infuriated contemporary left-wing critics. The Europe that the old 'criollos' looked to is of course not to be mistaken with that other Europe where poor Italian and Eastern European immigrants came from to reconfigure the new Argentina that she so despairs of:

> Cabe preguntarse por qué hay personas que niegan carácter nacional a la obra de Borges, y afirman que su literatura no refleja el país. […] Borges escribe […] sobre la Argentina de su añoranza. Si lo hiciera sobre la realidad nacional que hoy vivimos tendría que limitarse a temas, casas, hablares y psicologías de italianos, que constituyen la escencia de la argentinidad del siglo XX. Es natural que a los nacionalistas, casi todos recién llegados al país, les ofenda la nostalgia de Borges por una patria que no les perteneció y que ellos han contribuido a borrar. (p. 126)

With these sweeping comments about the impoverished quality of Argentine culture as a result of Italian immigration and a certain consequent nationalism Jurado asserts her own views regarding immigration and Italian-style fascist politics (pp. 115–17). In so doing, she achieves the perpetuation of the image of Borges as an elitist writer, which was clearly already in circulation at the time. As we shall see, with the help of Emir Rodríguez Monegal, this view of Borges will dominate the following thirty years, tapping into anxieties of the Argentine left-wing intelligentsia during the 1970s and fitting in with the agendas of the military Juntas. The nationalism that Jurado attacks in her book seems to be Peronism, a social and political phenomenon which she perceives as being largely constituted by elements from an immigrant working class, with no regard for what she perceives as a high culture cultivated by the criollo founders of the 'patria'. The tension arising from the emerging dichotomy of the so-called original Argentines, also called 'criollos', and a modern Argentina, newly defined by its melting-pot reconfiguration, is taken up and explored in great depth by Williamson. Williamson writes from a completely different position from Jurado, ideologically, chronologically, culturally and geographically, but the conflict between old criollo values and new Argentine ones, is of similar, if not greater strength in his work.[48]

Although Alicia Jurado's biography is no longer as widely circulated as it once was, its importance cannot be denied, both as an early critical work and as a sign

---

[48] Williamson uses the metaphor of the sword and dagger, which he makes a motif throughout his biography *Borges: A Life*, to refer to this conflict.

of its time. Considering that hers was the only biography of Borges available for the following twenty years in Argentina (the Spanish translation of Rodríguez Monegal's biography was published in 1987), it could be assumed that it was consulted exclusively and widely.[49] In a review of its third edition (1996), Cristina Parodi calls it 'el clásico libro de Alicia Jurado,' which is underlined by the fact that the new edition 'reproduce las anteriores [...] sin alterar el texto original.'[50] Moreover, as a pioneer of the Borges biography, *Genio y Figura de Jorge Luis Borges* has been consulted and cited and Alicia Jurado's analyses, opinions and memories sought by many subsequent biographers.[51]

The fact that Jurado's biography was being read by contemporary critics is evidenced by references in a variety of publications: as early as 1965, writer and influential Peronist intellectual Arturo Jauretche refers to Jurado as Borges's biographer in 'Moraleja de Borges: su "guerrero y su cautiva".'[52] Two years later, Ana María Barrenechea also cites Jurado in her influential *La expresión de la irrealidad en la obra de Jorge Luis Borges* (1967).[53] Most relevantly, Emir Rodríguez Monegal picks up her thread of Borges's love for all things British and, as we shall see next, manages to perpetuate the myth of Borges as an incurable Anglophile in his *Borges. A Literary Biography* (1978). There are a dozen references to Jurado's biography in María Esther Vázquez's *Borges. Esplendor y Derrota* (1996), where she is referred to as 'su [Borges's] amiga de toda la vida.'[54] Here, for example, Jurado's version of Borges's infamous 'promotion' out of the Miguel Cané Library to inspector of poultry by the Peronist government in 1946 is mentioned. More recently, Edwin Williamson mentions Jurado in his acknowledgements as one of the people who were kind enough to share their memories of Borges with him, some of which appear in his book.

Jurado's opinions have traditionally appeared in newspapers like *La Nación* and *La Prensa*,[55] and she is an active member of the Academia Argentina de

---

[49] There are three editions of Jurado's book and various print runs: the second edition followed the first only two years later, in 1966, with a further print run the following year and in 1980. The third edition dates from 1996, of which there has been at least one more print run in 1997.
[50] Cristina Parodi, 'Alicia Jurado, *Genio y figura de Jorge Luis Borges*', *Variaciones Borges*, 4 (1997), 239–40 (p. 239).
[51] Alejandro Vaccaro, for example, cites both *Genio y Figura de Jorge Luis Borges* and Rodríguez Monegal's *Borges: Una biografía literaria* as 'soporte para mi trabajo' in *Borges. Vida y literatura* (Buenos Aires: Edhasa, 2006), p. 11.
[52] Arturo Jauretche, 'Moraleja de Borges: su "guerrero y su cautiva"', *Marcha* 1259 (1965), in *Antiborges*, ed. by Martín Lafforgue (Buenos Aires: Javier Vergara, 1999), pp. 169–78 (p. 176).
[53] Ana María Barrenechea, *La expresión de la irrealidad en la obra de Jorge Luis Borges* (Buenos Aires: Paidós, 1967), p. 10.
[54] María Esther Vázquez, *Borges: Esplendor y derrota* (Barcelona: Tusquets, 1996), p. 296.
[55] See for example Maximiliano Seitz, 'Por qué Borges nunca obtuvo el premio Nobel', *La Nación*, 21 August 1999, online at www.lanacion.com.ar/nota.asp?nota_id=150373 [last accessed 27 September 2013].

Letras. Apart from the publication of its third edition in 1996, the fact that 'porteño' libraries contain copies of *Genio y Figura de Jorge Luis Borges* shows that the book is still in circulation: the website of the 'Red de Contenidos Digitales del Patrimonio Cultural' of the Ministry of Culture of the City of Buenos Aires shows that all the municipal libraries of the city hold copies of *Genio y Figura de Jorge Luis Borges*. Among these, Biblioteca Miguel Cané (a small neighbourhood library where Borges worked in the late 1930s, which has become something of a tourist attraction) holds three copies.[56] It is no wonder, then, that the view of Borges as an elitist, foreign-loving writer, has been so strong for so long in the Argentine imaginary.

(ii) Emir Rodríguez Monegal's Borges: Una biografía literaria *(1987)*

Uruguayan literary critic Emir Rodríguez Monegal knew Borges and his oeuvre well and he has been himself constructed as an authority: his biography has been extensively referred to by most subsequent biographers and by Borges scholars who have taken on the complex job of trying to approach the ultimate Borges truth through the added layer of Rodríguez Monegal's biography. Monegal's book was first published in English as *Jorge Luis Borges: A Literary Biography* in 1978. The edition considered here is a 1993 reprint of Homero Alsina Thavenet's 1987 Spanish translation. This remarkable nine-year gap between the English publication and the translation meant that subsequent biographers would have had to go to the English original for information. It was they who, by extensively quoting it made this book a seminal work and of Monegal the most recognized authority in the field. Knowledge of the English language as a prerequisite for consulting the literary biography of Argentina's most iconic writer clearly perpetuates the myth of the elite, foreign loving, Anglophile writer, first introduced by Alicia Jurado, who had pointed out that Borges 'piensa como un latino, pero expone como un sajón.'[57] She continues:

> Es preciso señalar como rasgo muy notable la patente influencia del idioma inglés y de sus escritores, perceptible en ciertos anglicismos [...] sobre todo en la construcción típicamente inglesa de los párrafos [...] ha eliminado la verborragia, las disgresiones y la multiplicidad de cláusulas secundarias que suelen resultar tan fatigosas en el idioma español escrito. (p. 136)

---

[56] Online at http://www.acceder.gov.ar/es/buscador/td:Libros.1/all:genio%20y%20figura%20de%20jorge%20luis%20borges [last accessed 27 September 2013]. The Biblioteca Nacional contains nine copies of the book (and only one of Rodríguez Monegal's biography of Borges). The central catalogue of the libraries of the Facultad de Filosofía y Letras, Universidad de Buenos Aires, contains seven copies of various editions of this biography (all other copies of various biographies of the author put together amount to a similar number), online at http://opac.filo.uba.ar/.
[57] Jurado, *Genio y figura*, p. 136.

After clearly stating her personal preference for the English language over the tiresome quality of written Spanish, Jurado drives home the point with her analysis of Borges's humour, which is apparently only available to those able to grasp and enjoy the British variety, underlining 'los procedimientos que emplea en su sobrio humorismo [...] principalmente [...] el *humour* británico, basado casi siempre en el *understatement*'(p. 136). Borges's particular interest in Anglo-Saxon, English and American literatures is evident from his published work and also from his use of English words in some of his poems and stories.[58] However, Jurado and Rodríguez Monegal's construction of Borges as an Anglophile rests on the assumption that Borges considered British culture, for example, to be superior to Argentine culture. Judging by the assertions of these two early biographers, one would expect Borges to have actually written a significant proportion of his oeuvre in English, which is clearly not the case.

In a style different to Jurado's, and through less formalist literary analyses, Rodríguez Monegal chooses to develop and perpetuate the myth of the Anglophile by creating a text which incorporates elements from both Borges's personal history and his work. In exploring the links between his story 'Historia del guerrero y de la cautiva' and the writer's own family mythology, for example, Rodríguez Monegal describes the journey of the archetypal civilization versus barbarism narrative of the white woman kidnapped by savages and assimilated into their culture, entwining it with tales attributed to Borges's English grandmother, Fanny. Rodríguez Monegal ventures even further, interpreting the symbolic value of the story as a metaphor for Fanny's own sense of isolation and entrapment. At this point, the theme of England as the epitome of civilization is taken up. Rodríguez Monegal presents Fanny Haslam as a civilized lady trapped in a world of violence, chaos and barbarism:

> Hasta cierto punto, el cuento revela su sentido secreto: también Fanny Haslam era una cautiva. Aunque se había casado con un caballero argentino, aunque había podido conservar su idioma y hasta transmitirlo a sus hijos y nietos, era todavía cautiva en una tierra primitiva y violenta, aprisionada para siempre en un mundo que era dominado por una lengua extranjera.[59]

---

[58] It is a well-known fact that Borges taught himself Anglo-Saxon, although this is more a sign of his interest in the Scandinavian sagas than in British culture itself. Between 1965 and 1967, he wrote *Introducción a la literatura inglesa* and *Literaturas germánicas medievales* (which includes 'Literatura de la Inglaterra Sajona') with María Esther Vázquez and *Introducción a la literatura norteamericana* with Esther Zemborain de Torres Duggan. In 1978 he wrote *Breve antología anglosajona* with María Kodama. These are all collected in *Obras Completas en Colaboración* (Buenos Aires: Emecé, 1998). His admiration for writers like Whitman, Shakespeare, Chesterton and Stevenson (to name just a few English language writers) is also well-known.

[59] Emir Rodríguez Monegal, *Borges. Una biografía literaria*, trans. by Homero Alsina Thevenet (México: Fondo de Cultura Económica, 1993), p. 14.

This appraisal shows that the narrative is constructed from arguably prevailing prejudices and preconceptions, even though the tone is one of revealed truth ('el cuento revela su sentido secreto'). In this context, the biographer offers a certain interpretation which can be contrasted, for example, with subsequent interviews in which Borges often referred to his grandmother as a very brave, no-nonsense woman, who does not come across as the helpless Victorian lady who needs rescuing from foreign lands, thus reinforcing the idea that such images are constructed in the narrative, rather than uncovered or revealed as irrefutable fact. The way the figure of Fanny Haslam and her relationship with Borges are constructed in this biography contributes to the perception of Borges as an Anglophile, who, in Rodríguez Monegal's view, 'habría de permanecer siempre [...] bajo la influencia británica'(p. 14).

The tone of these pages taps into a wider South American prejudice of English (together with French) as the language of culture, erudition and refinement, which finds expression in comments such as: 'la abuela inglesa que tenía la llave para el mundo de lo inglés y de los libros ingleses: el mundo de la cultura'(p. 19); or 'no es extraño, entonces, que para Georgie el español quedase asociado a una forma más primitiva o elemental de la vida, mientras el inglés daba acceso a un nivel superior' (p. 23). The impact of Borges's mixed heritage on the shaping of his cultural identity comes across as problematic in *Borges: Una biografía literaria*.[60] This results from the construction of a certain psychological configuration for Borges in which Spanish and English heritages are allegedly experienced as unreconcileable: in his analysis of Borges's 'La biblioteca de Babel', for example, Monegal suggests that the story 'contiene rasgos del trauma causado por el doble código lingüístico' (p. 29). It is one way of interpreting multiculturalism that may seem rather surprising bearing in mind that in the Buenos Aires of the first half of the twentieth century, cultural mix was the norm for a great number of families, as the result of mass immigration. Evidence of the creative possibilities opened by this experience appear very frequently in the Borgesian oeuvre and it is equally possible to offer positive interpretations of 'la discordia de sus dos linajes.'[61] Once again, this thread will be picked up in a more balanced analysis by Williamson. Considering the weight of Rodriguez Monegal's influence, especially on subsequent biographers, as we shall see below, it is fair to argue the critical importance of these pages in the construction of Borges as an incurable Anglophile.

Borges's bilingualism is related to another myth that Rodriguez Monegal's biography is instrumental in perpetuating: that of a bookish writer removed from the world. Monegal writes that 'desde el comienzo, el idioma inglés quedó

---

[60] 'Georgie se veía confrontado por el abismo cultural que separaba en su familia al lado paterno del materno [...] los dos bandos de su familia.' Rodríguez Monegal, *Borges*, p. 16.
[61] Borges, 'El sur', *OCI*, p. 524.

inseparablemente vinculado al placer de leer. Para Georgie, ése fue el código que le dio acceso al mundo de los libros.'[62] To depict the isolation that resulted from this bookishness, Monegal replaces the widely used metaphor of the ivory tower with the more Borgesian labyrinth. He does this, for example, in the section 'El habitante del laberinto', where he comes to the conclusion that 'al identificarse a sí mismo con el Minotauro, Georgie estaba allanando el camino a la futura mitología de Borges. En la época probablemente sintió [...] que él era un poco como Asterión' (p. 47). This image of Borges living in the world of books is built in this case through Rodríguez Monegal's methodology: he has taken the basic historical details of Borges's family, such as dates of birth, places of residence and he has put them together with the 'Autobiographical Essay' (published in *The New Yorker* in 1970).[63] To this basic recipe, he has added what he interprets to be the writer's references to his family in his creative work, and he has filled in the gaps with material taken from interviews and conversations. Crucially, however, it is the particular way in which these pieces are put together and combined with the biographer's analysis of the finished picture which achieves the construction of Borges as a writer in an ivory tower. This is illustrated by comments such as: 'la biblioteca se convirtió en su mundo' (p. 67) or, referring to Borges's prologue to *Evaristo Carriego*: 'allí contrasta el mundo de los libros con el mundo real que tenía tanta dificultad en dominar' (p. 67). The final paragraph of the biography leaves the reader with this particular image of Borges:

> Poco a poco Borges pasó a vivir dentro de un espacio mágico, totalmente vacío y gris, donde el tiempo no cuenta [...] Protegido y aislado por la ceguera, en un laberinto construido sólidamente por Madre, Borges se queda inmóvil [...] Todo en su derredor está quieto, excepto su imaginación [...] Anciano, ciego, frágil, Borges alcanza el centro solitario del laberinto. (pp. 436–37)

Beyond the text of the biography itself, this construction is reinforced by paratextual elements like the cover design, where the sadness and solitude predominant in Borges's life is illustrated by an effective juxtaposition of images (Fig. 1). On the front cover of the edition studied here, a black and white close-up photograph of Borges with an expression of sorrow has been reshaped in order to fit the convex surface of a fountain pen nib, with its tip dipped in what appears as red ink, although the brightness of the colour suggests it is blood. The signing of the name of Jorge Luis Borges on a surface that resembles the Argentine flag appears interrupted. The impression thus created is one of a suffering writer imprisoned inside a pen, bleeding through its tip as it inscribes his identity on to a symbol of 'Argentineness'. This conveys a sense of Borges's superiority with

---

[62] Rodríguez Monegal, *Borges*, p. 19.
[63] Rodríguez Monegal, *Borges*, pp. 464–71. Notably, the 'Autobiographical Essay' was published in English and edited and translated by Borges's American friend Norman Thomas Di Giovanni.

FIGURE 1. Emir Rodríguez Monegal, *Borges: Una biografía literaria*, trans. by Homero Alsina Thevenet (México: Fondo de Cultura Económica, 1993). Reproduced with permission of Fondo de Cultura Económica.

respect to his country (as he appears to have the authority to 'spell out' Argentine identity), and it gives the impression that his relationship with Argentina was forced and painful. Both the tight fit of the photograph within the nib and the deep, solid line of the frame, suggest a self-contained universe from which there is no easy escape. Thus, Rodríguez Monegal's agenda, namely to construct a mythical figure who inhabits a fictional world detached from the realities of his country and whose life can only be understood through the interpretation of his work, makes its first impact in the space of the paratext.

This is carried through to a further paratextual element: immediately after crossing the threshold of the cover, the reader is confronted by Rodríguez Monegal's dedication to Borges's fictional women: 'a todas las hermanas de Teodolina Villar y Beatriz Viterbo' (p. 7), accentuating the flavour of 'fictional factuality' of his narration of Borges's life, as it intersects with that of his characters. The body of the text itself consists of a great number of — in many cases extensive — quotations from Borges's vast oeuvre. The chronology of his life is linked to these quotations and it expands into a critical analysis, following the more or less regular pattern of fact-quotation-analysis-biographer's conjecture or conclusion. In terms of narrative technique, lexical choices such as 'museo', 'panteón', and 'mito', which abound in the first two sections of the biography, suggest the veneration of a past that has been constructed out of a selection of objects of memorabilia and oral accounts. Similarly, many of the section headings are akin to fiction, with an abundance of metaphors in some cases, such as 'Un espejo deformado ante la realidad', 'La pluma y la espada', for example. Indeed in many cases, they are more or less direct references to Borgesian tropes, as is the case of 'El habitante del laberinto', mentioned above, or 'La biblioteca infinita'.

The first chapter opens with a quote from *Evaristo Carriego* (1930), about the supposed origins of Borges's bookishness, and the well-known story of a young Georgie growing up in the library whilst the exciting life of the 'compadritos' went on on the other side of the spear-headed fence. It is interesting that Rodríguez Monegal chooses to start his literary biography by putting forward a fictional quote as evidence of what is generally perceived to be one of the writer's best-known traits. The words 'imaginario/a' and 'real' occur in the first paragraphs of the first chapter in equal measure, as if Rodríguez Monegal wanted to announce a certain awareness of the coexistence of both realms in Borges's perception of his own life: 'Borges [...] fue el habitante de un mundo imaginario creado por libros escritos en inglés, y también el de un mundo real, un barrio de Buenos Aires' (p. 9). As he turns his attention to Borges's ancestry, the poem 'Isidoro Acevedo' not only provides information about the warrior Acevedo, but also reminds the reader that the memory of Borges himself, which in any case is fictional, relies on 'fraudes de la palabra' (p. 9), that is, they are made up, narrated. That Acevedo 'died as a hero' comes not from historical documents, but from the poem. The most striking detail, the point at which fact and fiction blend, is the phrase 'El poema documenta' (p. 10): to what extent can poems document, one wonders. It is perhaps amusingly ironic in this context that among the verses that Rodríguez Monegal chooses to illustrate the hero's death, are: 'y la inventiva fiebre le falseó la cara del día, / congregó los ardientes documentos de su memoria / para fraguar su sueño' (p. 10).

The Spanish version of the biography concludes with the ultimate praise for Rodríguez Monegal himself: this comes in the shape of a postscript dated 1985, which reproduces a statement by Borges on occasion of *Jorge Luis Borges. A Literary Biography* being awarded the 1983 'Premio Comisso de Biografía Literaria':

> No conozco la biografía de Rodríguez Monegal. Sé que es un buen amigo y un excelente escritor. Sé que sus biografías no condescienden a trivialidades ni a conjeturas psicológicas. No he leído su libro porque el tema no me interesa o, quizá, porque me interesa demasiado.
> No me ha sometido nunca a interrogatorios. Tampoco a mis amigos. Ha ejecutado su obra a su modo. Éste es su mérito. (p. 443)

Although Borges claims not to have read the book, such a statement is invaluable as it lends the biography immense kudos. Rodríguez Monegal's inscription in his own work corroborates the idea posed by the 'genre' of literary biography itself: both the author-biographer and the author-biographed are vehemently put forward as legitimising forces of origin. Borges's words serve as a link to other biographies, in which the habit of making psychological conjectures has since been taken up by his former girlfriend Estela Canto, his good friend María Esther Vázquez, and more recently, Williamson, whose biography contains some strong elements of it. By juxtaposing words related to fact-finding ('no me ha sometido nunca a interrogatorios') and to artistic performance ('ejecutar'), Borges reinforces the idea that Rodríguez Monegal's account of his life is far from factual: like the word 'ejecutar' itself, it moves from the connotation of an act of extermination to that of an act of unique creation. Thus, Borges points out, instead of gathering documentary evidence or quoting from witness statements — as biographers would normally do, Rodríguez Monegal has constructed his own fiction of Borges in his own style. Rodríguez Monegal makes no apology, then, for 'writing, or inventing, a literary biography of Borges,'[64] and Borges's approval justifies his choice.

By virtue of having been introduced in the English and in the Spanish-speaking markets separately and at different times, Rodríguez Monegal's influence on other

---

[64] Emir Rodríguez Monegal, 'Borges and Derrida Apothecaries', originally published as 'Borges y Derrida boticarios' in *Maldoror*, 21 (1985), translated and reproduced in *Borges and his Successors: the Borgesian Impact on Literature and the Arts*, by Edna Aizenberg (Columbia: University of Missouri Press, 1990), pp. 128–38 (p. 128).

Borges biographers and scholars is vast, a comprehensive assessment of which exceeds the scope of this chapter. I will provide a few examples. In 1990, Borges expert Evelyn Fishburn includes Emir Rodríguez Monegal as an entry in her *Dictionary of Borges* (1990), where his *Literary Biography* is referred to as 'the best biography to date.'[65] In accordance with the Borgesian trope of a story within a story, Borges scholar Daniel Balderston cites a reference to Estela Canto in Rodríguez Monegal's *Literary Biography* in an article about Canto's *Borges a contraluz*, which, in turn, makes reference to Rodríguez Monegal, in 1996.[66] Subsequently, six other articles cite or refer to Rodríguez Monegal's biography in *Variaciones Borges* between 1997 and 2000.[67] In *Georgie* (1996), Argentine biographer and collector of Borgesiana, Alejandro Vaccaro comments on Rodríguez Monegal's excess of interpretation: 'Las conjeturas que lleva a cabo Emir Rodríguez Monegal en su biografía [...] no son otra cosa que una demostración más de lo excesivamente interpretativo que resulta su trabajo.'[68] However, the fact that he has studied the work closely shows in his careful refutations and corrections based on intensive documentary research.

María Esther Vázquez does the opposite: she chooses to concentrate on Rodríguez Monegal's interpretations and conjeturas in order to justify or legitimize her own. She refers to, rather than cites, Rodríguez Monegal, thus giving the impression that his solid influence and authority in the field are to be taken for granted. She also reproduces some of the rather loaded nicknames that Rodríguez Monegal created for Borges, such as 'El Gran Desconstructor' and 'anciano gurú', as well as carefully selected anecdotes which are reproduced in detail. One of these is the amusing story that tells of how Rodríguez Monegal fell for one of Borges's playful artifices: 'Borges juega con el lector, ya que ofrece bajo la engañosa apariencia de una crítica bibliográfica a una novela, [...] una pieza de ficción.'[69] Vázquez refers to the fictional *The Approach to Al-Mu'tasim*,[70] which Rodríguez Monegal 'pidió a una librería de Londres.'[71] This anecdote illustrates

---

[65] Evelyn Fishburn and Psiche Hughes, *A Dictionary of Borges* (London: Duckworth, 1990), p. 206. Rodríguez Monegal's is the only biography of Borges mentioned in this book.

[66] Daniel Balderston, "Beatriz Viterbo c'est moi': Angular Vision in Estela Canto's *Borges a Contraluz*', *Variaciones Borges*, 1 (1996), 133–39 (pp. 137–38).

[67] Sergio Pastormelo, 'Borges crítico', *Variaciones Borges*, 3 (1997), 6–16; Umberto Eco, 'Between La Mancha and Babel', *VB*, 4 (1997), 51–62; Fabiana Sabsay-Herrera, 'Para la prehistoria de H. Bustos Domecq', *VB*, 5 (1998), 106–22; Jorge Hernández Martín, 'Textual Polyphony and Skaz in *Seis problemas* by Bustos Domecq', *VB*, 6 (1998), 13–32; Juan Arana, 'Las primeras inquietudes filosóficas de Borges', *VB*, 7 (1999), 6–27 and Alfonso García Morales, 'Jorge Luis Borges, autor del *Martín Fierro*', *VB*, 10 (2000), 29–64.

[68] Alejandro Vaccaro, *Georgie, 1899–1930: Una vida de Jorge Luis Borges* (Buenos Aires: Editorial Proa/Alberto Casares, 1996), pp. 109–10.

[69] Vázquez, *Borges*, pp. 154–5.

[70] Jorge Luis Borges, 'El Acercamiento a Almotásim', *Historia de la Eternidad*, *OCI*, pp. 414–18.

[71] Vázquez, *Borges*, p 155.

Rodríguez Monegal's general conception of the blurred boundary between fact and fiction which characterizes his belief that Borges the man can be reached through his work. Vázquez devotes a whole section of her ninth chapter to herself, which opens with a severe complaint about the inaccuracy of Rodríguez Monegal's work concerning her personally, and the nature of her relationship with Borges. She takes Rodríguez Monegal as an almost absolute authority on Borges, but sets the limit where the exposure extends to her: 'Emir Rodríguez Monegal [...] comete varias inexactitudes que lamentablemente han sido repetidas por algunos biógrafos posteriores' (p. 255). More recently, Williamson lists Rodríguez Monegal's *Literary Biography* in his bibliography and cites a couple of anecdotes that appear in it, in his own *Borges: A Life* (2004).[72]

In his review of *Borges. A Literary Biography*, John King writes that Rodríguez Monegal's work 'could be subtitled, without much exaggeration, "Borges y yo".'[73] King remarks on how Rodríguez Monegal's own personal trajectory could be charted in his account of Borges's life: 'Just as the two histories run parallel and begin to overlap, so fiction and reality begin to blend'(p. 246). This review constitutes a very accurate description of the position Rodríguez Monegal assumes within his work: his autobiographical inscription and blending of fact and fiction, as this section demonstrated. The reception and extensive circulation of Rodríguez Monegal's work — which, as we have seen, is evident in a number of references in biographical and critical works — have contributed to the perpetuation of the construction of an Anglophile Borges who could be 'recognized and appreciated by only a few initiates'(p. 246), delineated by Jurado and renarrated by Rodríguez Monegal. Other biographers have also entwined their own life stories in their accounts of the life of Borges, constructing other, more intimate, Borgeses. As we shall see next, it is also the case of Estela Canto's *Borges a contraluz* (1989) and María Esther Vázquez's *Borges. Esplendor y derrota* (1996).

(iii) Estela Canto's Borges a contraluz *(1989)*

When Argentine writer, translator and committed communist Estela Canto met a middle-aged Borges, she maintains that he immediately fell in love with her. Their unusual, on and off, relationship spanned the decade between 1944 and 1955. This was also the first period of Peronist rule, a time of great emotional turmoil in the writer's life, according to Canto.[74] Canto draws her legitimization as biographer by putting herself forward as the ultimate Beatrice and thus taking

---

[72] See Williamson, *Borges*, pp. 342 and 371.
[73] John King, 'Review: Literary Biography in Argentina', *Latin American Research Review*, vol. 18, No. 1 (1983), 246–53 (p. 246).
[74] Williamson explores this psychological turmoil in *Borges*, p. 286.

the position of revealer of Borges-the-sexual-being, even though, as other biographers claim, Borges was infatuated with and loved many women. However, the uniqueness of Estela Canto's work, which is half-way between a biography and a memoir, lies in the open discussion of Borges's sexuality, from which Borges emerges as an impotent lover, so desperate and prone to suicide that he seeks the help of a psychoanalyst.

The cover of *Borges a contraluz* (Fig. 2) shows a classic black and white posed close-up of the writer deep in thought. He is an old, blind man and the photograph makes the viewer very aware of his unseeing eyes. As the next chapter explores, it is interesting that this particular image of the elderly writer was chosen to illustrate an account which pivots around a relationship that took place when he was middle-aged.[75] The shadow that falls on a portion of the profile evokes the title: 'a contraluz', which has been translated into English as 'in silhouette', bringing to mind the image of a lover standing by a window at night, giving a sense of intimacy, consistent with Canto's approach to her account. The blurb on the back cover presents it as 'el testimonio de los años más intensos de la relación entre ellos, las cartas de amor que él le escribiera, así como los comentarios sobre el texto que Borges estaba gestando en ese tiempo y que luego le dedicaría ['El Aleph'].'[76] The fact that this is a book as much about Estela Canto as it is about Borges is corroborated by her own assertion: 'Hablo aquí del Borges vivo, del hombre que conocí' (back cover).

The book presents important documentary evidence in the form of photographs and letters. The choice and use of these documents is creative and effective, and it serves a dual function: to inspire a certain aura of sacredness, and at the same time, to weave the author herself into the story she is telling. The letters are addressed to her in Borges's neat, regular handwriting and they all bear his signature. Treasured by Canto, these are testimonies of their love affair, which is ultimately the main subject of this book. The author is also generous with photographs from her personal collection, especially those which include her, for example, those in which she is taking leisurely walks with Borges in Buenos Aires, the backdrop to their affair. This is significant, as it reinforces the role of the writer's mother as censor, which Canto stresses was a significant element in relation to Borges as a sexual being. Estela Canto describes Leonor Acevedo's unavoidable presence in their relationship as unbearable, as Borges seemed incapable of standing up to her prejudices and traditional values. For example, Borges is alleged to have telephoned his mother every time he and Estela were

---

[75] This choice of cover photograph contrasts with the Brazilian edition *Borges à Contraluz* (São Paulo: Illuminuras, 1991), which bears the photograph of the couple which appears on page 214 of the edition considered here. This contrast between other images of Borges circulated in Argentina and abroad is examined in Chapter 2 of the present study.

[76] Estela Canto, *Borges a contraluz* (Madrid: Espasa Calpe, 1989), back cover.

FIGURE 2. Estela Canto, *Borges a contraluz* (Madrid: Espasa Calpe, 1989). Reproduced with permission of Grupo Planeta.

out, as his mother did not allow them to be alone in his apartment and would sit with them if Estela came to visit. Williamson later explores the relationship between Borges and his mother in his biography and links it to the conflict that he identifies as that of the sword and the dagger, or tradition versus desire.

Narrated mainly in the first person, *Borges a contraluz* is an obvious example of autobiographical inscription, where Borges is the other main character in the narration of Canto's own story. The book has no bibliography, no sources are cited — other than letters which are reproduced — and the only two or three footnotes are explanatory notes rather than references. There are a few quotations mainly from Borges's poetry, where Canto enjoys finding what she considers to be references to herself. The narration of the main events in the writer's life constitute the narration of a narration, as Canto relays mostly what she has heard, interspersed with passages written in a florid and grandiloquent style: 'Una cárcel infinita y cambiante como las olas, las formas que creemos idénticas repeticiones de otras formas, la extensión limitada por una geometría impuesta. Tenía que querer a su ciudad: no tenía nada más. Era el mandato' (p. 65).

In Canto's work the interweaving of the life of Borges the man and Borges the author with his work, together with his relationship with her, is bold and unapologetic: the reader is expected to believe the relationship narrated. Her literary analyses of various pieces by Borges reveal her position regarding authorship and her mimetic conception of literature. Among the stories that Canto analyzes are 'Funes el memorioso', 'El zahir', 'El Aleph', 'La escritura del dios' and 'La intrusa', which are also chapter headings in the biography. In her introduction, she announces that she will be revealing the various truths about Borges's character to which only she appears to hold the key:

> Borges ha dado las claves para penetrar en el laberinto que era su carácter. Una es *El Aleph*; otra, *El Zahír*; otra, *La escritura del dios*, que inventó una mañana que estábamos en el Jardín Zoológico, junto a una jaula [...] Hay otras claves [...] La clave de estas claves son dos o tres de las cartas que me escribió. (p. 13)

In attempting to place herself so close to the heart and mind of the author, Canto seems to be claiming her share in part of the creative process, thus merging her own autobiographical impulse with the writing of Borges's work itself, as she appears to imply that some of the most renowned texts would not have been written had it not been for her inspiring (omni)presence.[77] She not only considers the emotional being called Borges whom she knew the very core from which his work emanates, she also emphasises her position right next to that core. Following

---

[77] This is explored by Daniel Balderston in "*Beatriz Viterbo c'est moi*': Angular Vision in Estela Canto's *Borges a contraluz*', later published in Spanish in *Borges: Realidades y simulacros*. Subsequent references are to the Spanish version.

in Rodríguez Monegal's steps, her belief in the power of the texts to reveal the essence of the author dominates her interpretations:

> He elegido el cuento *Funes el Memorioso*, escrito por Borges antes de conocerme [...] Funes es una confesión, una imagen de la forma en que se veía a sí mismo [...] Hay aquí una especie de compasión que, sin querer, se le escapa al autor. En toda su literatura Borges cuida meticulosa, casi obsesivamente, que la compasión no asome.[78]

This analysis also perpetuates Alicia Jurado's claim that there is no passion in Borges's stories. The strength of this image can be surmised by the presence of the comment itself in a book which is all about passion.

Following Canto's death in 1994, an article in *La Nación* referred to her unashamed account of intimate details such as the lack of physicality of her relationship with Borges: 'Canto se atreve a emitir las opiniones más audaces, más sinceras y originales que se hayan publicado sobre su amigo.'[79] If Canto expected to come across as bold in her interrogation of the figure of a national 'monument' by bringing to the fore Borges as a sexual being, her book achieved its objective.[80] Daniel Balderston underlines the importance of this biography as he explores the question of Estela Canto's autobiographical impulse in 'Beatriz Viterbo *c'est moi*: Visión angular en *Borges a contraluz* de Estela Canto', and comes to the conclusion that 'su propio libro sin duda será visto en el futuro como una contribución mucho más significativa para la comprensión de Borges que el de Monegal.'[81] Later, Balderston again took up Canto's thread on Borges's sexuality in his article 'La "dialéctica fecal": pánico homosexual y el origen de la escritura en Borges', where he mentions that '[e]n su libro (1989) Canto ofrece un análisis fascinante de los enigmas de la sexualidad en Borges.'[82] The conclusions that Balderston comes to in this article are very different from Canto's. Nevertheless, it can be argued that Balderston's reference to her book indicates that she inaugurated a new era in the assessment of Borges's life story, as her psychological approach was later taken up, albeit in a different style, by Williamson more than a decade later.

The value of Canto's contribution lies in her challenging of the myth of Borges as detached from the world of experience, which accompanies the revision and

---

[78] Canto, *Borges*, pp. 161–62.
[79] *La Nación*, 3 June 1994. Cited in León Tenenbaum, *Buenos Aires, tiempo de Borges* (Buenos Aires: Ediciones turísticas, 2001), pp. 81–82.
[80] María Rosa Lojo, for example, refers to *Borges a contraluz* as 'libro polémico que se propuso, entre otros objetivos, develar penosas intimidades de su biografiado (como sus problemas afectivos y sexuales)' in 'Una mujer con vocación de rebeldía', *La Nación*, 11 August 1999, online at www.lanacion.com.ar/nota.asp?nota_id=214648 [last accessed 27 September 2013].
[81] Daniel Balderston, 'Beatriz Viterbo *c'est moi*', p. 115.
[82] Daniel Balderston, *El deseo, enorme cicatriz luminosa: ensayos sobre homosexualidades latinoamericanas* (Beatriz Viterbo Editora, 2004), note to p. 62, p. 75.

revalorization, in the 1990s, of Borges's youth. The extent of the impact of her work can be seen in Argentine director Javier Torre's decision to base his film *Un amor de Borges* (2000) on her book. The release of the film motivated various articles in the Argentine press about Canto and her 'interpretaciones desprejuiciadas sobre el autor de *Ficciones*.'[83] In *Borges: A Life* Williamson relies on *Borges a Contraluz* for his account of the relationship with Canto, which he considers pivotal at this stage of Borges's development both as a man and as a writer.[84] The fact that Borges dedicated 'El Aleph' to Canto, even though Williamson claims that it is a story about Norah Lange, places her in the role of Beatrice. Williamson bases his theory of Borges's quest for a muse that will allow him to write that page that will justify him as a writer on this allegory, which comes across very strongly in his biography.[85] Here, the figure of Beatrice condenses Borges's source of inspiration and his object of desire. In fact, Williamson chooses the title 'The New Beatrice' for the chapter in which he describes the writer's relationship with Canto. The fact that it studies closely *Borges a contraluz* speaks of the impact of her account in respect of Borges's sexuality.

Another significant aspect of Borges's life which Canto refers to in her biography is the importance of Buenos Aires, both as a backdrop to their relationship and as central to Borges's own life and oeuvre. In *Buenos Aires, tiempo de Borges* (2001), León Tenenbaum welcomes 'toda la información urbana que Estela Canto ofrece de sus paseos y encuentros con Borges y de las inclinaciones y preferencias de éste que registraría luego en sus obras' and he devotes a section of his book to her biography.[86] This focus on the writer's intimate experience of the city contributes to a change in the Borges image which gradually becomes less detached from his environment, both natural and emotional. Estela Canto's *Borges a Contraluz* plays an important part in this construction, of Borges as a national monument and an 'ordinary' man. The next section examines how it falls to another female biographer to continue this transition in the construction of Borges.

---

[83] Hugo Beccacece, 'Un personaje de película', *La Nación*, 5 September 2000, online at http://www.lanacion.com.ar/31672-un-personaje-de-pelicula. See also Julia Montesoro, 'Jean Pierre Noher es Borges enamorado', *La Nación*, 5 September 2000, online at www.lanacion.com.ar/nota.asp?nota_id=31673 [both last accessed 27 September 2013].
[84] Williamson, *Borges*, p. 519.
[85] See Williamson's chapter 'The New Beatrice', as above, pp. 275–90.
[86] León Tenenbaum, *Buenos Aires, tiempo de Borges* (Buenos Aires: Ediciones turísticas, 2001), p. 81.

(iv) María Esther Vázquez's Borges. Esplendor y derrota *(1996)*

A regular contributor in the national daily *La Nación*, Argentine writer María Esther Vázquez met Borges at the Biblioteca Nacional, when he was in his fifties, already an established and well respected writer. She worked and travelled with him and they had many friends in common. Rodrigo Fresán has pointed out that her book 'se inscribe en la serie de obras escritas por las-mujeres-que-supieron-frecuentar-a-Borges".'[87] In 1984 she wrote *Borges, sus días y su tiempo*, a biographical collection of interviews entwined with comments by Vázquez and prefaced by Borges himself, and which is referred to often in *Borges: Esplendor y derrota*, not only as a source of factual information, but also for the anecdotal contribution of the experience of writing.

The cover of *Borges: Esplendor y derrota* shows a smiling middle-aged Borges, a portrait which picks up the image of Alicia Jurado's Borges as warm-hearted and friendly (Indeed the photograph also appears in Alicia Jurado's biography, Fig. 3). It is quite an uncommon image, compared with the more widely circulated and therefore more familiar, image of a serious, gloomy Borges who is deep in thought. Unlike those, this photograph has no shadows: all brightness and liveliness, it suggests a gregarious, fun-loving Borges who appears to be enjoying a social occasion. This image, which is consistent with the description of Borges's personality that Vázquez offers in her biography, emphasises the contrast between the early, 'happy' Borges and the elderly 'defeated' Borges whose sad demise Vázquez mourns at the end of the book. In her review of *Borges. Esplendor y derrota*, Annick Louis refers to Borges in this photograph as 'erigido por la revolución libertadora en "escritor nacional" y nombrado director de la biblioteca, es feliz, y hasta ha embellecido.'[88] This emphasises an implicit alignment of Vázquez with Borges's, and Jurado's anti-Peronism. In terms of the layout of the biography itself, Vázquez's can be considered a precursor of the pictorialization of the Borges biography, a commercial decision that will be imitated in other items of biographical interest.[89] Apart from a great number of photographs from her personal collection, which attest to her friendship with the writer at the time of his greatest public exposure, her chapters are headed with images, as she approaches her story of Borges's life through a combination of image and text.

---

[87] Rodrigo Fresán, 'Una guía de las biografías de Borges escritas en la Argentina', *Página/12*, 16 January 2005, online at http://www.pagina12.com.ar/diario/suplementos/radar/subnotas/1953-296-2005-01-16.html [last accessed 27 September 2013].
[88] Annick Louis, 'Nota bibliográfica: María Esther Vázquez, *Borges. Esplendor y derrota*', *Variaciones Borges*, 2 (1996), 223–28 (p. 227).
[89] Consider, for example, *El factor Borges: Nueve ensayos ilustrados*, by Alan Pauls (Buenos Aires: Fondo de Cultura Económica, 2000); or *Borges: Una biografía en imágenes*, by Alejandro Vaccaro (Buenos Aires: Ediciones B, 2005).

FIGURE 3. Alicia Jurado, *Genio y Figura de Jorge Luis Borges* (Buenos Aires: EUDEBA, 1964), pp. 2–3. Reproduced with permission of EUDEBA. The same photograph was used in the cover design of María Esther Vázquez's *Borges: Esplendor y derrota*.

A degree of autobiographical inscription, as we have seen with the previous three biographies, is immediately apparent on the back cover of Vázquez's book: 'Este es el relato minucioso, matizado con novedosas y a veces polémicas anécdotas, sustentado a la vez por una sólida investigación, de una dilatada y privilegiada amistad: la que unió hasta el final a Vázquez con Borges.'[90] The friendship between biographer and subject legitimises the book, but it also links it, in the minds of Argentine readers, with Vázquez's continuing production as a writer and her presence in the press. This, in turn, reinforces her position as enemy of Borges's widow, María Kodama: consider, for example, articles such as

---

[90] Vázquez, *Borges*, back cover.

'Reeditarán una obra de Borges con Vázquez: El texto es de 1966 y será publicado por Emecé, luego de una disputa judicial entre Vázquez y Kodama.'[91] This antagonism is also later explored by Juan Gasparini in *La posesión póstuma* (2000), and perpetuated by Kodama's virulent reaction to Gasparini's book, which resulted in her taking legal action against him.[92] It is also clearly delineated in *Borges: Esplendor y derrota*, as we shall see.[93] The Borges presented by Vázquez is a victim of circumstances which lead him to a life that ends in defeat. Her book is summarized in its last lines:

> Borges triunfó y se vio envuelto en el esplendor de la fama, de los halagos, de los premios. Eso lo hizo feliz. Y, sin embargo, fue incapaz de lograr un amor entero en el momento adecuado.
> Más allá del esplendor, encontró la derrota.[94]

Vázquez's agenda is clearly to denounce what she perceives as the appropriation of Borges by the wrong people: her attack is on the figure of Borges's widow and heir María Kodama and her entourage, which she threads through the narration of Borges's life in terms of decline and fall, lamenting the loss of the great man. Shortly before his death in 1986, María Kodama and Borges were married in a ceremony in Paraguay in which the writer was not present due to ill health. The ceremony made Kodama Borges's most immediate relative. The wedding was perceived as Kodama's opportunism, even though Borges had already named her as his sole heir in his revised will in 1985. Vázquez's account of the wedding, for which she chooses the title 'Casamiento y muerte', shows how highly suspicious she was of Kodama and her motives. Here, Vázquez uses words such as 'sorpresivamente', 'insólitos' and 'rareza' to refer to the circumstances surrounding the marriage; and she ends the section by citing the opinion of Borges's sister, Norah, published in a French newspaper: 'La famille accepte ce malefice en silence, ce marriage a quelque chose de diabolique' (pp. 326–27). In *Borges: A Life*, Williamson refers to Vázquez's biography as he narrates her relationship with Borges, although her name does not appear in his acknowledgements. In a more nuanced analysis, Williamson considers that

---

[91] Juan Manuel Bordón, *Clarín*, 10 September 2008, online at http://edant.clarin.com/diario/2008/09/10/sociedad/s-01756834.htm [last accessed 27 September 2013].
[92] The result of the trial, after which Gasparini was found innocent of libel, and other instances of legal actions initiated by Kodama against other writers and journalists, were reported by the main newspapers, for example: Mariano Blejman, 'Un testamento que deja dudas', *Página/12*, 9 October 2004, online at www.pagina12.com.ar/diario/cultura/index-2004-10-09.html; or Ana Prieto, 'La viuda, la elegida, la guardiana', *Clarín*, 7 October 2006, online at www.clarin.com/suplementos/cultura/2006/10/07/u-01285316.htm [both last accessed 27 September 2013].
[93] Juan Gasparini, 'La otra María Kodama', *La posesión póstuma* (Madrid: Foca, 2000), pp. 14–32.
[94] Vázquez, *Borges*, p. 337.

Borges's latter years were greatly enriched by the love of Kodama, thus reversing Vázquez's 'decline and fall' storyline.

As a measure of Vázquez's reception and impact, I have mentioned her presence in the press, which I shall return to later, with regard to her comments on Williamson's *Borges: A Life*. Annick Louis believes that the contribution of Vázquez's biography lies in that it is 'una excelente exposición de los saberes que circulan actualmente en el círculo de adeptos a la obra del escritor.'[95] However, she regrets the image of a defeated, emotionally impoverished writer, which emerges in Vázquez's work and which Louis claims 'responde también a una concepción cultural y a una moda, ya que se inscribe en una tendencia actual del género biográfico: la de intentar descalificar a los grandes escritores a partir de su vida privada' (p. 228). In this sense, following in Canto's footsteps, the Borges constructed by Vázquez comes across as an 'ordinary' human being who is susceptible to emotional turmoil. At the same time, however, her theme of 'apogee and defeat' suggests a sense of historical significance, in the same way as ancient civilizations or movements are described in historical accounts. Thus, in these two biographies, Borges appears to be in transition from a national monument which stands above and beyond the realities of the nation, to a mere mortal who is vulnerable to emotional defeat. It is perhaps the interpretation of this transition, which, as Louis points out above, appears to some to be an attempt to lessen Borges's greatness that has earned Williamson some negative reviews, as we shall see in the next section.

(v) Edwin Williamson's Borges: A Life (2004)

Other biographies of Borges had already been written in English by foreigners, but none as controversial as Williamson's.[96] Its analysis of the Borgesian oeuvre pivots around the affective upheaval allegedly suffered by the writer in his relationships both familial and amorous. The biography revolves around two main metaphors: the sword of honour and the dagger of desire. Thus, Borges's quest for a definition of his identity and, consequently, of his position in terms of an object of desire, is referred to as the conflict between the sword and the dagger. Everything to do with the writer's mother, criollo values, civilization, tradition, control is represented by the sword; the rest is represented by the dagger: the father, barbarism, anarchism, the avant-garde, desire: 'he was creating a parallel between his inner conflict of sword and dagger and the quintessential Argentine conflict of "civilization" and "barbarism".'[97] In terms

---

[95] Louis, 'Nota bibliográfica', p. 226.
[96] James Woodall's *The Man in the Mirror of the Book* (1996) and Donald Yates's *Jorge Luis Borges: Life, Work and Criticism* (1985).
[97] Williamson, *Borges*, p. 211.

of his poetic voice, Williamson sees Borges's life as a quest for a unifying principle in the person of a woman who would love him. The Borgesian oeuvre is seen through this Dantean pattern, which takes Borges from failed relationship to failed relationship until he finally finds his true Beatrice in Kodama: 'The particular terms of this Dantean myth can be reconstructed from an array of allusions and symbols in Borges's writing' (p. 243). The Borges that emerges is a tortured soul whose life appears greatly influenced by family values. As a consequence, he struggles to form meaningful relationships, which, in Williamson's view, enhances the interest of his work. The undermining of a great mind by reference to these alleged inabilities has received more attention than the real strength of this biography, which is Williamson's analysis of the historico-political context of Borges's life and the author's engagement with it.

Following the Rodríguez Monegal tradition of literary biography, Williamson delves into the depths of Borges's oeuvre in search of clues about Borges the man, as announced in the blurb: 'By correlating this new biographical information with Borges's literary texts, Edwin Williamson reconstructs the dynamics of his inner world — the conflicts, desires and obsessions that drove the man and shaped his work' (front-cover flap). Consistent with his purpose of interpreting Borges's life story through the prism of his emotional life, the intertitles in Williamson's biography contain words denoting feelings, such as 'isolation' or 'false hopes'. Each of the five parts of the biography is headed by a title with a lyrical quality, with loaded references to the famous poetry of Rimbaud: 'A Season in Hell', for example. There is the plainly factual: 'Geneva (1914–1919)', as well as the more dramatic: 'The rule of Mother'. This has the effect of emphasizing the less than clear-cut boundary between fact and fiction while, at the same time, helping to carry the narrative forward.

The whole front cover of Williamson's book (Fig. 4) is a photo of Borges as an old blind man, with a faintly melancholic expression on his face. It is a posed picture, in which parts of his face and body are shadowed. He appears surrounded by solid, dark furniture, giving an impression of rigidity and seriousness. This image does not relate directly to the content of the biography: the reader finds a solitary old man surrounded by shadows where he or she would expect to see the image of a young man, possibly in love. The blurb contains carefully written, extended, generous praise, by highly respected and renowned writers and literary critics from various countries such as John Updike, Mario Vargas Llosa and Harold Bloom. Williamson finds himself in the uncomfortable position of a university critic tackling a 'lesser genre', as the academic community seem to be dismissive about biography-writing. In an interview published in *Clarín* in 2006, Williamson explains the mistrust by the academic world of the 'genre' of literary biography as based on the notion of 'biographical fallacy' expounded by American New Criticism in the 1940s and

FIGURE 4. Edwin Williamson, *Borges: A Life* (London: Viking Penguin, 2004). Reproduced with permission of Penguin Group.

1950s.[98] On the other hand, the fact that Williamson's work received praise from fiction writers and literary critics indicates the kind of erudite audience the biography did appeal to.

In contrast with the other four biographers studied here, Williamson is arguably an 'outsider' in relation to Borges insofar as he is neither a compatriot or a colleague or friend, and he did not know the writer personally. Thus, he enjoys a certain cultural distance from Borges's context. Approaching Borges as object of study, rather than writing about a personal relationship affords Williamson the advantage of critical distance. It could be argued, of course, that in comparison to the biographies mentioned above, he lacks the possibility of legitimising his work by positioning himself within the story. Furthermore, Williamson's long academic trajectory in the field of Spanish and Latin American Studies may have played against him in terms of the reception of his work particularly in Argentina. Crucially, Argentine reviews of his biography, which, at points, were unfavourable, have made *Borges: A Life* famously controversial. Alejandro Vaccaro dismisses Williamson's biography as written by 'este hombre de Escocia' who comes to 'decirnos cómo interpretar la vida de Borges.'[99] Writing in *Página/12*, Rodrigo Fresán flagrantly misspells the author's name and calls the biography a travel guide which he considers unnecessary for Argentines.[100] These comments, I argue, constitute a valuable indicator of a certain Argentine possessiveness of Borges as a 'national treasure', rather than of the quality of Williamson's work.

Reviews in the Argentine media refer to Williamson as 'catedrático de Oxford', or, simply, as 'académico inglés' or 'catedrático escocés', which makes him even more alien and less entitled to an opinion of the local writer. This goes against a certain Argentine snobbish preference for all things British, and dismisses the (perhaps unrealistic) expectation of an erudite work capable of revealing a truth that is only reserved to the very few. This may be the reason for the disappointment expressed in the negative reviews, which found the biography to be lacking in insight of the deepest nuances of Borges's work in the Argentine

---

[98] 'Todavía hay una desconfianza en el género de la biografía literaria entre muchos críticos universitarios, algo que los críticos norteamericanos de los años 40 y 50 llamaron la *falacia biográfica*.' Matías Repar, 'A Borges le incomodaba su reputación de escritor frígido', *Clarín*, 13 May 2006, online at www.Clarin.com/diario/2006/05/13/sociedad/s-06201.htm [last accessed 27 September 2013].

[99] Alejandro Vaccaro, 'Un trabajo bochornoso', *Clarín*, 13 May 2006, online at http://edant.clarin.com/diario/2006/05/13/sociedad/s-06201.htm [last accessed 27 September 2013].

[100] 'Un libro correcto y funcional y pertinente para el lector en inglés, pero por completo innecesario para nosotros [...] está más cerca de la guía de turismo que del mapa del tesoro.' Rodrigo Fresán, 'No-Ficciones', *Página/12*, 16 January 2005, online at www.pagina12.com.ar/diario/suplementos/radar/9-1953-2005-01-16.html [last accessed 27 September 2013].

context.[101] This is rather surprising, given that Williamson's can be considered one of the most comprehensive studies of the historico-political context of Borges's life. At the same time, however, Williamson's work seems to have touched a nationalistic nerve and triggered a certain national pride and protectiveness of Borges as an Argentine icon, that is, the success story that makes all Argentines winners.[102]

In a letter to the editor of *La Nación*, María Esther Vázquez complains of Williamson's contrivance of a fantasy love life for Borges, offers corrections — some of which are based on her own take on the author's life — and closes with: 'Lo que natura no da, Oxford no presta,'[103] which is a very clear stab at the marketing of Williamson as a prestigious academic. Three days later, another letter appeared, by Edgardo Krebs, who points out what he considers to be errors of interpretation, fact and custom, referring to Williamson as a foreigner and condemning his Freudian analysis.[104] Williamson defends himself addressing his reply to both critics and duly justifying his choice of facts by his intensive and thorough research, and urging readers to read his book in order to make up their own minds. He explicitly rejects that his was a 'Freudian analysis' and explains that what he has tried to do is 'situar ciertos símbolos poéticos […] en un contexto de experiencia personal para así poder llegar a un sentido de la dinámica del mundo interior del escritor,' which he claims, is 'tarea propia de un biógrafo literario.'[105]

Other reviews remark on what I believe is the most valuable contribution of Williamson's work to the field of Borges studies, which is the appropriately clear and concise analysis of the historical and political context of Borges's life and work. The paramount importance of this careful study of the various relevant moments in Argentine history is that it seriously undermines the existing myths of Borges as a writer in an ivory tower, and places him, quite clearly, in the position of a relatively more *engagé* writer. This image of an impassioned Borges, both as a writer and as a politicised young man, comes across in one of Williamson's public discussions of the author in a BBC radio programme in

---

[101] Edgardo Krebs, 'Borges en inglés: problema de traducción', *La Nación*, 14 November 2004, online at www.lanacion.com.ar/nota.asp?nota_id=653713 [last accessed 27 September 2013].
[102] This particular construction of Borges as internationally recognized success-story is examined in further detail in Chapter 2.
[103] María Esther Vázquez, 'Los amores de Borges', Cartas de lectores, *La Nación*, 16 October 2004, online at www.lanacion.com.ar/nota.asp?nota_id=645355 [last accessed 27 September 2013].
[104] Edgardo Krebs, 'Borges', Cartas de lectores, *La Nación*, 19 October 2004, online at www.lanacion. com.ar/nota .asp?nota_id=646152 [last accessed 27 September 2013].
[105] Edwin Williamson, 'Los amores de Borges', 'Cartas de lectores', *La Nación*, 31 October 2004, online at www. lanacion.com.ar/nota.asp?nota_id=649821 [last accessed 27 September 2013].

January 2007, in which he said that Borges 'has a reputation of being a political conservative. In fact, nothing could be further from the truth.'[106] As presenter Melvyn Bragg pressed him on Borges's support of military regimes in Argentina, Chile and Spain, Williamson insisted that 'you have to see that in the context of his whole political development, in fact, Borges [...] saw himself as a public intellectual' who, in 'every major juncture in Argentine history [...] took a public position.'[107] These comments aptly summarize his depiction of the writer in *Borges: A Life*, which includes, for example, the detailed portrayal of a politicised young Borges who espoused what Williamson terms 'democratic *criollismo*' and who played an important role in Hipólito Irigoyen's reelection campaign in 1928.[108] The possibility of this reappraisal of Borges is due to Williamson's cultural distance, which allows him to achieve a certain objectivity that may not have been available to Argentine biographers, thus reinforcing the significant influence of the historical and political context in which those biographies were written.

Borges: A Life has been widely cited in many of the articles that appear in *Variaciones Borges*, and it has been in the international public eye, probably more than any other work on Borges of its type. In the case of Argentina, crucially, the reception of *Borges: A Life* is a valuable tool for the evaluation of the central role of the figure of Borges as cultural signifier: the protectiveness expressed by the various Borges specialists mentioned above speaks of the strength of the writer as a protected national treasure.

Conclusion

The purpose of this chapter was to demonstrate that what are generally perceived to be truths revealed in biographies are actually a set of constructs. The comparative analysis of the five biographies considered, and the different cultural and historical contexts of their production show that each of these biographies constructs a Borges that responds to a set of discourses prevalent at that time.

The journey from the two pioneering works, Alicia Jurado's *Genio y Figura de Jorge Luis Borges* and Emir Rodríguez Monegal's *Borges. Una Biografía Literaria*, through Estela Canto's *Borges a Contraluz*, María Esther Vázquez's *Borges. Esplendor y Derrota* to Edwin Williamson's *Borges: A Life*, allows us to trace the

---

[106] Williamson takes part in a discussion of Borges with presenter Melvyn Bragg, Evelyn Fishburn and Efraín Kristal, in 'Jorge Luis Borges', *In Our Time with Melvyn Bragg*, BBC Radio 4, 04 January 2007, online at http://www.bbc.co.uk/programmes/b0076182 [last accessed 27 September 2013], 36′26″–36′32″.
[107] Williamson, *In Our Time*, 36′35″–37′01″.
[108] Consider, for example, Williamson's 'Revenge and Defeat' and 'A New Dawn in Iceland', in *Borges*, pp. 160–74 and pp. 416–27, respectively.

changing face of Jorge Luis Borges. But, perhaps most tellingly, this survey of the agendas and motivations behind the construction of different images of the writer, allows us to form a picture of the context behind them. Jurado's conservative Borges responds to the political debates going on in the 1960s. It reveals the emerging reconfiguration of Argentina and the insertion, after the last large wave of immigration of the early twentieth century, of first generation Argentines in the institutional, cultural and political life of the country. It was also written as a reaction to the rise of Peronism. Rodríguez Monegal's depiction of the old wise man inhabiting his own fictional labyrinth perpetuates Jurado's image of the elitist writer and extends his reputation as an Anglophile. Perhaps this is a result of Rodríguez Monegal's own positioning within North American academia and the debates surrounding the idea of popular culture as opposed to high culture. Estela Canto introduces the idea of a sexual Borges, which Williamson then explores in greater depth. María Esther Vázquez is a good example of appropriation of the 'national writer' and it epitomizes Argentine reaction to his death in Geneva, finding someone to blame in the figure of María Kodama. I believe that after Vázquez, a less antagonistic image of Borges emerges, one that it is possible to reappropriate differently, as I demonstrate in the last two chapters. With its in-depth analysis of a more politicized Borges, Williamson's biography is a sign of its times: the old myths can now be set aside to approach Borges in a more moderate way.

An appraisal of the reception of these five biographies provides a sense of the extent of the circulation of the constructions of Borges within Argentina and in academic circles internationally, through coverage in the Argentine media and citations in relevant academic publications. It also corroborates Genette's notion of the power of the paratext as mediator of our experience of both Borges's oeuvre and the biographies themselves.

The next chapter continues the examination of the making of Borges as an icon considering its visual aspect. There follows a more detailed exploration of the particular cultural and historical contexts and the commercial, political and media discourses that constructed the author throughout the 1960s, 1970s and 1980s in order to study closely the motivations for the parallel processes of development of an Argentine cultural identity through that of the literary icon.

CHAPTER 2

Portrait of the Artist as an Old Man: Images of Borges

Introduction

> detrás del rostro que
> nos mira no hay nadie.
> Anverso sin reverso
>
> Jorge Luis Borges, 'Cambridge'

'Si ... lo dice' is a formula that is often completed by '... es palabra santa,' a phrase mostly used to suggest that the words of whoever has spoken are to be taken as gospel. 'Si Borges lo dice' was the phrase chosen as a title for an article published in *Somos* magazine (Fig. 5) in 1982 about the recent publication of *Borges el memorioso*, a book containing a selection of conversations between the writer and the famous radio presenter Antonio Carrizo which had been broadcast in 1979.[1] This is only one of several books of this type in existence, which is testimony to the great number of radio interviews that Borges gave in his later life.[2] The photograph that precedes the article in *Somos* takes up three-quarters of the page and shows Borges surrounded by books. The elderly writer appears dignified, impeccably dressed in a suit and tie, with his hands resting on his now iconic walking-stick. The juxtaposition of the image of the elderly writer, the old books and the title creates the semblance of a figure of authority whose words are to be taken as sacred. Furthermore, the angle from which the photograph is taken, which places the viewer slightly beneath the subject, together with the fact that

---

[1] *Borges el memorioso: Conversaciones de Jorge Luis Borges con Antonio Carrizo* (Mexico and Buenos Aires: Fondo de Cultura Económica, 1982). The original interviews were broadcast as part of the programme 'La vida y el canto' which for many decades aired in Buenos Aires's commercial Radio Rivadavia between 12 and 3.30 pm.

[2] Consider, for example, Jorge Luis Borges and Osvaldo Ferrari, *Borges en diálogo* (Buenos Aires: Sudamericana, 1985), which contains interviews broadcast by state radio Radio Municipal de Buenos Aires.

FIGURE 5. 'Si Borges lo dice', *Revista Somos*, 10 September 1982, p. 2. Image courtesy of Archivo del diario *Clarín*. Reproduced by permission.

Borges's unseeing gaze seems lost outside the frame of the image, contribute to producing a sense that one is in the presence of a figure worthy of veneration. This type of image is the one that instantly comes to mind whenever the name of Borges is mentioned: it is the purpose of this chapter to examine what has made it iconic.

The image of Borges in old age, which circulated in the 1960s, 1970s and early 1980s, perpetuated the notion of the writer as an old man, with an emphasis on his blindness to create the figure of a venerable sage who inhabits a realm that is detached from that of the nation's reality. This made this image into an object of 'cultural worship', a national cultural treasure which could potentially remain unchanged over the generations, offering solidity to the ideal of a traditional Argentine culture. This process runs parallel to the development of the Borges image in biographical accounts analysed in the previous chapter.

I will examine the motivations behind the construction of the author as a national 'cultural treasure' by exploring the mechanisms whereby the image of the writer has been detached from its merely representational nature in order to become a mirror, a repository for desires and expectations associated with the quest for Argentina's cultural identity. It could be argued, in this sense, that Argentine culture takes up the space previously occupied by the 'original', historical man in order to become the general referent of the cultural icon. I will begin with a delineation of the concept of icon and its relationship with some of the main issues related with portraiture and photography. I will then proceed with a brief examination of the role of images in the construction of identity in Borges's work. A summary of the ideas underlying my analysis of photographic images of Borges between the 1960s and the early 1980s in Argentina will follow. I will then examine a selection of portraits of the author on the covers of books in order to plot the development and perpetuation of the image of Borges as an old man, which dominates the imaginary of Argentine consumers. I will also consider the efforts to challenge the predominance of the image of Borges as an old blind sage around the time of his centenary in 1999, and comment on what such efforts actually achieved. The points discussed will provide a framework for the assessment of the writer's relationship with the Argentine media and the latter's role in the construction and, most relevantly, the perpetuation of his image during the last twenty-five years of his life. I shall then refer to portraits taken by two photographers from the U.S.A. in order to show, by contrast, that the main motivations behind the construction of the author as an old blind sage by Argentine photographers appear to be culturally specific to Argentina.

The focus of this chapter is on photographic portraits of Borges: it studies the impact and effect of the circulation, primarily, of posed photographs where the writer's upper body and particularly his face constitute the focal point. This type of image has been the publishers' preferred choice for book covers — again, a connection to the study of the biographies.[3] The appearance of a writer's portrait on a book cover — be it a book written by him or about him — symbolizes a direct connection between the man and his work.[4] Also, as we shall see, the impact of the iconic face of Borges can be compared to that of Hollywood stars, and this is further corroborated by the distortions of the writer's physiognomy

---

[3] It is pertinent to underline, at this point, that, as David Ellis points out, even though 'the initial assumption of biographers is that photographs will illustrate their text,' the 'relationship between words and images is seldom that simple,' as the decision actually lies with the publisher and is largely based on economic factors. David Ellis, 'Images of D.H. Lawrence: On the Use of Photographs in Biography', in Graham Clarke (ed.), *The Portrait in Photography* (London: Reaktion Books, 1992), p. 155.

[4] I refer here to the book as an object to which symbolic value and meaning are attributed: as part of its paratext, the image of the writer affects the reader's preconceptions about the content, in this case, the immediate association with the idea of the old blind sage that appears on the cover.

achieved by the particularly powerful expressiveness of a series of caricatures that have been based on his portraits. These cartoons have appeared in a variety of memorabilia and merchandise, such as stamps and bookshop carrier bags. Most significantly, and consistent with Robert Hariman and John Lucaites's analysis of iconic photographs,[5] they have constituted a form of appropriation of the image of Borges that particularly links politics and popular culture in Argentine comic strips produced in the 1980s, which the next chapter analyses.

The concept of 'icon' that this study, and particularly this chapter are based upon draws from a variety of sources: portraiture in general and portrait photography in particular, and film studies. Related to these practices are issues of subjectivity and cultural processes of signification which have been the concern of contemporary philosophy, sociology and cultural theory. Thus, my definition of 'icon' incorporates Barthes's early considerations of cultural products as 'myths', that is, the process of mythification understood as the construction of a powerful narrative which condenses a variety of socially significant meanings.[6] However, even though 'icon' and 'myth' have been used as synonymous, I do not consider them to be so.[7] Instead, I argue that the icon condenses (literally makes 'portable' and easily repeatable) the meanings that the myth narrates. The next two sections consider the main issues related to portraiture which are relevant to this chapter and provide a more detailed definition of the concept of icon.

Portraiture: Representation, 'Realism' and Subjectivity

Portraiture, understood as the 'delineation of a person, especially of the face, made from life, by drawing, painting, photography, engraving'[8] or the 'deliberate replication of a singular image for wide public distribution,'[9] is a practice that extends as far back as the ancient world.[10] This linking of pictorial representation of a subject with the intention of wide circulation yields, as Shearer West suggests, a rich array of engagements with social, psychological, and artistic practices and expectations.[11] Catherine Soussloff also underlines the notable adherence to

---

[5] Robert Hariman and John Louis Lucaites, *No Caption Needed: Iconic Photographs, Public Culture, and Liberal Democracy* (Chicago and London: The University of Chicago Press, 2007), pp. 5-6. Hariman and Lucaites concentrate on iconic images as a form of public art in the US.
[6] Roland Barthes, *Mythologies*, sel. and trans. by Annette Lavers (London: Vintage, 1993).
[7] Juan José Sebreli, for example, uses 'mito' and 'ícono' (as well as 'ídolo') as synonyms in *Comediantes y Mártires: Ensayo contra los mitos* (Buenos Aires: Debate, 2008).
[8] Shearer West, *Portraiture* (Oxford: OUP, 2004), p. 11.
[9] Richard Brilliant, *Portraiture* (London: Reaktion Books, 1991) p. 47.
[10] Brilliant mentions instances in Ancient Egypt and Imperial Rome in *Portraiture*, p. 47, and West refers to ancient Peru in *Portraiture*, p. 13.
[11] West, *Portraiture*, p. 11.

portraiture of issues of identity in art, as resemblance and desire lie at the core of processes of recognition between viewers of the portrait, the artist, and the subject.[12] With the advent of photography in the nineteenth century, soon followed by its industrialization, the issues surrounding artistic representation in portraiture were further complicated by mechanization and mass reproduction.[13] The photographic portrait in particular, as Graham Clark underlines, 'for all its literal realism [...] denotes, above all, the problematics of identity, and exists within a series of cultural codes.'[14]

The notion of 'literal realism' associated with photographs stems from its 'indexicality', that is the presence of the subject photographed in the image.[15] As a practice which is predominantly a form of documentation, photography has motivated debates surrounding the question of mimetic 'truth' or 'likeness' that are still ongoing today. Semioticians like Umberto Eco have discussed iconicity and indexicality to refer to the different types of relationship between the image and the thing or person it depicts.[16] The discussions of the varying degrees of 'reality' or 'veracity' in photography in Roland Barthes's *Camera Lucida* (1980) and Susan Sontag's *On Photography* (1977) are well-known.[17] In *Symbolic Exchange and Death* (1976), Jean Baudrillard talked of 'hyperreality' in relation to the floundering of 'reality' as a consequence of endless repetition by media such as photography.[18] It is also worth highlighting Pierre Bourdieu's exploration of photography as an eminently social practice which is structured and systematic in *Photography: A Middle Brow Art* (1965). In it, Bourdieu argued that it is naïve to believe that photographs are a direct representation of the real as this 'is only ever conveyed through socially conditioned forms of perception' and it owes its

---

[12] Catherine M. Soussloff, *The Subject in Art: Portraiture and the Birth of the Modern* (Durham: Duke University Press, 2006), p. 83.
[13] For an early exploration of these issues see Walter Benjamin's 'Kleine Geschichte der Photografie' (1931), where the discussions surrounding the 'aura' and reproducibility of a work of art, later developed in his seminal *The Work of Art in the Age of Mechanical Reproduction* (1936), were first introduced. Walter Benjamin, 'A Small History of Photography', in *One-Way Street and Other Writings*, trans. by Edmund Jephcott and Kingsly Shorter (London: Verso, 1978). For an exploration of the intersections of writing, the 'aura' and photography in Benjamin, see Carolin Duttlinger, 'Imaginary Encounters: Walter Benjamin and the Aura of Photography' in *Poetics Today*, 29:1 (Spring 2008), 79–101.
[14] Clarke, *The Portrait in Photography*, p. 4.
[15] Indexicality is a notion first developed as part of the triadic conception of the sign and the sign-function by semiotician Charles Sanders Peirce in the first half of the twentieth century. It refers to a material relationship between a sign and what it represents.
[16] See, for example, Umberto Eco, *A Theory of Semiotics* (Bloomington: Indiana University Press, 1979).
[17] Roland Barthes, *Camera Lucida: Reflections on Photography*, trans. by Richard Howard (London: Vintage, 2000); Susan Sontag, *On Photography* (London: Penguin, 1979).
[18] Jean Baudrillard, *Symbolic Exchange and Death*, trans. by Iain Hamilton Grant (London: Sage, 1993), p. 71.

objective appearance to 'conformity with rules which define its syntax within its social use.'[19]

Bearing in mind the complexity and ramifications of the various debates surrounding portrait photography, I would like to concentrate on the relationship between the image and the viewer, that is, on the culturally determined transaction that takes place as the photographic image of Borges is consumed by Argentines and how this transaction constructs the writer as an icon.

From Image to Icon: Borges as *chora*

In 'The Face of Garbo' (1955), Barthes wrote about the impact of the close-up image of the famous Hollywood star, describing Garbo's face as a mask.[20] Cultural critic Kobena Mercer later enhanced this analysis by defining the face of a star as a space of social inscription, an 'aesthetic surface where society writes large its own preoccupations.'[21] Following on from Richard Dyer's work on stardom in the late 1970s,[22] Christine Gledhill later explained the cultural relevance of a star as a social signifier which expresses the intimacies of individual personality, inviting desire and identification while it conveys cultural meanings and ideological values.[23] I argue that, inasmuch as Borges has become an 'industrial marketing device' and 'an emblem of national celebrity' (Gledhill), Borges's iconicity is akin to that of stardom. In this context, the most significant trait that iconic figures from other cultural fields share with film stars is the role of their physiognomy as a 'screen face'. This face thus constitutes the locus of viewers' projected ideas and fantasies, a 'screen within a screen'.[24]

This concept of a famous face as a surface onto which certain ideas and feelings are 'reinscribed' has its origin in early Christian icons.[25] Catherine Sousloff refers

---

[19] Pierre Bourdieu, 'The Social Definition of Photography', in *Photography: A Middle Brow Art*, trans. by Shaun Whiteside (Stanford: Stanford University Press, 1990), p. 77
[20] Roland Barthes, 'The Face of Garbo', in Susan Sontag (ed.), *A Roland Barthes Reader* (London: Vintage, 1993), pp. 82–84.
[21] Kobena Mercer, 'Monster Metaphors: Notes on Michael Jackson's *Thriller*', in Julia Thomas (ed.), *Reading Images* (New York: Palgrave, 2001), p. 31.
[22] See Richard Dyer, *Stars* (London: British Film Institute, 1979).
[23] Christine Gledhill (ed.), *Stardom, Industry of Desire*, (Abingdon: Routledge, 1991), p xiii.
[24] Brian Gallagher, 'Greta Garbo is Sad: Some Historical Reflections on the Paradoxes of Stardom in the American Film Industry, 1910–1960', in *Images: A Journal of Film and Popular Culture*, 3 (Spring 1997), online at www.imagesjournal.com/issue03/infocus/stars5.htm [last accessed 27 September 2013]. It is important to bear in mind that, as Richard Dyer argues, 'star images are always extensive, multimedia, intertextual' and they are 'produced by the media industries.' Richard Dyer, *Film Stars and Society* (London: Routledge, 2004), pp. 3–4.
[25] Sousloff argues that 'the portrait more clearly than any other genre of representation elicits the question of who it reinscribes, more emphatically than any other kind of image', in *The Subject in Art*, p. 3.

to 'icon' as a 'foundational mimetic image,' which goes beyond portraying or narrating by being itself 'in the deepest theological sense holy' (p. 10). This aspect of religiosity is one of the core components of the iconic image of Borges. For centuries (since the early Byzantine icons), the icon has been conceived not as the representation of a physical God, but that of immanence itself. Sousloff cites as an example a medieval icon in a church in Istanbul, which bears an inscription describing it as *chora*. This significant word, meaning 'land, space or container' (p. 11), has also been interpreted as 'receptacle' and 'imprint-bearer' in contemporary studies of space by French thinkers.[26] The notion of icon that I apply to Borges brings together the ancient religiosity (and its accompanying veneration) associated with early Christian icons and the highly socially symbolic nature of stardom which is so current. These two concepts have in common a sense of 'chora', as both film stars and religious images constitute receptacles for the projection of their viewers' (worshippers') impressions and desires. In Sousloff's words, 'the icon demonstrates most clearly how the history of portraiture necessarily entails a viewer who projects his otherwise invisible God, onto or into the portrait, yet [...] the believer also inevitably projects himself onto the image' (p. 11).

According to Sousloff, the genealogy of the modern subject in visual representation can be traced back to the so-called Vienna school of artists and historians in the first years of the twentieth century. The Viennese art historians delivered the 'alternative to naming the subject in the portrait [...]: when I see another represented in the portrait I see my social context and myself, including my history,' thus laying the foundations for the later development of a more complex theory of the modern subject by Continental philosophy and Lacanian psychoanalysis.[27] This is in contrast with the notion of resemblance as indexical, as the significance of the portrait goes beyond mere reproduction of an exterior reality. Sousloff refers to this 'excess to resemblance' as iconic, as it 'resides in the projection of interiority onto the depicted person' (p. 8).

This is a function of the gaze, which is one of psychoanalytic theory's main contributions to photography criticism. It lies behind the particularly powerful role of photographic images in the construction and reaffirmation of a sense of identity.[28] For Psychoanalysis, Liz Wells explains, 'images offer fantasy resolutions for subjective angst' by offering points of identification.[29] These points of

---

[26] For a discussion of the use of '*chora*' in contemporary French philosophy, particularly its definition as 'receptacle' and 'imprint-bearer', see Elizabeth Grosz, *Space, Time and Perversion* (London and New York: Routledge, 1995).
[27] Soussloff, *The Subject in Art*, p. 3.
[28] Derrick Price and Liz Wells, 'Thinking about Photography', in Liz Wells (ed.), *Photography: A Critical Introduction* (London and New York: Routledge, 2005), pp. 9–63 (p. 36).
[29] Liz Wells, 'On and Beyond the White Walls: Photography as Art', *Photography*, pp. 245–94 (pp. 282–83).

identification include properties or attributes of the seen other, which are assimilated in order to be 'transformed, wholly or partially, after the model which the other' provides (p. 282). Thus, the Argentine gaze (as constituted by a collective of more or less consistent trends which is in constant resignification) seeks in the image of Borges traits which can offer a delineation of a cultural identity. It can be argued that these 'model' elements that his image offers to effect this identification are knowledge and stability.

Consistent with Bourdieu's analysis, Price and Wells point out that images are 'embedded in particular cultural circumstances and therefore reflect specific assumptions and expectations.'[30] In this sense, Hariman and Lucaites defined iconic images as those '*appearing in print, electronic, or digital media that are widely recognized and remembered, [...] activate strong emotional identification or response, and are reproduced across a range of media, genres, or topics.*'[31] Their study, which focuses on photojournalistic images, binds iconicity with historical significance, which is another major component of the definition of Borges as icon. Thus, in the Argentine context, with its fragmented and unclear genealogy (Pons), the author is constructed as historically and culturally coherent and stable.[32]

The iconic image of Borges constitutes the locus for the condensation of a variety of meanings related to national identity: partly a mythical, sacred narrative, which exists outside time and partly a surface for the projection of cultural anxieties in constant evolution. The analysis of 'visual methods of communication'[33] on which this chapter pivots is based on the aspects of visual discourse discussed above and the way in which these relate to one another. Most relevantly, however, the making of Borges as an icon cannot be considered independently from the context of the historical development of Argentina, particularly in the 1960s, 1970s and early 1980s, as the construction of Borges as a venerable old man responds to the discursive practices prevalent at the time. This period is marked by a dislocated sense of identity and disorientation caused by constant change and uncertainty. In this sense, Hariman and Lucaites explain, 'the iconic photograph acquires public appeal and normative power as it provides embodied depictions of important abstractions operative within the public discourse of a historical period.'[34] The following analysis of a selection of Borgesian texts demonstrates the importance of these issues, where history and iconicity converge, throughout his oeuvre.

---

[30] Price and Wells, 'Thinking', p. 35.
[31] Hariman and Lucaites, *No Caption Needed*, p. 27, italics in the original.
[32] Pons, 'El mito', pp. 20–21.
[33] Derrick Price and Liz Wells, 'Thinking about photography', in *Photography: A Critical Introduction*, by Liz Wells (London and New York: Routledge, 2005), pp. 9–63 (p. 35).
[34] Hariman and Lucaites, *No Caption Needed*, pp. 198–9.

'*Vi interminables ojos inmediatos escrutándose en mí como en un espejo*':[35]
Image and Identity in Borges

I will refer to five texts written by Borges at various stages of his literary career in order to illustrate his strong conception of visual images as fundamental to the construction of a narrative when defining individual and national identity. These are 'El Aleph' (1945), 'L'Illusion Comique' (1955), 'El simulacro' (1960), 'Cambridge' (1969) and 'Utopía de un hombre que está cansado' (1975). I will subsequently connect these ideas with the construction of the image of the writer himself in photographs.

One of Borges's best-known stories, 'El Aleph' explores the visual quality of the construction of identity and the ineffability of seeing — and therefore knowing — everything. Even before considering the fantastic visions conjured up by the magical object called the 'Aleph' in a darkroom/cellar, Borges manages to evoke vivid pictures of characters and places which leave an unforgettable trace in the reader's mind. The story opens with the poignancy of an absence, which is first manifest in the changing of a billboard, as the world moves on without Beatriz Viterbo, recently deceased. As part of his grieving process, the protagonist — named Borges — feels the need to seek out his beloved in the materiality of her photographs and he decides to continue with his customary visits to her house. This, to him, now represents the pantheon of her memories, where he can almost touch her and possess her with his gaze (the only way that is now available to him). Borges is shown into an anteroom, where he waits to see Beatriz's cousin, Carlos Argentino Daneri. Here, he can appropriate Beatriz's image, the narrative of her life strung together in a capricious photographic montage:

> De nuevo estudiaría las circunstancias de sus muchos retratos. Beatriz Viterbo, de perfil, en colores; Beatriz, con antifaz, en los carnavales de 1921; la primera comunión de Beatriz; Beatriz, el día de su boda con Roberto Alessandri; Beatriz, poco después del divorcio, en un almuerzo del Club Hípico; Beatriz, en Quilmes, con Delia San Marco Porcel y Carlos Argentino; Beatriz con el pekinés que le regaló Villegas Haedo; Beatriz, de frente y de tres cuartos, sonriendo, con la mano en el mentón. (p. 617)

A story reminiscent of the Dantean descent into hell, 'El Aleph' also reminds us of the Sartrean idea that hell is other people. In it, Daneri, who is also a writer, invites Borges to descend to the cellar of the house where Beatriz used to live, so that he can experience seeing the whole universe through a tiny crystal object called the Aleph. Amongst the spectacles this fantastical object has in store for him, perhaps the most disturbing is that of infinite eyes looking at him, and in doing so, seeing themselves, as in a mirror: 'vi interminables ojos inmediatos escrutándose en mí como en un espejo' (p. 624). A short while later, as he

---

[35] *OCI*, p. 624.

descends into an underground station, the horror really dawns on him: the idea that all humanity has now become familiar and that the Aleph may have condemned him to the curse of the gaze. This extreme perceptual experience, together with the power of the materiality of printed photographs ironically illustrates the writer's own fate, as his image, repeatedly reproduced and published, became a mirror in which the Argentine people expect to see their own identity. In the story, the illusion of immediacy created by the tangibility of the photograph is explored through the juxtaposition of the empty lifelessness of the vase and the piano, and the ever so alive image of Beatriz:

> El niño estaba, como siempre, en el sótano, revelando fotografías. Junto al jarrón sin una flor, en el piano inútil, sonreía (más intemporal que anacrónico) el gran retrato de Beatriz, en torpes colores. No podía vernos nadie; en una desesperación de ternura me aproximé al retrato y le dije:
>
> — Beatriz, Beatriz Elena, Beatriz Elena Viterbo, Beatriz querida, Beatriz perdida para siempre, soy yo, soy Borges. (p. 623)

As he addresses the photograph of his beloved, invoking Beatriz in the intimacy of the little room, Borges utters his own name: it is by looking at her that he can identify himself. Similarly, I argue, it is by looking at the image of Borges and ascribing to it the imagined values of a national cultural identity that Argentine society as a collective seeks to identify itself. In this sense, following the Freudian idea of the myth as a collective dream, it can be said that the mythical quality of Borges's iconic image lies in that it embodies an ideal which, as Pons suggests, 'la gente hace lo posible para que la realidad se le parezca.'[36] In this sense, the strong presence of the medium of photography in 'El Aleph' appears prophetic.

The importance of the visual in the definition of a culture is reinforced in 'El Aleph' by the exploration of the nature of national literary tradition in the context of the story. This is made explicit in the choice of the middle name of the pompous poet Daneri: 'Argentino'. Daneri was awarded the polemic 'Premio Nacional de Literatura'[37] for a selection of 'trozos argentinos' (p. 626) from his vast poem 'La Tierra', which he was only able to write by looking at the Aleph. Thus, as a parable of the impossibility of expressing simultaneity with language, 'El Aleph' underlines the fundamental role of visual perception in the delineation of a sense of 'Argentineness'. The controversy surrounding the 'Premio Nacional' constitutes the first public manifestation of Borges's long and complex relationship with Argentine critics and fellow writers in terms of the definition

---

[36] María Cristina Pons, 'El mito: un sueño colectivo', in *Delirios de grandeza. Los mitos argentinos: memoria, identidad, cultura*, ed. by María Cristina Pons and Claudia Soria (Rosario: Beatriz Viterbo, 2005), pp. 11–37 (p. 19).

[37] Borges's *El jardín de senderos que se bifurcan* was entered for the actual contest of the same name in 1942, but it did not win, which generated very public reactions both on the part of his supporters and his detractors.

of a 'national' literature.[38] It is interesting that the chosen fictional environment for this polemic is a study of the construction of identity in the interaction of linguistic and visual discourses as 'El Aleph'.

The role of images in the fictionalisation of national history in the context of national politics is more explicit in 'L'Illusion Comique'. This unusually aggressive piece which welcomed the fall of Perón following a coup d'état that became known as 'Revolución Libertadora', was published in *Sur* in December 1955. Here, historical events are described as fiction, in particular those of 17th October 1945, when president Perón was arrested and subsequently freed thanks to the people's demand: 'El 17 de octubre de 1945 se simuló que un coronel había sido arrestado y secuestrado y que el pueblo de Buenos Aires lo rescataba.'[39] Language related to advertising and propaganda is chosen to define the methods used by the dictator to control the masses: Perón is referred to as a name or an effigy, and images related to representation, simulation and performance abound: 'todos [...] sabían o sentían que se trataba de una ficción escénica' (p. 10). These fictions, continues the narrator, 'no podían ser creídas y eran creídas' (p. 10), highlighting the remarkable power of the manipulation of images which tap into the expectations of a people who needed something to believe in. The piece underlines the efficacy of the method of propaganda used by the regime which consisted in using portraits of the charismatic leaders: 'bandas de partidarios apoyados por la policía empapelaron la ciudad de retratos del dictador y de su mujer' (p. 9). Eva, the president's wife, who had died three years earlier, would become one of the most iconic figures in Argentine history. Referred to as 'abanderada de los pobres,' synonymous with the Argentine working class, her portrait was worshipped — and still is today — as the effigy of a saint.[40] Borges's examination of the power of iconic figures in the process of formation of national identity appears to pre-empt the writer's own iconization as a national cultural referent.

The quasi-religious fervour provoked by the image of Eva Perón is picked up in Borges's 1960 prose piece 'El simulacro', which describes the spectacle of a re-enactment of her wake. According to Margaret Schwartz, the story invites a postmodern reading as a 'meditation on the copy's usurpation of the original, on the emptiness behind the mask.'[41] Its last sentence, which Schwartz sees as a 'metaphysical punch-line', reflects on the iconic nature of the figures of the

---

[38] This polemic is explored in the first chapter of Lafforgue's *Antiborges*.
[39] Jorge Luis Borges, 'L'Illusion Comique', *Sur*, 23 (1955), 9–10 (p. 9).
[40] Tomás Eloy Martínez captures this deification in his novel *Santa Evita* (1995). I have personally attended more than one wake in Buenos Aires where the portrait of Eva Perón was hung above the coffin, along with that of the Sacred Heart of Jesus and the Virgin Mary.
[41] Margaret Schwartz, 'Dissimulations: Negation, the Proper Name, and the Corpse in Borges's "El simulacro"', *Variaciones Borges*, 24 (2007), 93–111 (p. 98).

Perones. Borges's text presents these figures as simulacra which served as aesthetic surfaces where the working classes projected their expectations in order to construct their mythology:

> El enlutado no era Perón, y la muñeca rubia no era la mujer Eva Duarte, pero tampoco Perón era Perón ni Eva era Eva sino desconocidos o anónimos (cuyo nombre secreto y cuyo rostro verdadero ignoramos) que figuraron, para el crédulo amor de los arrabales, una crasa mitología.[42]

During the actual historical time that 'El simulacro' refers to, the images of Juan Domingo and Eva Perón were attributed with the characteristics of the people, even though the reality of the historical figures was completely different from their daily-life experiences: Perón was called 'El primer trabajador', for example, even though he had a career in the military and had no real working-class experience. Eva was famous for her sumptuous gowns and hair-dos which the average working woman could only dream of. The working class was badly in need of being represented by government and these figures were able to lend it a sense of identity. The last words of the story refer to the representation of a representation ('figurar una mitología'), where the word 'figurar', which suggests simulation, appears to hold the key to the piece: something which signifies another, or the exterior of a body which makes it different from others, an image which echoes the word 'muñeca' above.

Written by a mature Borges and published in *Elogio de la sombra* (1969), whose prologue announces the addition of the theme of old age to his usual tropes,[43] Borges's poem 'Cambridge' speaks of a world of depthless images.[44] Words usually associated to the discovery of the meaning behind things ('puertas'; 'rostro'; 'moneda') are juxtaposed with images of surface ('anverso sin reverso') and fragmentation ('Formas inconstantes'; 'espejos rotos'). The sense of depthlessness is reinforced by the image of doors leading nowhere, not even the void (pp. 358–59), and also that of a disembodied face looking at us, like the head on a coin that cannot be flipped (p. 359). This face, together with the broken mirrors, does not lead us to the discovery of a hidden essence: instead, it reflects our own anxieties, desires and quest for identity. It is the face of an icon. The last two lines echo the repetition of 'como en los sueños' above (pp. 358–59), and reinforce the fluid and fragmentary nature of dreams, where identity is something in constant construction: 'Somos ese quimérico museo de formas inconstantes, / ese montón de espejos rotos' (p. 359). The saturation of pictorial information caused by the circulation of the photographic image of Jorge Luis Borges as an

---

[42] *OCII*, p. 167.
[43] 'A los espejos, laberintos y espadas que ya prevé mi resignado lector se han agregado dos temas nuevos: la vejez y la ética.' *OCII*, p. 353.
[44] *OCII*, pp. 358–59.

old blind sage results in a similar loss of depth, where a simulacrum has come to fill the space left by the gradual disappearance of the 'original' Borges: 'Detrás del rostro que nos mira no hay nadie. / Anverso sin reverso' (p. 359).

The strength of fictionalisations of national history and their perpetuation through reproduced images is once again taken up in 'Utopía de un hombre que está cansado' (1975). Here, Borges flagrantly chooses to mistranslate the Latin phrase central to the philosophy of George Berkeley,[45] as the nameless protagonist remembers the world that he has come from:

> Las imágenes y la letra impresa eran más reales que las cosas. Sólo lo publicado era verdadero. *Esse est percipi* (ser es ser retratado) era el principio, el medio y el fin de nuestro singular concepto del mundo.[46]

Taking Berkeley's idea that to be is 'to perceive', not just one step further, to 'to be perceived', but beyond, to 'to be portrayed', Borges draws attention to the centrality of representations by media discourse in contemporary history. It is an example of what Richard Brilliant has referred to as the imprinting of 'the consolidated image' of public figures and celebrities 'on the minds of their people' by means of the 'effective combination of mechanical or electronic reproduction and tendentious redundancy.'[47] It is also a fitting reflection of Borges's own protagonism in the Argentine media and his construction by media discourses at the time this story was written, as we shall see later.

These five pieces, written over a period of thirty years, illustrate Borges's approach to the way in which images construct identity and create the illusion that they are perceived as 'more real' than what they represent. The vivid depictions of performance and fictionalisation considered above are all described in the context of twentieth-century Argentina in relation to the particular way in which certain 'national' traits are perceived and projected. In particular, the need for people to construct effigies upon which their demands for a just society could be inscribed, as was the case with the Perones; or, in the case of Borges, the quest for an Argentine cultural tradition which could lend the nation cultural cohesion. It seems impossible to imagine what Borges and the Perones might have had in common, especially given Borges's visceral dislike of these figures and everything related to their politics, as is evident in 'L'Illusion Comique'. However, it could be argued that the process whereby the image of Borges is constructed as iconic

---

[45] This philosophy is referred to implicitly or explicitly throughout Borges's work, starting from his early essays. He re-evaluates the concept of idealism in 'Tlön, Uqbar, Orbis Tertius', for example, as analysed in Marina Martín,'Borges, perplejo defensor del idealismo', in 'Dossier: Borges: Perplejidades filosóficas', *Variaciones Borges*, 13 (2002), 7–21. Amongst others, Zulma Mateos also explores this philosophy in the works of Borges in *La filosofía en la obra de J.L. Borges* (Buenos Aires: Biblos, 1998).
[46] *OCIII*, p. 54.
[47] Richard Brilliant, *Portraiture* (London: Reaktion Books, 1991), pp. 47–48.

has points of contact with the way in which the images of Perón and Evita were constructed.

María Cristina Pons's Jungian view of the myth is that of the 'collective conscience' of frustrations, fears and hopes; and a locus for the articulation of a lack.[48] It is this fundamental characteristic of the myth that constitutes one of the main components of the icon: when collective anxieties, hopes and needs are condensed in a single visual representation, the myth becomes constituent of the icon. Eva Perón, for example, is seen as eternal and saintly, while at the same time, she is the embodiment of all things working class; but, most importantly, she has a voice to express its needs and expectations. In 'El simulacro' Borges understood that in order to be that voice, Eva had to be an empty vessel which could convey these hopes and fears.

However, where the image of Eva Perón's iconic status is founded on the idea of transgression and change, Borges's relies on its power to provide Argentina with a sense of traditional national cohesion. This illustrates Pons's observation that 'es notoria la contradicción entre los mitos encarnados en transgresores/as que se veneran y la condena a la "transgresión" desde un principio de autoridad y verticalismo (machista) que se percibe como sinónimo de estabilidad, de orden, de nación' (p. 28). The construction and circulation of the image of Borges as a perpetual old blind sage speaks of an attitude of veneration of the figure within Argentine culture. The social and political turmoil experienced in Argentina in the twentieth century, which brought about a redefinition of its identity, required a referent outside of these historical changes which could provide a sense of stability and solidity. This echoes the nationalistic agendas of successive military and democratic regimes which contributed to the emergence of an imagined need for unity and definition which ran contrary to the multicultural and plurilingual nature of Argentine society: instead of embracing diversity, they attempted to quash it.[49]

The next section examines the historical context in which the photographic image of Borges developed into an icon, tracing a trajectory which has proven to be similar to those of iconic images earlier described in Borges's own work.

---

[48] Pons, 'El mito', p. 17.
[49] The prohibition of foreign names is an example of this attempt to erase diversity: Article 3 of the 'Ley 18.248 del nombre de las personas naturales' (promulgated on 10th June, 1969) states that 'no podrán inscribirse […] los nombres extranjeros, salvo los castellanizados por el uso.' This law still applies in Argentina today. Online at www.gob.gba.gov.ar/portal/documentos/ley18248.pdf [last accessed 27 September 2013].

Constructing Borges in the Post-Perón Years

The social and political struggles that marked Argentina for most of the twentieth century motivated the delineation of a new profile of Argentine society. This transformation had started with the rapid increase of the country's population as a consequence of mass immigration, particularly in the last two decades of the nineteenth century.[50] By the middle of the twentieth century, foreign immigration was combined with internal migration to Buenos Aires. David Rock explains: 'Migrants arrived from the pampas, from the interior, and from neighbouring Latin American states, and a half million new European immigrants were admitted between 1947 and 1951.'[51] The influx of these waves of immigration, particularly in Buenos Aires, resulted in most of the university students being from immigrant backgrounds around the middle of the century, for example. Migrants also 'swelled the numbers of new urban workers in industry, transportation, and services, becoming the backbone of the swift upward surge in union membership during Perón's first years as president' (p. 283). Juan José Sebreli points out that, combined with a nineteenth-century cultural tradition which had installed the need to construct symbols of nationhood (mainly through the system of state education), this new multiculturalism motivated a new form of 'hero cult':

> La necesidad de inventarse una historia heroica que diera fundamento y estabilidad al incipiente Estado nacional y, a la vez, frenara el peligro de disgregarse, temido por las clases dirigentes frente a las oleadas inmigratorias, llevó a organizar una escuela pública donde se inculcaba una verdadera 'religión cívica', con sus símbolos, ritos y ceremonias.[52]

Rock uses words like 'deadlock' and 'stalemate' to describe Argentina between 1955 and 1982 — the period which this chapter focuses on.[53] The perceived lack of solutions for the country's many problems resulted in a situation of instability and turmoil, of change without progress. The main issues that contributed to a prevailing sense of unrest during this period can be summarized as 'chronic inflation and recurrent cycles of recession and recovery'; 'social and political divisions' which 'grew increasingly tense and violent' and 'progressive

---

[50] As David Rock points out: 'The nation's population increased from an estimated 1.1 million in 1857 to approximately 3.3 million by 1890 [...] the population of the city and province of Buenos Aires almost sextupled,' in *Argentina 1516–1982* (London: Tauris, 1986), p. 132.
[51] Rock, *Argentina*, p. 283.
[52] Sebreli, *Comediantes y Mártires*, p. 29.
[53] In *Argentina 1516–1982*, Rock broadly identifies the period between the depression of the 1930s and the Malvinas War in 1982 as one of 'progressive' and 'unchecked' decline. Rock's book is relevant to this chapter as it concentrates on the sense of uncertainty and turmoil predominant in the post-Perón years. Borges is not considered in relation to the 1982 war in this study. The 1976–1983 dictatorship and the transition to democracy in the mid-80s are considered in Chapter 3.

institutional decay' (p. 320). Rock refers to the country's social problems as 'extreme' and seemingly 'ineradicable' and blames the erratic behaviour of the economy for the political instability that prevailed: 'as the economy waxed and waned, regimes came and went' (pp. 320–21).[54]

Another significant aspect of this period is Argentina's impoverished sense of international standing, coming to terms with its new situation as a 'second-rank nation in Latin America [...] unable to find a stable international position and [...] largely isolated in the world community' (p. 320). Rock places particular emphasis on the gradual erosion of the high living standards that Argentines had enjoyed in contrast with those of the rest of Latin America. Bearing in mind that one of Argentina's most characteristic collective fantasies relates to Europe as the locus of legitimisation for cultural accomplishment, this period is characterized by a tension between a definition of an identity in 'local' terms and the need for international recognition. In this context, the circulation of photographs of an internationally successful and recognised Borges may be explained by the fact that these images were in a position to provide a sense of cultural reassurance.[55]

One of the main motivations for the consumption of the image of Borges is the desire for self-assurance in the acquisition of a sense of identity, which is marked by the projection of some of the more or less consistent elements, or 'grand narratives' of what it means to be Argentine. According to Cristina Pons, these constitute the country's 'foundational myths'.[56] Among them is a sense of superiority with respect to the rest of Latin America, which is related to the idea that Argentina was destined for greatness. These foundational myths compensate for the absence of a clearly defined origin. Thus, the delineation of an Argentine identity is a search for a cultural father-figure which oscillates between local and foreign models.

The attribution of these symbolic meanings to the figure of Borges over an extended period of time and in a variety of contexts has resulted in the image becoming an icon. American cultural theorist Paula Rabinowitz considers that an image becomes an icon when it has been 'composed, revised, circulated, and reissued in various venues until whatever reality its subject first possessed has been drained away.'[57] According to this approach, it could be argued that Borges's

---

[54] Torcuato S. Di Tella provides an outline of the socio-political instability which was particularly predominant in Argentina and its consequent violent atmosphere in 'The sixties and Seventies', *History of Political Parties in Twentieth-Century Latin America* (New Brunswick and London: Transaction, 2004), pp. 99–120 (pp. 108–11).

[55] Cf. Wells's claim that a sense of 'self-location' can be 'acquired through the contemplation of the phographic image' in 'On and Beyond the White Wall', p. 283.

[56] Pons, 'El mito', pp. 18–19.

[57] Paula Rabinowitz, *They Must be Represented: The Politics of Documentary* (London: Verso, 1994), p. 86, cited in *Photography*, by Liz Wells (London and New York: Routledge, 2005), p. 47.

iconicity is partly due to its wide circulation and repeated reproduction in a variety of media. However, I would stress that even though the 'reality' of Borges the subject at the time of exposure has been drained out of his photographs, it has not been completely exhausted: it remains as a trace. This trace, called 'indexicality', is where the authority of the image lies. As mentioned above, this, combined with 'the symbolic value invested in it' makes the photographic image of Borges iconic.[58] This explains why the visual is such a pivotal aspect of the construction of the icon: the image of Borges conveys a certain presence, a trace of the actual, historical man, which produces the illusion that by contemplating his image, the viewer is, in fact, in the presence of the man.

The images analysed here demonstrate that when associated with an aura of sacredness afforded to it by the conjunction of other constructions of the author, the indexicality of Borges's portrait becomes a powerful conveyor of meanings associated with identity construction. As we have seen, Borges explores this in 'El Aleph', where the protagonist considers the photographs of his recently deceased friend Beatriz Viterbo. Similarly, in the case of Borges himself, his image is the locus for a projected desire to possess certain attributes of the writer. Alan Pauls notes this in his discussion of Borges's perceived erudition:

> El saber [...] se lo asocia con la gravedad, con el tedio, con la disciplina [...] La única cara del saber que irradia algún *glamour* es la cara 'capitalista': la fase de adquisición, de acumulación de información y conocimiento. Pero es inaccesible. El resto — el *ejercicio* del saber, esa momificación en vida — mejor perderlo que encontrarlo [...] Pero lo que espera del otro lado del saber [...] es un poco de 'autoridad'.[59]

When the image of Borges is printed on a book cover which consumers can acquire, this facilitates the appropriation of the authority associated with his knowledge. The next section explores how the appropriation of Borges's visual image, commercialised together with his oeuvre and criticism on the covers of books, perpetuates the construction of Borges as an authority and unifying cultural force throughout the last decades of the twentieth century.

Photographs of Borges on the Covers of Books

Umberto Eco considers iconic photographs as condensers of discourse which refer us to other images which have preceded them or imitated them subsequently.[60] Such is the case of a certain type of portrait of Borges where the

---

[58] Price and Wells, 'Thinking', p. 47.
[59] Alan Pauls, 'Loca erudición', in *El factor Borges: Nueve ensayos ilustrados* (Buenos Aires: Fondo de Cultura Económica, 2000), pp. 141–56 (p. 142).
[60] Umberto Eco, 'Una fotografía', *La estrategia de la ilusión*, trans. by Edgardo Oviedo (Buenos Aires: Lumen, 1992), pp. 293–98 (p. 296).

writer appears as an old blind sage worthy of veneration. This image was constructed during the latter part of his life and it was perpetuated by its continuing circulation in the media and on the covers of books. The covers of the biographies considered in Chapter 1 are examples of this. It is difficult to distinguish between different portraits of a mature, post-1960s Borges: there have been so many circulated that it feels as though they have all become one. Images of the type printed on reams of newspaper and magazine paper during the 1970s and 1980s have continued to appear on the covers of books written by him and about him (Fig. 6). These usually show an elderly writer with a serious expression and posing formally against a dark background which often includes books. Those pictures taken indoors tend to contain an internal source of light and black and white versions of these portraits generally seem to have been preferred to colour, even to sepia. This could be understood as a publisher's decision to maintain costs to a minimum. However, even the few instances of use of colour photographs favour hues of brown and grey. The fact that as long as we are able to recognize these elements it makes little or no difference whether we are looking at one or a variety of different photographs, shows that this type of photograph has become iconic. The image of an old Borges appears to be a single one, a montage made up of the vestiges of an original, fragmented Borges which, in Baudrillard's words, 'persist here and there.'[61] We are confronted by a variety of images, but we only perceive one which contains elements of the historical Borges, such as his recognizable facial features. Most relevantly, as has been discussed so far, we recognize those values that have been attributed to his image.

When portraits of a mature Borges appear on the covers of books, the image grows stronger. This is not only because books are more likely than newspapers or magazines to remain in a library; but also due to the fact that the presence of a photograph on a book's cover establishes an immediate link between the work and a particular image of the man. The wide circulation of the photographic image of an elderly Borges creates the mistaken impression that the whole corpus of his literary production began in his seventies. This is likely to be due to the launch of Borges into the international limelight in the 1960s, which is marked by the award of his first international prize in 1961 for *Ficciones*.[62] This collection of short stories, as well as much of his best-known work, of course, was written in the 1940s, and it is work from this period that was first chosen for translation into other European languages, and eventually, into English. Claudio Canaparo

---

[61] Jean Baudrillard, *Simulacra and Simulation*, trans. by Sheila Faria Glaser (Michigan: The University of Michigan Press, 1994), p. 1.

[62] The first French translations of Borges's work can be traced back to the early 1950s, which, Edwin Williamson explains, 'can be taken as the true origin of the immense reputation Borges would eventually gain abroad.' Borges was awarded the International Publishers' Prize (jointly with Samuel Beckett) for *Ficciones* in May 1961. Williamson, *Borges*, pp. 345–46.

FIGURE 6. A selection of front and back covers of books by and about Borges. From the top, left to right: Estela Canto, *Borges a contraluz* (Madrid: Espasa Calpe, 1989); Jorge Luis Borges, *Ficciones* (Buenos Aires: Emecé, 1996) (back cover); Evelyn Fishburn (ed.), *Borges and Europe Revisited* (London: Institute of Latin American Studies, 1998); Pilar Bravo and Mario Paoletti, *Borges Verbal* (Buenos Aires: Emecé, 1999); Edwin Williamson, *Borges: A Life* (London: Viking Penguin, 2004); León Tenenbaum, *Buenos Aires. Tiempo de Borges* (Buenos Aires: Ediciones Turísticas, 2001). All images reproduced with permission of the copyright holders.

has traced the history of the publication of *Ficciones* which launched Borges to a wider readership: 'A partir de 1956 [...] los libros de Borges comienzan a ser distribuidos, al menos en el mercado hispanohablante, fuera del círculo reducido de los lectores de *Sur* y de las otras pequeñas editoriales.'[63] Thus, a book originally published in 1944 was launched to a wider market more than a decade later, and reached international acclaim almost twenty years after the stories were written. Next, we will see how this image which ties the elderly writer with his early work was perpetuated, as age became one of the most distinctive traits of the construction of Borges as a figure of reverence.

Argentine Surrealist Grete Stern photographed the writer in 1951 and this image is reproduced on the cover and inside the 1964 edition of Alicia Jurado's *Genio y Figura de Jorge Luis Borges* (Fig. 7). Stern's portrait, showing an amiable, relaxed and gregarious Borges sitting on a café chair, as if the photograph had been taken during a chat with friends, has, however, circulated significantly less than later portraits depicting him as an elderly man. After Stern, just about every photographer worth his or her salt produced images of Borges. Sara Facio, for example, is one of the best known Argentines to have photographed the writer in the 1970s and early 1980s.[64]

Sara Facio's *Jorge Luis Borges en Buenos Aires* (2005) is a good example of the perpetuation of the image of the writer as an old wise man. Here, the photographer, writer and curator skilfully juxtaposes her portraits of the author with quotations from his poetry and images of Buenos Aires. This creates a phototextual image of a profoundly porteño Borges whilst, at the same time, it reinforces the idea of wisdom associated with the writer. This aura of wisdom is also evoked by the setting of some of the photographs (taken in the Biblioteca Nacional, for example), in which Borges appears surrounded by books. The fact that most of the photographs are taken at an angle, so that Borges's unseeing eyes appear to be directed beyond the camera, produces the effect of an intellectual lost in thought. Thus, this particular way of photographing blindness suggests certain 'Borgesian' associations to other, perhaps inner or perhaps distant, realms,

---

[63] Claudio Canaparo, 'De Bibliographica Ratio. Un comentario acerca de 'lo Borgiano' como narración historiográfica. Las *Ficciones* de Josefina Ludmer', in *Jorge Luis Borges: Intervenciones sobre pensamiento y literatura*, ed. by William Rowe, Claudio Canaparo and Annick Louis (Buenos Aires: Paidós, 2000), pp. 199–247 (p. 242).

[64] It is worth mentioning here Eduardo Comesaña, a principally journalistic photographer who worked for a few of Buenos Aires's popular weekly magazines such as *Siete Días*. Comesaña is not as prestigious as Facio or Raota (famous for his photographs of working-class life, his photograph of Borges in his seventies has been used for the covers of books like Evelyn Fishburn's *Borges and Europe Revisited*). However, he has taken many well-known photographs of Borges, amongst which is the one used for the cover of Estela Canto's *Borges a contraluz*. He currently runs a photographic agency and archive which makes these photographs available for sale for publication, online at www.comesana.com [last accessed 27 September 2013].

FIGURE 7. Borges by Grete Stern (1951) on the cover and on pages 6–7 of Alicia Jurado's *Genio y Figura de Jorge Luis Borges* (Buenos Aires: EUDEBA, 1964). Reproduced by permission of EUDEBA.

particularly, the world of ideas. Thus, Borges's blindness — which was, and continues to be, a fact well known by the Argentine public — is portrayed not as a way of exposing a disability which may elicit pity or condescension but, instead, as a link to a world of sapiency not normally accessible to the 'ordinary' Argentine. This technique has allowed most Argentine photographers to give their portraits of Borges a certain air of dreaminess and introspection that turns his blindness into an essential component of his sagelike image.

In Facio's book, the paratextual spaces of the prologue and the back cover show that her approach does not vary hugely from that of most literary biographers. In the prologue, which is structured as a selection of reminiscences and anecdotes involving herself and Borges, Facio fulfils her autobiographical impulse as she concludes with the legitimising phrase 'Éste es el Borges que conocí,'[65] which is almost identical to Estela Canto's 'Hablo aquí del Borges vivo, del hombre que conocí.'[66] The blurb on the back cover repeats the biographical mantra of the revelation of the real man, as seen in the examples of literary biographies in the previous chapter, claiming that its aim is to 'lograr una aproximación al mundo real del personaje a través de la representación gráfica más testimonial, espontánea e íntima que se conoce: la fotografía'.[67] Borges's work is quoted in an attempt to provide factual evidence of that real context that is promised in this book: 'Los textos, siempre del autor […] tratan de situar las imágenes en el tiempo y sus circunstancias' (back cover).

However, it is in the juxtaposition of the portraits with photographs of urban landscapes and close-ups of certain objects, including the obligatory books, a painting and photographs of photographs, that the photographer is able to narrate this image of a Borges intimately linked to Buenos Aires. This composition shows an august Borges, who, surrounded by objects of great traditional value, such as the portraits of his illustrious ancestors, appears as a greatly respectable figure. The fact that the photographs are printed in black and white also suggests an aura of history and tradition, as if Borges were also one of the objects of cultural worth.

The photographs reproduced in this book, which date from between 1963 and 1980, have also been exhibited in Buenos Aires and abroad and some have been used to illustrate many other books, as is the case of Pilar Bravo and Mario Paoletti's *Borges Verbal* (1999) (Fig. 6, centre right) and Alejandro Vaccaro's *Borges: Una biografía en imágenes* (2005) amongst others. Facio's iconic portrait of Argentine writer Julio Cortázar (Fig. 8) is amongst the best known images of this author.[68] This photograph, where he appears with a cigarette in his mouth,

---

[65] Sara Facio, *Jorge Luis Borges en Buenos Aires* (Buenos Aires: La Azotea, 2005), p. 12.
[66] Canto, *Borges a contraluz*, p. 9.
[67] Facio, *Jorge Luis Borges*, back cover.
[68] Available at http://commons.wikimedia.org/wiki/File:Cort%C3%A1zar.jpg [last accessed 27 September 2013].

FIGURE 8. Julio Cortázar at age 53, in 1967, by Sara Facio. Available online at http://upload.wikimedia.org/wikipedia/commons/1/19/Cort%C3%A1zar.jpg [last accessed 27 September 2013].

captures his renowned playfulness and contributes to the generalized impression of the author as eternally young. Cortázar was fifty-three when this photograph was taken, in 1967. Compared to photographs of Borges also taken by Facio when the writer was sixty-three,[69] the ten-year age difference between the two seems considerably greater. Cortázar's youthful, relaxed pose against a bright white background contrasts with Borges's, who appears formal and more serious sitting up against the old fashioned dark seat.

---

[69] Cf. Facio's portrait of Borges at the Biblioteca Nacional taken in 1963, in *Jorge Luis Borges en Buenos Aires*, p. 14.

The case of Borges's *Autobiografía* (Fig. 9) is a further example of the portrayal of the author as an old sightless sage: published in 1999 by El Ateneo, this was the first time the complete text of Borges's *Autobiographical Essay* became available in Spanish in Buenos Aires since its original publication in instalments in English in American magazine *The New Yorker* in 1970. The original black and white photograph on the dust-cover was taken by Argentine artist Ronald Shakespear in 1964. It shows an elderly Borges with a hand on a desktop globe which, due to the way the photograph is lit, gives the impression of being on fire. Borges's face is brightly lit by the glow emanating from above. In contrast, his back is in darkness. The side of the face that can be seen shows an eye whose socket appears empty, like that of a statue. The sepia tones chosen for the cover design evoke photographs from old times. All these elements suggest a god-like sage. This semblance is echoed in Martín Lafforgue's introduction to *Antiborges* (1999),

> Jorge Luis Borges ha ingresado [...] al exclusivo panteón de los mitos nacionales. Es el nuevo ídolo de un Olimpo en el que se codea con muchas de las figuras que en vida supo abominar [...] Así, como objeto, se lo consagra y

FIGURE 9. 'Borges en la Biblioteca Nacional', by Ronald Shakespear, 1967, on the cover of *Autobiografía*, designed by Lorenzo Shakespear, 1999. Reproduced with permission of Ronald Shakespear.

consume [...] Las agencias gubernamentales se lo disputan. La opinion pública lo reverencia.⁷⁰

Lafforgue's book contains a valuable selection of texts whose range illustrates the critical but also political and ideological debates surrounding Borges which spans most of the twentieth century (1926–1996).⁷¹ It boasts an inverted black and white photograph of Borges in his seventies on its cover (Fig. 10), against a red background. This audacious subversion of the image of Borges in the manner of the 'Anti-Christ' has a comic effect, which is consistent with the intentions of the book: to explore 'nuevos mapas de lectura [...] en un sentido si no necesariamente contrario, por lo menos diferente del de esta sofocante hagiografía' (pp. 11–12). The image chosen to illustrate this departure would not have been as effective if Borges had not been generally perceived as worthy of reverence. The fact that both publishing houses — El Ateneo and Javier Vergara — chose this portrayal of the author corroborates the weight of his image as old and esteemed. Almost a decade later, the words of Rodrigo Fresán illustrate how current that preference for the image of an old Borges is in the twenty-first century: in a review of Adolfo Bioy Casares's *Borges* (2006), which shows a photograph of a young Bioy and a Borges in his thirties on its cover (Fig. 11),⁷² Fresán protests that it is too youthful and expresses a preference for 'una foto de portada "más de madurez"'.⁷³

The section that follows evaluates the consequences of efforts to renovate the Borges image by choosing cover photographs of the writer in his youth, as the image on Bioy's *Borges* illustrates.

'*El nuevo Borges*': Borges's Centenary and Retrograde Innovation

In the late 1990s, there were significant efforts to revive the image of a young Borges, with a proliferation of new editions of his early work and publication of previously unpublished material from his youth. This marketing strategy was motivated by the celebration of the centenary of the writer's birth in 1999. During this year, Josefina Ludmer notes, Borges was 'en la calle, la televisión, las exposiciones, los suplementos de los domingos, las encuestas de

---

⁷⁰ Lafforgue, Antiborges, p. 11.
⁷¹ The earliest text dates from 1926 and the latest, from 1996.
⁷² There is a very similar photo which appears to be part of the same series, in Alicia Jurado's *Genio y Figura de Jorge Luis Borges* (p. 119) captioned 'Mar del Plata, 1943'. According to Emir Rodríguez Monegal, the photograph may have been taken in the garden of Victoria Ocampo's San Isidro house in 1932, when Borges and Bioy first met (it is reproduced in *Borges: Una biografía literaria*, page unnumbered).
⁷³ Rodrigo Fresán, 'Caro Diario. Adivina quién viene a comer', *Página/12*, 13 May 2007, online at www.pagina12.com.ar/diario/suplementos/radar/9-3806-2007-05-13.html [last accessed 27 September 2013].

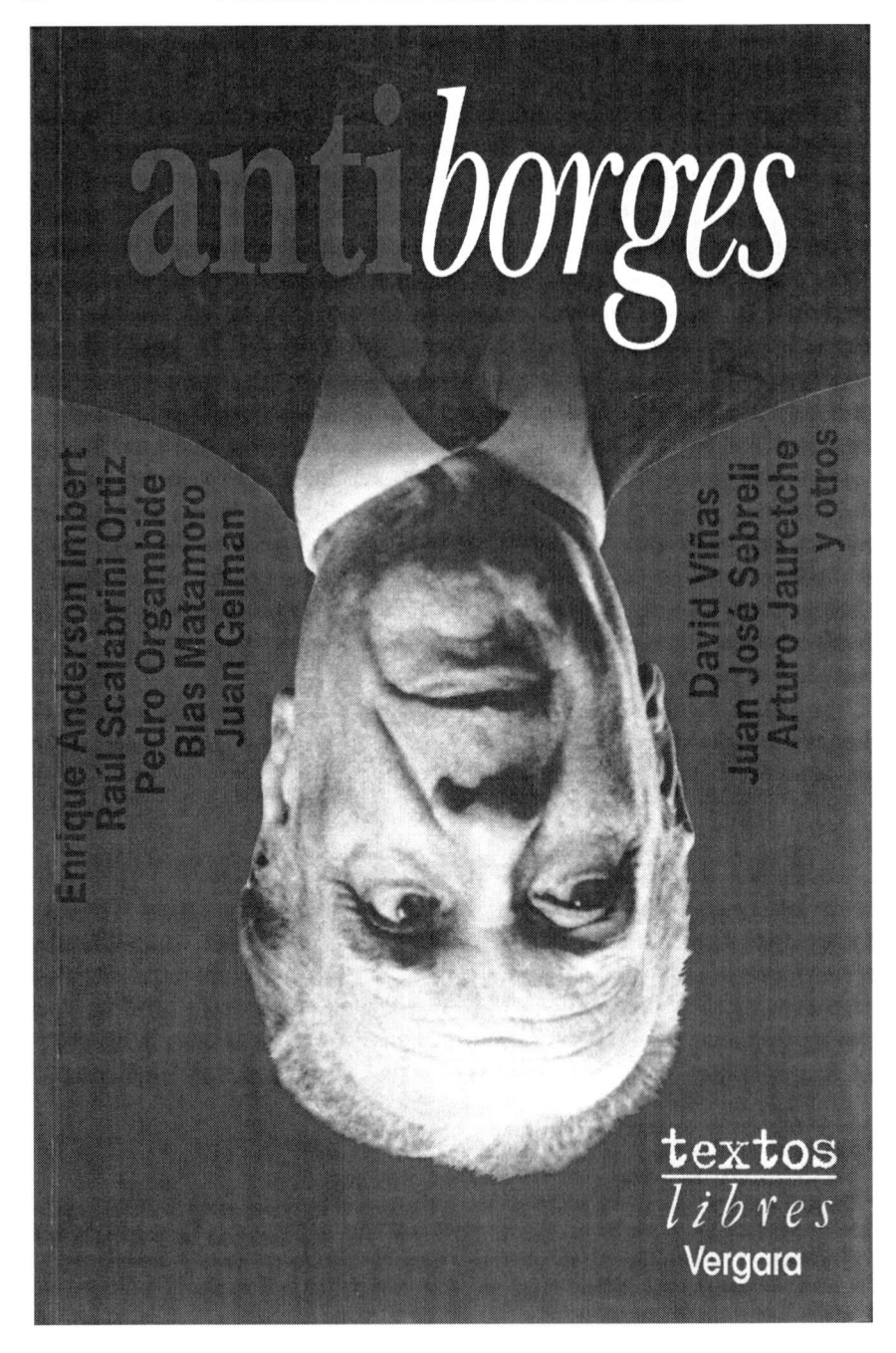

FIGURE 10. Cover of Lafforgue's *Antiborges*, designed by Raquel Cané, 1999. Reproduced with permission of the copyright holder.

FIGURE 11. Cover of Adolfo Bioy Casares's *Borges* (2006).
Image courtesy of Ediciones Destino.

opinión.'⁷⁴ Graciela Montaldo describes the attempted renovation of the Borges image as a contributing factor to the creation of a new demand, as the author became a trademark which constituted a new mode of circulation for 'high culture' in a globalized marketplace.⁷⁵ However, I argue that the elements of the new that the design of the Borges trademark incorporates, have not succeeded in creating a new writer. Instead, these have resulted in a consolidation of the image of the traditional, monument-like elder that had circulated during the previous decades.

As part of the commercial decision to re-launch the Borges image, portraits from the 1920s and 1930s made a comeback. Publishing house Emecé in particular used photographs from this period in collections as diverse — in terms of content — as *Cartas del Fervor, Textos recobrados* and *Borges en Sur*, which were all published between 1997 and 1999 (Figs. 12–14). These efforts accompany a re-valuation of Borges's earlier work, with a shift of focus from Borges as the highly intellectual creator of cosmogonies to that of the *flanêur porteño*. Importantly, the latter entails a strong attachment to the Buenos Aires of the first decades of the twentieth century and its socio-political configurations. However, despite the significant change of perspective that is noticeable in criticism, this choice of images of a young Borges constitutes a visual reinforcement of the notion of age and tradition, as they are themselves perceived as 'old', that is the photos are themselves now old documents. In *Hyperreality and Global Culture*, Nick Perry calls this strategy 'retrograde innovation.'⁷⁶ Perry argues that advertising discourse has shifted 'towards the cultural codes through which meanings are generated' and that meaning is now to be attached to the name, rather than the particular product itself. The same can be said of the physiognomy of Borges, for which the advertiser must ensure a privileged position, assuming that 'the resulting sign value in the culture will translate into exchange value on the market' (p. 38).

Cover designers in the advertising departments of publishing houses are thus faced with the task of tapping into the traditional name of Borges, the timeless Argentine bard, whilst appearing to offer a 'new' product. The choice of portraits of a young Borges establishes a connection with the original date of production of the texts to be sold while, at the same time, it reminds consumers of the Borges to which they are accustomed. These photographs bear the marks of their age:

---

⁷⁴ Josefina Ludmer, '¿Cómo salir de Borges?', in *Jorge Luis Borges: Intervenciones*, ed. by Rowe, Canaparo and Louis, p. 289.
⁷⁵ Graciela Montaldo, 'Borges, Aira y la literatura para multitudes', in *Boletín* 6 (1998), p. 12. Cited in Jeffrey Ceñedo, 'Un nuevo Borges: Literatura y globalización en América Latina', *Iberoamericana. América Latina-España-Portugal*, VI (2006), 43–61 (p. 44).
⁷⁶ This is in the context of Perry's discussion of Benetton advertising in 'Post-Pictures and Ec(h)o effects' in *Hyperreality and Global Culture* (London and New York: Routledge, 1998), pp. 38–9.

FIGURE 12. Cover of one of the books published by Emecé between 1997 and 1999. Original photograph from 1919. *Jorge Luis Borges: Cartas del fervor: correspondencia con Maurice Abramowicz y Jacobo Sureda (1919–1928)*, ed. by Cristóbal Pera (Barcelona: Emecé, 1999). Reproduced with permission of the copyright holder.

FIGURE 13. Cover of one of the books published by Emecé between 1997 and 1999. Original photograph from 1943. *Borges En Sur 1931–1980*, ed. by Sara Luisa del Carril and Mercedes Rubio de Socchi (Buenos Aires: Emecé, 1999). Reproduced with permission of the copyright holder.

FIGURE 14. Cover of one of the books published by Emecé between 1997 and 1999. Original photograph from 1919. *Jorge Luis Borges: Textos recobrados 1919–1929*, ed. by Sara Luisa del Carril (Buenos Aires: Emecé, 1997). Reproduced with permission of the copyright holder.

they are grainy and most of them are either sepia or black and white. In the case of *Borges en Sur* (Fig. 13), the portrait has had its background removed. This gives the impression of a Borges detached from a specific time and a place, so that his face and attire show him in his early forties, but the lack of a definite setting makes him appear timeless: old and present at the same time. But where Perry talks about relocating depictions that would otherwise have been considered traditional within a different discursive context, we may think of the 'new' Borges image within the traditional context of the book cover, triggering associations to tradition and age. This is because, by being displayed in the same spaces as the traditional images of an elderly Borges, these young images have inherited, retrospectively, the same set of meanings. This juxtaposition of the original discursive context of the photograph with that of the book cover taps into the cultural codes that generate the meanings of reverence, tradition and prestige.

The fact that post-centenary biographies and other studies of Borges have subsequently returned to cover designs bearing the traditional depiction of the elderly writer attests to the strength of this image. It is the case of books as diverse as the mainly anecdotal *El Señor Borges* (2004), written by Borges's maid, Fanny Uveda de Robledo, and Vaccaro's predominantly pictorial *Borges. Una biografía en imágenes* (2005). Even Williamson's biography, which explores the earlier part of Borges's youth in Buenos Aires, has on its cover a portrait in sepia — as seen in the previous chapter — in which Borges is old, blind and sitting in a library (Fig. 4).

The meanings condensed in the photographic image of Borges in old age have also been appropriated by the Argentine media. This, which is considered next, contributed to Borges being erected as a monument to national culture and a figure of international prestige.

'*El anciano gurú*': Borges in the Argentine Press

It may not be surprising that the image of Borges that has circulated most widely is that of an elderly writer, given the fact that he was in his sixties when he acquired greatest exposure as a public figure and his work gained international renown. However, the generalized perception of Borges as a blind sage stems from a complex combination of the cultural, historical and editorial contexts in which this particular type of image has been disseminated. Alan Pauls laments the narrow definition of Borges's bookishness that dominated much of the criticism of the previous decades:

> Años, décadas enteras dedicadas a pensar en la erudición de Borges, o no a pensarla sino a darla por sentada, a confundirla con los valores con que la asocia el sentido común — 'cultura', 'elitismo', 'hermetismo', 'academicismo'.[77]

---

[77] Pauls, 'Loca erudición', p. 141.

As Pauls suggests, it is worth reflecting on the connotations that common sense has associated with this erudition, mainly constructed by Argentine media discourses. Thus, Borges was constructed as a figure far removed from the experience of the 'average' Argentine, a writer who inhabited a separate sphere. This sphere was in turn considered a space for the production of a type of literature to which only a chosen few had access.

In *Autobiografía*, Borges claims that: 'Hasta que fui publicado en francés yo era casi invisible, no sólo en el exterior sino también en Buenos Aires.'[78] The construction of Borges in the Argentine press as internationally prestigious taps into one of the most widespread Argentine myths regarding its perceived 'Europeanness'. María Cristina Pons explains: 'Desde nuestros orígenes prosperó la idea o el inconfesable deseo de que éramos lo más europeo de América Latina, y así quisimos creerlo y hacerlo creer.'[79] This, in turn, relates to the tragedy of what Argentina expected to become but which it did not manage to become. In this context, continues Pons, Argentine myths constitute 'símbolos y síntomas de un país que muestra una imperiosa necesidad de figurar en el mundo' (p. 34). As we shall see, this will become evident in the reporting of Borges's public exposure abroad in the Argentine press, which reinforced the construction of the 'cultural success story' that forms a fundamental part of his image.

The International Publishers' Prize prompted the translation of his work into English, thus opening up the North American market, instantly extending Borges's international recognition.[80] In Borges's own words, 'a consecuencia de ese premio, de la noche a la mañana mis libros brotaron como hongos por todo el mundo occidental.'[81] As a consequence, 1961 saw the beginning of Borges as a public figure, as the last twenty-five years of his life were documented in a vast number of photographs, as well as in audiovisual material such as interviews and documentaries. His increased public exposure was also due to his position as director of Argentina's National Library and his many public lectures in Buenos Aires, the interior and abroad. Emir Rodríguez Monegal's biography describes the phenomenon of the international wise man of letters, which the most circulated images encapsulate, under the apt title 'El anciano gurú':

---

[78] Jorge Luis Borges and Norman Thomas Di Giovanni, *Autobiografía* (Buenos Aires, El ateneo, 1999), pp. 141–42. Translations into French appeared as early as 1939, but the first complete selection of stories was published by Gallimard in 1951. See Jaime Alazraki, 'Recepción de Borges en los EE.UU.' in *El siglo de Borges: vol. I: Retrospectiva-Presente-Futuro*, ed. by Alfonso de Toro y Fernando de Toro (Madrid: Iberoamericana; Frankfurt am Main: Vervuert, 1999), pp. 337–38.

[79] Pons, 'El mito', p. 34.

[80] Alazraki provides an overview of the reception of the Borgesian oeuvre in the United States in 'Recepción de Borges en los EE.UU.'.

[81] Borges, *Autobiografía*, p. 142.

> En Parma o en Jerusalén, en Dublín o en Madrid, Borges fue entrevistado hasta el aturdimiento, fue agasajado y aclamado, fue rodeado y hasta abrumado por la adulación. En todos lados se prestó pasivamente a ese culto público [...] Delgado, frágil, tan blanco que a la distancia se hacía difícil saber si estaba de pie o si realmente flotaba, Borges parecía hecho de acero [...] Lo aceptaba todo. Su imagen pública ya no le pertenecía, y él se dejaba hacer como si las cosas le ocurriesen al otro, a 'Borges'.[82]

Borges appears at once vulnerable and made of steel, a worshipped figure who seems above his admirers and at the same time interacts with the young generation: 'Aquel hombre tímido [...] se había convertido en el decano de las letras hispanoamericanas, el gurú para una nueva generación' (p. 409). This portrayal is consistent with Juan José Sebreli's description of contemporary popular heroes as Olympian gods: 'superiores y a la vez iguales a los simples mortales.'[83] As an icon, Borges needs to be constructed as outside of history but also accessible, super-human and human at the same time.

A revered Borges, portrayed as an elderly man, also evokes a traditional, conservative writer in an ivory tower. This image started to develop in Argentina in the late 1960s and it was reaffirmed during the 1970s and 1980s. Between 1962 and 1986, Borges was closely scrutinized and much of what he did or said publicly was captured on camera. Williamson refers to this ravenous obsession of the Argentine press to record everything Borges said and did as 'monstrous fame'.[84] By the mid-1970s, Williamson explains, Borges possessed 'a magical aura that drew total strangers to him' as he was 'regularly stopped in the street by admirers who wanted to shake his hand or ask for his autograph' (p. 423).

Many journalists have said that Borges was a pleasure to interview and that he seemed eager to receive those who were prepared to accompany him and play the role of both amanuenses and fellow *flâneurs*. American academic Ted Lyons, for example, writes that 'for nearly sixty years, Jorge Luis Borges freely and congenially granted hundreds of interviews,' and that the writer 'willingly shared his time and words.'[85] Interviews generally took place in his apartment on Maipú street or during a stroll around the surrounding 'barrio', or at the Biblioteca Nacional when Borges worked there. There are also interviews that took place in television studios both in Argentina and abroad.[86]

---

[82] Rodríguez Monegal, *Borges: Una biografía literaria*, p. 411.
[83] Sebreli, *Comediantes y Mártires*, p. 22.
[84] Williamson, *Borges*, pp. 418–24.
[85] Ted Lyon, 'Jorge Luis Borges and the Interview as Literary Genre', *Latin American Literary Review*, vol. 22, No. 44 (1994), pp. 74–89 (p. 1).
[86] Consider, for example, 'A fondo', Joaquín Soler Serrano's interview for *Televisión Española* in 1980, or 'Tiempo de Borges', Borges interviewed by Raúl Horacio Burzaco for *ATC*, 28 June 1985. *Audiovideoteca de Buenos Aires*, Centro Cultural Recoleta, Gobierno de la Ciudad de Buenos Aires, AEVR2038C, 31′23″.

Photographs of interviews of Borges by students, academics, professional photographers and young journalists abound on the Internet, in personal blogs and within the writer's various fan pages on the social network Facebook, for example.[87] American photographer Richard Avedon saw his visit to the writer mirrored in writer Paul Theroux's story of his own experience four years later:

> I read an account by Paul Theroux of his visit to Borges. It was my visit: the dim light, the trip to the bookcase, Kipling, the Anglo-Saxon recital. In some way, it seemed Borges had no visitors. People who came from the outside could exist for him only if they were made part of his familiar inner world, the world of poets and ancients who were already his true companions.[88]

Avedon experienced his visit to the writer as an invitation into a different, self-contained world, although, interestingly, as we shall see, the photographs he took of him the following year do not necessarily convey such sense of isolation. There are also many photographs and video recordings of interviews which have been broadcast or published in various formats, some of which are collages of photographs from a variety of sources. Many of these have been gathered in assorted documentaries that are easily accessible online.[89] This wealth of material attests to a Borges who obviously felt comfortable in his role of interviewee.

Borges appeared in Argentina's audiovisual media over three decades. First, he was shown in news programmes as part of the cultural scene of Buenos Aires, and, progressively, interviews were broadcast on radio and television which seemed to want to dissect every inch of the writer. Newsreel footage from 1969 of 'Argentina al Día' and 'EPA' (shown in Argentine cinemas in the 1960s and 1970s) contain images of Borges in an advertisement for a literary contest for Argentine writers organized by Editorial Planeta. These images in particular are shown together with publicity for private and state-run ventures, all of which are portrayed as supporting a respect for tradition and the safeguarding of the national cultural patrimony by people who work 'para la gran familia argentina', a 'sociedad dinámica y creadora en constante evolución.'[90] The style in which this

---

[87] Consider, for example: http://oyeborges.blogspot.co.uk/2012/04/aquella-increible-entrevista-con-jorge.html; https://www.facebook.com/photo.php?fbid=10151796001410491&set=pb.57195065490.-2207520000.1379936048.&type=3&theater or https://www.facebook.com/photo.php?fbid=10201037304478803&set=a.3260761081901.2161649.1353406794&type=3&theater [last accessed 27 September 2013].
[88] Richard Avedon, 'Borrowed Dogs', *Richard Avedon Portraits, 2002,* online at www.richardavedon.com/data/web/richard_avedon_borrowed_dogs.pdf [last accessed 27 September 2013], p. 4.
[89] See, for example www.youtube.com/watch?v=coc3Wtqn6I8 [last accessed 27 September 2013].
[90] *Argentina al día* 697 and *EPA* 467, Audiovisual section of the state archive 'Archivo General de la Nación', Ministerio del Interior, República Argentina, 1969. This archive does not follow a coherent system for the classification of audiovisual material.

is presented, which is similar to other news footage of the time, suggests that as cultural custodian Borges plays a vital role in the grand plan for Argentina to become a powerful modern nation. As mentioned before, this 'manifest destiny' for greatness is, according to María Cristina Pons, one of Argentina's 'foundation myths', a grand narrative which gives the nation a sense of belonging and identity. This is a position, she maintains, of which the country as a collective is constantly mindful.[91] Borges would play a fundamental role in the perpetuation of this foundational myth throughout the following fifteen years, as the next section explores.

The 1970s and Early 1980s and Venerable Borges

The 1970s and early 1980s were troubled times for Argentina, as the political situation seemed to worsen day by day. Political turmoil, marked by violent clashes between guerrillas and the state, was felt both nationally and internationally. During the military dictatorship of 1976–1983, general human rights abuses and the killing and disappearance of public figures, both Argentine and foreign, motivated international reactions.[92] 1977 saw the first marches of the 'Madres de Plaza de Mayo', which brought the conflict into the public eye, especially internationally. As mentioned before, this was also a time of great popularity for Borges and the Argentine press regularly reported interviews which had been broadcast both at home and in the foreign media.[93]

These articles were often accompanied by either a small portrait or a photograph of Borges in conversation, as shown in Figures 15–17. The basic elements of these famous photographs are the white hair, trade-mark suit and tie, and, although not always used, the equally iconic walking-stick, all against a backdrop of books or solid, dark furniture. Another crucial feature is the emphasis on his blindness, which is made 'visible' through the choice of angle: most portraits of Borges as an old man clearly show that his eyes are not able to focus even though they are either directed at or at an angle to the camera. The use of these images complements the depiction in the articles they accompany,

---

[91] Pons, *Delirios de grandeza*, pp. 18–19.
[92] Only in 1977, for example, the Foreign Secretary, César Guzzetti was seriously wounded in a guerrilla attack; the leader of the guerrilla group Montoneros, Julio Roqué, was killed in a clash with police forces; among the 'public' disappeared during 1977 were the union leader Oscar Smith, the Venezuelan Ambassador, Héctor Hidalgo Solá and two French nuns. Writer and journalist Rodolf Walsh was ambushed and murdered by a special military group. The director of newspaper *La Opinión* was also detained and tortured.
[93] Consider, amongst many others: 'Difundiose una entrevista a J.L. Borges en Italia', *La Nación*, 21 September 1971; 'Borges en la TV Italiana', *La Razón*, 22 September 1971; 'Borges, en la TV Francesa', *La Razón*, 28 March 1979; 'Programa de la BBC sobre Borges', *La Nación*, 29 April 1979); and 'Si Borges lo dice', *Somos*, 10 September 1982. I am indebted to Agustín Maurín for access to the archives of *Clarín* in Buenos Aires.

FIGURE 15. *Diario Popular*, 2 November 1980. Image courtesy of Archivo del diario *Clarín*. Reproduced with permission.

Buenos Aires, miércoles 8 de agosto de 1984 ★ CLARÍN

Borges, también estrella en la radio norteamericana

Página 4 ★ ESPECTÁCULOS

El escritor Jorge Luis Borges: sus textos se difunden por los emisoras radioles estadounidenses.

La red de estaciones de radio no comerciales de Estados Unidos difunde actualmente un ciclo dedicado al escritor argentino Jorge Luis Borges. Se leen algunos de sus textos, se define su personalidad y se relata la influencia que Borges ha tenido y tiene en la literatura del mundo occidental.

NUEVA YORK (AP). — Una singular amalgama de recuerdos de juventud, de misteriosas fantasías filosóficas surge de un programa de la radio pública nacional de Estados Unidos dedicado al escritor argentino Jorge Luis Borges.

Las voces de locutores y actores y la del mismo Borges comparten abstracciones de universos míticos y tigres imaginarios con una prosa inglesa que hace honor a la galanura, con que el autor de El Aleph, Ficciones y centenares de otros cuentos y ensayos las plasmó en el original español.

Otros escritores, como el uruguayo Emir Rodríguez Monegal y el norteamericano Alastair Reid, ofrecen breves facetas personales del hombre de letras argentino.

El programa, subtitulado La risa del universo, es el segundo de una serie de trece producidos para la red de estaciones de radio no comerciales del país con el título general de "Rostros, espejos, máscaras —Ficción latinoamericana del siglo XX". Cada uno de los segmentos está dedicado a una gran figura de la literatura contemporánea de esa región. El primero honró al colombiano Gabriel García Márquez.

En un bosquejo biográfico del hombre de letras argentino, la locutora del programa dice que "El padre de Borges, ciego a los 30 años, transmitiría su ceguera hereditaria a su hijo, consciente de que se perdería la vista, adquirió una enorme avidez por la lectura, especialmente la de la enciclopedia que había en la biblioteca de su padre..."

En un pasaje que probablemente, sin intención de los productores, resulta risueño para el oyente de habla hispana, un actor de voz perfectamente impostada y con el fondo musical de un viejo tango tocado con guitarra, recita en un inglés de pureza shakesperiana este fragmento de un ensayo de Borges:

"... Recortados contra el fondo azul de paredes o de un cielo abierto, dos maleantes de trajes negros ajustados y zapatos de gruesos tacos bailan una danza mortal, un ballet de dagas que se rozan hasta que un clavel aparece en la oreja de uno de ellos cuando un cuchillo encuentra su marca en él y pone fin a la danza sin acompañamiento en el piso con su muerte. Satisfecho, el otro ajusta su sombrero de copa alta y pasa sus últimos años recordando la historia de aquel duelo leal... Esa es en resumen la historia de nuestro viejo arrabal argentino..."

Para deleite de estudiosos de la obra del escritor argentino en un idioma distinto del original, el programa ofrece este ejemplo de pensamientos típicamente borgeanos trasladados con evidente admiración y afecto al inglés:

"Una siniestra sociedad secreta imaginada por Borges ha inventado el planeta Tlon mediante el simple procedimiento de insertar información acerca de él en las enciclopedias terráqueas. A su debido tiempo, si el tiempo en verdad existe, la Tierra será suplantada por Tlon, un escalofriante doble de la Tierra que abarca incluso las escuelas contradictorias de la filosofía, que de acuerdo con Borges es una rama importante de la literatura fantástica".

"Otra de esas escuelas declara que la totalidad del tiempo ya ha ocurrido y que la vida, nuestra vida, es un vago recuerdo de un tenue reflejo, fallas indudables y fragmentadas de un proceso irrevocable. Otra sostiene que la historia del universo, que contiene la historia de nuestras vidas, y los detalles más infinitesimales, es el designio producido por un dios menor a fin de comunicarse... con un demonio. Otra afirma que el universo es comparable con esos sistemas de código en los que los símbolos tienen significados en los cuales solamente lo que ocurre cada tricentésima noche es verídico. Otra piensa que cuando dormimos estamos despiertos en alguna otra parte..."

"Y así cada hombre es dos hombres...", dice el propio Borges, y habla de sí mismo como si tuviera una segunda personalidad: "Yo vivo, yo me dejo vivir para que Borges pueda tramar su literatura... Y esa literatura me justifica".

FIGURE 16. *Clarín*, 8 August 1984. Image courtesy of Archivo del diario *Clarín*. Reproduced with permission.

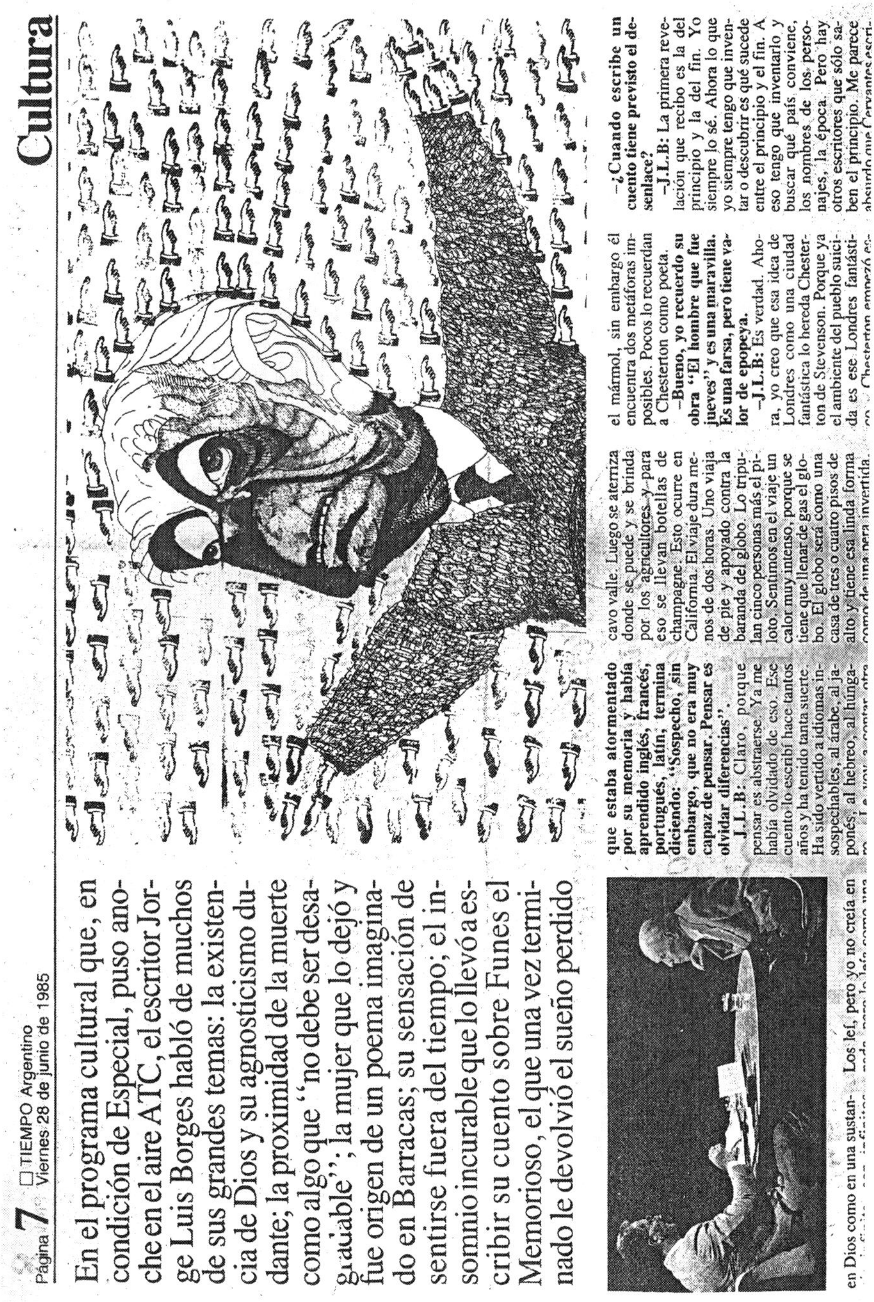

Página 7 □ TIEMPO Argentino
Viernes 28 de junio de 1985

Cultura

En el programa cultural que, en condición de Especial, puso anoche en el aire ATC, el escritor Jorge Luis Borges habló de muchos de sus grandes temas: la existencia de Dios y su agnosticismo dudante; la proximidad de la muerte como algo que "no debe ser desagradable"; la mujer que lo dejó y fue origen de un poema imaginado en Barracas; su sensación de sentirse fuera del tiempo; el insomnio incurable que lo llevó a escribir su cuento sobre Funes el Memorioso, el que una vez terminado le devolvió el sueño perdido

en Dios como en una sustan-

Los leí, pero yo no creía en

que estaba atormentado por su memoria y había aprendido inglés, francés, portugués, latín, termina diciendo: "Sospecho, sin embargo, que no era muy capaz de pensar. Pensar es olvidar diferencias".

J.L.B: Claro, porque pensar es abstraerse. Ya me había olvidado de eso. Ese cuento lo escribí hace tantos años y ha tenido tanta suerte. Ha sido vertido a idiomas insospechables, al árabe, al japonés, al hebreo, al húngaro...

cavo valle. Luego se aterriza donde se puede y se brinda por los agricultores y para eso se llevan botellas de champagne. Esto ocurre en California. El viaje dura menos de dos horas. Uno viaja de pie y apoyado contra la baranda del globo. Lo tripulan cinco personas más el piloto. Sentimos en el viaje un calor muy intenso, porque se tiene que llenar de gas el globo. El globo será como una casa de tres o cuatro pisos de alto y tiene esa linda forma como de una pera invertida.

el mármol, sin embargo él encuentra dos metáforas imposibles. Pocos lo recuerdan a Chesterton como poeta.

–Bueno, yo recuerdo su obra "El hombre que fue jueves" y es una maravilla. Es una farsa, pero tiene valor de epopeya.

–J.L.B: Es verdad. Ahora, yo creo que esa idea de Londres como una ciudad fantástica lo hereda Chesterton de Stevenson. Porque ya el ambiente del pueblo suicida es ese Londres fantástico... Chesterton empezó es-

–¿Cuando escribe un cuento tiene previsto el desenlace?

–J.L.B: La primera revelación que recibo es la del principio y la del fin. Yo siempre lo sé. Ahora lo que yo siempre tengo que inventar o descubrir es qué sucede entre el principio y el fin. A eso tengo que inventarlo y buscar qué país conviene, los nombres de los personajes, la época. Pero hay otros escritores que sólo saben el principio. Me parece absurdo que Cervantes escri-

FIGURE 17. Raúl Burzaco interviews Borges for state television, 'Tiempo de Borges', *Tiempo Argentino*, 28 June 1985. Image courtesy of Archivo del diario *Clarín*. Reproduced with permission.

of a Borges who has become an object of cultural worship. On 25th August 1979, for example, Hellén Ferro writes in *Clarín*:

> En toda la literatura argentina solamente hay un escritor que en su vejez haya conocido la veneración nacional que su genio, pero también los medios de difusión, han conseguido para Jorge Luis Borges. [...] La fama de Borges es internacional [...] y transmisiones como las de Canal 11 tienen la virtud de llevar a la conciencia del pueblo que hombres como Borges [...] son algo importante para la argentinidad.[94]

The article (Fig. 18), which itself perpetuates the veneration that it refers to, is about an interview broadcast by Argentine TV's *Canal 11* on occasion of the writer's 80th birthday. It is testimony to the importance ascribed to the figure of Borges in the construction of a sense of 'Argentineness' by the media of the time. The regular appearance of Borges in the press — both popular and high-brow — in interviews at home and abroad shows his position as a legitimating cultural force, as Ferro points out in the same article (p. 11). Borges is thus portrayed as an 80-year-old 'monumento' (Ferro) which stands for the greatness of Argentine culture. A monument is an empty effigy set in stone, unlikely to change or evolve and worthy of veneration, which becomes metaphorical when a certain set of meanings is projected onto it. As Chapter 3 of this study argues, the solidity of this construction of Borges as a father figure, who is representative of a strong sense of tradition, is proven by the strength of the rebellion of the intellectuals of the New Generation. Thus, the early image of Borges constructed in Alicia Jurado's biography is perpetuated, solidifying the image of the old blind sage, enclosed in the labyrinth of his fictional cosmos.

The sense of Borges as a national figure of worship is reinforced by publications such as 'Todo Borges', a special issue of popular magazine *Gente* published in January 1977 which was dedicated entirely to the writer.[95] The magazine contains a great number of images of miscellaneous Borges-related documents, including newspaper articles, manuscripts, portraits, book covers and airport baggage claim tickets. The fact that not all of these are dated clearly adds a sense of timelessness, giving them a certain simultaneity which reinforces the figure of Borges as eternal and unchanging. Also, the inclusion of a great deal of foreign newspaper clippings and book covers in foreign languages contributes to the impression that Borges triumphs abroad, thus legitimating his acclaim at home.

On page 150 of 'Todo Borges' a photograph shows the writer posing for a portrait by painter Elbio Fernández. It is a scene in the fashion of the 1970s, as seen in the artist's clothes and in the decoration of the room. The only elements that appear to be oblivious to the trends of the decade are the presence of books

---

[94] Hellén Ferro, 'Una antología de frases borgeanas', 'Espectáculo', *Clarín*, 25 August 1979.
[95] 'Todo Borges', *Gente* (Buenos Aires: Atlántida, 1977).

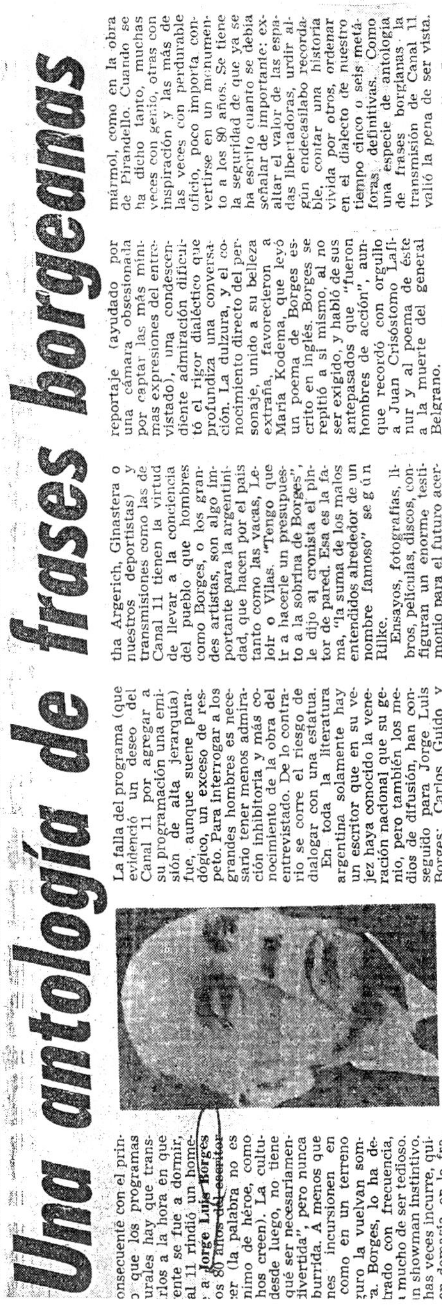

.RIN ★ Buenos Aires, sábado 25 de agosto de 1979 ESPECTACULO ★ Página 11

Una antología de frases borgeanas

onsecuente con el prin- que los programas urales hay que trans- rlos a la hora en que ente se fue a dormir, al 11 rindió un home- a Jorge Luis Borges os 80 años del escritor er (la palabra no es nimo de héroe, como hos creen). La cultu- desde luego, no tiene qué ser necesariamen- divertida", pero nunca burrida. A menos que nes incursionen en como en un terreno guro la vuelvan som- a. Borges, lo ha de- trado con frecuencia, mucho de ser tedioso. n showman instintivo. has veces incurre, qui- en demasía, en la fra- rillante antes que pro- la. Se divierte al es- arse y oye con irónica osidad lo que dicen de "otro Borges", el de la a que no acierta a ex- plicarse, como afirmó en un poema publicado en "Clarín" el jueves último.

Borges: cumpleaños y programa de televisión.

La falla del programa (que evidenció un deseo del Canal 11 por agregar a su programación una emisión de alta jerarquía) fue, aunque suene paradógico, un exceso de respeto. Para interrogar a los grandes hombres es necesario tener menos admiración inhibitoria y más conocimiento de la obra del entrevistado. De lo contrario se corre el riesgo de dialogar con una estatua.

En toda la literatura argentina solamente hay un escritor que en su vejez haya conocido la veneración nacional que su genio, pero también los medios de difusión, han conseguido para Jorge Luis Borges: Carlos Guido y Spano, al que los chicos de los colegios visitaban en su lecho patriarcal como a un héroe civil. La fama de Borges es internacional (como la de Martha Argerich, Ginastera o nuestros deportistas) y transmisiones como las de Canal 11 tienen la virtud de llevar a la conciencia del pueblo que hombres como Borges, o los grandes artistas, son algo importante para la argentinidad, que hacen por el país tanto como las vacas, Leloir o Vilas. "Tengo que ir a hacerle un presupuesto a la sobrina de Borges", le dijo al cronista el pintor de pared. Esa es la fama, "la suma de los malos entendidos alrededor de un nombre famoso" según Rilke.

Ensayos, fotografías, libros, películas, discos, configuran un enorme testimonio para el futuro acerca de uno de los grandes escritores actuales, al que todos los años **no le dan** el Premio Nobel, como dijo el propio Borges con encomiable humor. En el reportaje (ayudado por una cámara obsesionada por captar las más mínimas expresiones del entrevistado), una condescendiente admiración dificultó el rigor dialéctico que profundiza una conversación. La dulzura, y el conocimiento directo del personaje, unido a su belleza extraña, favorecieron a María Kodema, que leyó un poema de Borges escrito en inglés. Borges se repitió a sí mismo, al no ser exigido, y habló de sus antepasados que "fueron hombres de acción", aunque recordó con orgullo a Juan Crisóstomo Lafinur y al poema de éste a la muerte del general Belgrano.

Dijo lo de siempre, del excelente modo como lo ha dicho muchas otras veces. La admiración que el cronista, y muchos al igual que él, siente por ... la obra y ... mármol, como en la obra de Pirandello. Cuando se ha dicho tanto, muchas veces con genio, otras con inspiración y las más de las veces con perdurable oficio, poco importa convertirse en un monumento a los 80 años. Se tiene la seguridad de que ya se ha escrito cuanto se debía señalar de importante: exaltar el valor de las espadas libertadoras, urdir algún endecasílabo recordable, contar una historia vivida por otros, ordenar en el dialecto de nuestro tiempo cinco o seis metáforas definitivas. Como una especie de antología de frases borgianas la transmisión de Canal 11 valió la pena de ser vista.

Hellén Ferro

FIGURE 18. *Clarín*, 25 August 1979. Image courtesy of Archivo del diario *Clarín*. Reproduced with permission.

and Borges himself: his clothes and his walking-stick. The image of a 70-something Borges is captured in a fittingly Borgesian game of mirrors and reproduction, first in the artist's sketch and then in the photograph. The significance of this multi-layered image goes beyond the photograph itself, thus illustrating the mechanisms at work in the construction of a wider, more influential, image of the writer. A series of elements that lie outside the image include the publication where it appeared and its own contextual significations, especially the year of publication, which, in turn, has significance within Borges's historical life span, as discussed before. The caption, which includes a comment by the artist on the situation depicted in the photograph: 'Había luz a su alrededor,' lends the image an aura of saintliness, reinforcing the sense of Borges as a superior being.[96] In accordance with the title 'Todo Borges', this montage of memorabilia seems to promise access to the conveniently packaged and consumable writer. In this sense, it suggests that printed photographs of the writer have become 'fetishes', occupying the space of something unattainable but desired.[97] This is announced on the dustcover of this special issue, paraphrasing Whitman: 'Este libro es un hombre. Y el que toca este libro toca a un hombre.'[98]

During the 1970s and early 1980s Borges travelled extensively around Europe and the United States, and he often gave interviews which were promptly reported in Argentine newspapers (e.g. Fig. 16); this contributed to the construction of the image of Borges as cultural success story. As mentioned before, the reporting of Borges's international recognition amounts to the ostensive appropriation of the image of the writer as a triumph on behalf of the nation at large. Further proof of this is an article published in Clarín in 1980, where Borges is referred to as the epitome of the 'ordinary' Argentine. Here, the trait that defines Borges's 'Argentineness' is a paradoxical desire to be someone else in order to be able to know himself: 'Un chisporroteo suave, más cerca del circunspecto humor inglés que del ingenio español, mostró la deliciosa inteligencia de quien dio una de las más profundas definiciones del argentino medio: "Yo, que soñé ser otro".'[99]

Televised interviews of Borges also contributed to the construction of his image as a wise elder. Amongst the many that were originally broadcast at the time, some can be found in the video archive of Buenos Aires's television station *Canal 13*, which contains clips of a variety of interviews broadcast between 1980 and

---

[96] Elbio Fernández in 'Todo Borges', p. 150.
[97] Martin Lister explains that this occurs as a result of 'putting photographic indexicality and materiality together,' when 'we see the photograph as something which it is as important to hold, touch, feel and check for as it is to see, and which we sense has literally touched something that [...] has existed but is no more,' in 'Photography in the Age of Electronic Imaging', in *Photography*, by Liz Wells, pp. 297–336 (p. 332).
[98] 'Todo Borges', dustcover. Cf. Walt Whitman, 'So Long', *Leaves of Grass* (1860), ll. 55–58.
[99] Hellén Ferro, 'La televisión y un Borges para todos', *Clarín*, 27 August 1980.

1986.[100] Most of these show the writer wearing a suit and sitting in his green armchair, in his own sitting room, accompanied by his white cat, Beppo. The fact that the setting is always the same (as described by Avedon above) reinforces the idea of a holy man in his shrine, which interviewers visit in search of truth. He is an elderly man surrounded by books, and the room generally appears in darkness, which reinforces the idea of his blindness. Interviewers treat him with great respect, as is the case, on 23rd August 1980, of Lidia Satragno, better known as 'Pinky', a popular TV presenter who epitomized the middle class housewife of the time.[101] In the interview, she speaks slowly and carefully and smiles sweetly at Borges as if she was addressing her grandfather. The questions she asks are very similar to those asked by other reporters in the many other interviews, about death, old age, blindness and books. The answers that Borges provides are also repeated in various interviews, particularly the recitation of 'Poema de los dones', which he normally accompanies with a reflection on the other two blind directors of the Biblioteca Nacional (José Mármol and Paul Groussac).

'Tiempo de Borges' is another example of the elderly writer being interviewed at length on Argentine television. The programme, in which Borges is interviewed by Raúl Burzaco for the state-run television station *ATC*, was broadcast between 11.00 pm and 12.30 am on 27th June 1985.[102] Even though Burzaco has a different — slightly less reverential although always respectful — attitude to Borges, the fact that interviewer and interviewee are sitting at a plain table against a background of complete darkness gives the encounter an air of detachment from time and place. The viewer can see a table, two chairs, books, a glass of water, Burzaco and the reassuring image of an elderly, besuited Borges leaning on his walking stick (Fig. 17). Here Borges and Burzaco discuss a variety of subjects which are highly intellectual. The following day, a few extracts of this interview were published in the newspaper *Tiempo Argentino*, which Burzaco himself introduces by saying: 'Dialogar con Jorge Luis Borges supone una suerte de forzosa autosuperación, para ponerse "a la altura de …".'[103] thus reinforcing the image of the writer's erudition. The sense of Borges's protagonism in the construction of an Argentine culture is reinforced by the presence of the name of the country in the television channel (*ATC* stands for 'Argentina Televisora Color') and in the newspaper in which the article appeared.

---

[100] In 1979, a devastating fire destroyed earlier material. I am indebted to Mario Mattaruco, Head of Archive of *Canal 13*, for access to these sources in April 2008, as there is no ordinary provision for consultation of this archive by researchers.
[101] Archivo *Canal 13*, A-6641, TCS-00-46-12.
[102] Video footage found in the *Audiovideoteca de Buenos Aires*, Gobierno de la Ciudad de Buenos Aires, AEVR2038C 31'23".
[103] Raúl Burzaco, 'Tiempo de Borges', *Tiempo Argentino/Cultura*, 28 June 1985.

The strength of the construction of Borges as a figure worthy of reverence, a national treasure whose greatness is confirmed and legitimized by his success abroad, is emphasized when it is considered as an Argentine phenomenon. This becomes evident when it is compared to the image of the writer that foreign photographers constructed. The next section examines this contrast.

Borges's Reception in the USA and the Irreverence of American Photographers

In 1962, the publication of *Ficciones* and *Labyrinths* in the United States by Grove Press and New Directions respectively, inaugurated a period which Argentine academic Jaime Alazraki identifies as the highest point in the American reception of Borges, and which spans the 1960s and 1970s.[104] Apart from what he refers to as frenetic celebration of Borges's work in academic circles, Alazraki measures the extent of Borges as a dominant presence in the American literary scene by the constant appearance of translations of, or comments on, Borges's texts in important publications such as '*Time, Harper's Bazaar, Vogue, The Atlantic Monthly, The New Yorker, The New York Times, New American Review, Mundus Artium, The New York Review of Books, Salmagundi, The Antioch Review, Esquire, TriQuarterly,*' as well as on public radio and television (p. 343). Alazraki also underlines Borges's influence on contemporary American fiction and criticism. However, he hastens to point out Borges's appeal to an academic readership, to the average reader and to the professional writer alike. This, Alazraki claims, is where the uniqueness of Borges's success in the United States lies (p. 345).

In the 1960s, in the United States, *Time Magazine* portrayed Borges as 'the greatest living writer in the Spanish language,'[105] and gave *Ficciones* fourth place in a list of 'The Decade's Most Notable Books'.[106] In 1975, he was referred to as 'the most eminent living Argentine' by Hedley Donovan in 'South America: Notes on a New Continent'.[107] In an article published in 1977 in *The Boston Review*, Katherine Singer Kovacs highlights Borges's position as Argentina's main legitimating cultural force, both locally and abroad:

---

[104] Alazraki, 'Recepción de Borges en los EE.UU.', p. 343.
[105] 'Books: Greatest in Spanish', *Time Magazine*, 22 June 1962, online at www.time.com/time/magazine/article/0,9171,870003,00.html [last accessed 27 September 2013] (author unknown).
[106] 'Fiction: The Decade's Most Notable Books', *Time Magazine*, 26 December 1969 www.time.com/time/magazine/article/0,9171,941837,00.html [last accessed 27 September 2013] (author unknown).
[107] Hedley Donovan, 'Time Essay: South America: Notes on a New Continent', *Time Magazine*, 1 December 1975, online at www.time.com/time/magazine/article/0,9171,913779,00.html [last accessed 27 September 2013].

It is in the direct interest of the government to continue serving up Borges as a distraction, an icon, the ultimate Argentine success story. At home, his countrymen not only bask in the reflected glory of his international reputation, but they also receive assurances from their greatest writer that all is well in Argentina. Abroad, potential critics of the regime may be disarmed — after all, a government which has the support of Jorge Luis Borges can't be all that bad.[108]

Kovacs's article stresses the strength of Borges as an Argentine success story by suggesting that the appropriation of his figure on the part of the military dictatorship which governed Argentina between 1976 and 1983 was equivalent to Borges's condoning of their actions. This controversial perception of Borges as cultural father-figure who lent his support to a brutally repressive regime is contested in Chapter 3. Apart from the obvious recognition of Borges's greatness as a literary figure, the construction of his image in the United States lacked the component of the projections regarding the definition of a national cultural identity present in Argentina. This was replaced, in America, by an exploration of difference.

The portrayal of Borges abroad, in particular in portraits taken by American photographers, shows some variance in relation to those images produced and circulated in Argentina. These variations in the discourses condensed in them are achieved through an interrogation of certain elements of the figure of Borges, in particular the meanings associated with his blindness and his air of traditional respectability. I will refer to two photographs of Borges taken in New York by celebrated American photographers Diane Arbus in 1969 and Richard Avedon in 1976, to underline, by contrast, the uniformity of the image of the writer constructed in Argentina. Where Argentine photographers show Borges as a homogenizing force which lends coherence to an Argentine identity, the Borges of Arbus and Avedon tells a different story.

Avedon and Arbus were the same age, both based in New York and employed at some point by magazines such as *Harper's Bazaar* (which published Arbus's famous photograph of Borges in Central Park, as we shall see). They each chose to shoot Borges not because he was a literary monument, but in spite of it. According to Alazraki, Borges was considered a must-read among those who were 'intelectualmente informados y de alta curiosidad literaria.'[109] Arbus's biographer Patricia Bosworth wrote that the photographer was known to be a voracious reader, especially of Kafka, Rilke and Borges.[110] The 'great blind Argentine writer,' she claims, was Arbus's 'idol' (p. 287). However, apart from

---

[108] Katherine Singer Kovacs, 'Borges on the Right', *Boston Review*, Fall 1977, online at http://bostonreview.net/kovacs-borges-on-the-right [last accessed 27 September 2013].
[109] Alazraki, 'Recepción', p. 344.
[110] Patricia Bosworth, *Diane Arbus: A Biography* (New York: Norton, 1984), pp. 196–97.

the fact that both photographers knew his work, they felt, at a personal level, that photographing the blind writer allowed them to explore difference. Susan Sontag argues that Arbus's subjects 'are to remain exotic' and that 'her view is always from the outside.'[111] In Avedon's case, his decision to photograph the writer responded to a deep-seated fear of blindness: 'I photograph what I'm most afraid of, and Borges was blind.'[112] In the eyes of these American artists, Borges appeared as an interesting 'other', whose exoticism lay in his blindness and in the fact that he was a cultural outsider.

Diane Arbus was very active during the 1960s until her suicide in 1971. She is famous for her photographs of 'assorted monsters and borderline cases [...] people who are pathetic, pitiable, as well as repulsive,' as Sontag observes.[113] Her work never comes across as 'comfortable' or 'reassuring', but is, instead, 'reactive [...] against what is approved,' advancing 'life as a failure against life as a success' (p. 44). To anyone who knew her work, Arbus's decision to photograph Borges may appear puzzling: however, it is this photographer's exploration of difference rather than a wish to perpetuate Borges as homogenizing cultural force which differentiates her portrayal from that of her Argentine counterparts. Tomás Eloy Martínez comments that even when one of the important magazines 'le encomendaba un tema, lo importante para ella era el sujeto que le pondrían por delante: la extrañeza, la diferencia, el ínfimo temblor de realidad que apartaba a ese personaje de todos los otros.'[114]

Diane Arbus was asked to photograph Borges by *Harpers Bazaar*, which she did in New York's Central Park. The black and white portrait, in which a besuited Borges appears with both hands on his walking stick and surrounded only by trees, was published in March 1969 to illustrate three of his poems.[115] It has also been included in the book *Diane Arbus: Magazine Work* (2004). Tomás Eloy Martínez points out that the challenge in photographing Borges lay in that everyone knew his image, a challenge that Arbus overcame by producing an image that is like no other image of the writer: 'La iconografía de Borges es infinita: Diane Arbus, sin embargo, lo ve como nadie más, con los ojos muy abiertos, rebosantes de inteligencia, y los labios apagados por la amargura' (para. 13) (a sorrow that may have been related to his unhappy marriage to Elsa Astete: in fact, this is one of the few images in which Borges appears wearing a

---

[111] Susan Sontag, 'America, Seen Through Photographs, Darkly', *On Photography* (London: Penguin, 1979), pp. 27–47 (p. 42).
[112] Avedon, 'Borrowed Dogs', p. 4.
[113] Sontag, 'America', pp. 32–33.
[114] Tomás Eloy Martínez, 'Viaje a las tinieblas de Diane Arbus', *La Nación*, 28 May 2005, online at www.lanacion.com.ar/nota.asp?nota_id=707933 [last accessed 27 September 2013].
[115] Diane Arbus, 'Three Poems (Poems by Jorge Luis Borges)', *Harper's Bazaar*, New York, March 1969, pp. 238–39. Reproduced in Doone Arbus and Marvin Israel, *Diane Arbus: Magazine Work* (New York: Aperture, 2004), pp. 118–19.

wedding band). In Argentine photographs Borges seldom looks directly at the camera, and when he does, part of his face normally appears in shadows. This gives the impression of a traditional pose, where the subject does not appear to engage with the photographer. Conversely, Arbus's photograph shows Borges staring at the camera. Sontag points out that in Arbus's work this makes her subjects 'look even odder, even deranged,'[116] accentuating not a sense of authority but one of quirkiness.

In *The Ongoing Moment* (2005), Geoff Dyer examines Arbus's portrait of Borges in Central Park in relation to the issue of blindness. With the 'stark frontality and frankness' he argues are characteristic of her method, the photographer acted in defiance of criticisms that photographing the blind amounted to exploitation. In his description of the portrait, Dyer makes reference to the relationship between the subject and the camera, a key point in portraiture which blindness problematizes:

> Borges is placed in the exact center of the frame and stares directly at the camera, fully conscious of the process of which he is a part. His wrinkled hands rest on a walking stick [...] While the writer is in sharp focus, the trees behind him are blurred, isolating him from the visible world that frames — and defines our view of — him.[117]

Frontality explores the ethical dilemma of photographing the blind as a way of exploring difference, which had been a trope in the work of American photographers of the first part of the twentieth century. Dyer points out that Arbus's choice was due to the fact that the blind 'can't fake their expressions. They don't know what their expressions are, so there is no mask' (p. 44). Arguably, however, even when a subject is sighted, the 'mask' that they may imagine they put on may be perceived differently by the viewer. Borges's blindness appears obvious in images taken by Argentine photographers. In the case of Diane Arbus, it was not only shown but also interrogated and problematized.

Richard Avedon was a prolific fashion photographer whose work span more than five decades. Patricia Bosworth reminisces that 'everybody who entered Avedon's studio was some kind of star. And there was a sense of excitement, of titillation in that huge, white, lighted space.'[118] This was not the case when Avedon flew to Buenos Aires to meet Borges in 1975, only to find that the writer's mother had just died. The photographer later said that he had felt so overcome with emotion that he had found the resulting photographs 'empty'.[119]

---

[116] Sontag, 'America', p. 37.
[117] Geoff Dyer, *The Ongoing Moment* (New York: Pantheon, 2005), p. 42.
[118] Bosworth, *Diane Arbus*, p. 285.
[119] Avedon, 'Borrowed Dogs', p. 4.

The following year, Avedon photographed Borges again in New York.[120] This portrait has been exhibited numerous times and it is reproduced in the book *Richard Avedon: Evidence. 1944–1994* (1994). It departs most distinctly from other images of Borges in terms of his posture: it is very rare to see Borges leaning forward, as he does in this unusual photograph against Avedon's signature stark, white background. His clothes crease quite naturally, and although it appears posed, there is a certain sense of movement in the picture, as if he was about to stand up, or as if he had been caught in the middle of a lively conversation. Borges's expression is also unusual, quizzical, perhaps due to the crease on the bridge of his nose, and the particularly prominent pair of nostrils. From underneath noticeably protruding white eyebrows, he appears to be peering into a camera that looks at him slightly from above. Even though the writer appears serious and elderly, the brightness of the background, the absence of props or scenery and the angle of the shot show a Borges who appears 'not sage but vaguely comical in his complacent blindness.'[121]

Avedon's portrait of Borges does not convey a sense of reverence. Instead, it situates the photographer and his subject at an equal level, one at which two creative minds can interact, or indeed, it may even suggest that Borges is slightly subjected to Avedon's camera and his creativity, rather than the other way round. This is in marked contrast with the sense of respect and reverence that characterizes Argentine portrayals of the 'national' author. As such, it serves to underline the fact that the construction of Borges as an old sage responds to a specifically Argentine need to see him as a figure of veneration and an icon of national culture, whose image condenses expectations regarding the cohesion of national identity, as this chapter has shown.

Conclusion

This chapter has shown how the construction of the subject that is Borges is achieved in photographic images through the interaction between the physiognomy of the writer and the anxieties and expectations that consumers pour onto his image. Argentines scrutinize themselves in Borges as they do in a mirror. The image of Borges as a venerated wise elder provides a sense of cultural history and solidity against the background of socio-political fragmentation which marked the nation during most of the twentieth century. As a cultural father-figure, Borges represents cultural success legitimated by international

---

[120] Borges was photographed by Avedon in New York on 30 April 1976. The portrait is reproduced in Mary Shanahan (ed.), *Richard Avedon: Evidence. 1944–1994* (Random House: New York, 1994), p. 159.
[121] Dyer quotes American writer Adam Gopnik's comments on this photograph in *The Ongoing Moment*, p. 43.

public exposure. Jaime Alazraki illustrates Borges's permanence by referring to him as an Olympian hero:

> Borges deja de ser la figura llevada y traída por la crítica de su tiempo para situarse en el Olimpo de los clásicos donde ningún dardo lo puede alcanzar, donde infinitos lectores seguirán leyéndolo en bibliotecas, escuelas o espacios privados, en buenas o malas traducciones y donde sus textos están ya de una manera eterna [...] en el plano de lo imperecedero.[122]

As Hariman and Lucaites point out, the iconic photograph 'doesn't just draw on social knowledge enthymematically but refashions social forms to structure understanding [...] and organize collective memory.'[123] The next chapter delves into how 'these modes of imitation become particularly visible, yet also destabilized, as the photograph acquires a history of subsequent appropriation and commentary' (p. 33) in the shape of the drawing of Borges in comic strips. Here, the evolution of the image of Borges as a writer detached from the world of 'ordinary' Argentines and his troubled relationship with politics in the 1960s and 1970s will be analysed. This will be followed by a study of the reassessment of the figure of Borges through the appropriation of his image in comic strips of the mid-1980s, during Argentina's transition to democracy.

---

[122] Alazraki, 'Recepción', p. 355.
[123] Hariman and Lucaites, *No Caption Needed*, p. 33.

CHAPTER 3

~

Borges para sobrevivientes: Culture, Politics and Comic Strips of the 1980s

Introduction

> Un hombre se propone la tarea de dibujar el mundo. A lo largo de los años puebla un espacio con imágenes. [...] Poco antes de morir, descubre que ese paciente laberinto de líneas traza la imagen de su cara.
>
> J.L. Borges, 'Epílogo', *El Hacedor*.

The relationship between the physiognomy of the world and that of a person, as Borges suggests in his epilogue to *El Hacedor* (quoted above), centres on the search for identity. The man imagined by Borges, who embarked on the task of representing the world and spent his life filling it with images, comes to the end of his life and realizes that the representation of his world and that of his personal identity coincide. Used in juxtaposition with 'espacio', Borges's choice of the verb 'poblar' to describe the filling of a space with images suggests that the identity of a space is constructed, gradually, as it becomes inhabited. The fact that these 'inhabitants' are images, and that it is as a community that they are able to give meaning to the space, underline the importance of the visual in collective identity formation. This chapter continues to trace the quest of a national cultural identity for Argentina through the image of Jorge Luis Borges: its aim is to tease out the mechanisms that go into the construction of those individual images that, put together, make up the face of Borges and in doing so, also construct that of Argentina.

In an article about Borges's view of the interrelation between literature and history, Saúl Sosnowski writes that history is constructed to make sense of conflict, availing itself of much the same strategies as those used by literature. The process of historical signification, Sosnowski adds, also builds up what he refers to as 'una malla cohesiva que se llamará pueblo o nación.'[1] This sense of cohesive

---

[1] Saúl Sosnowski, 'Memorias de Borges (Artificios de la historia)', *Variaciones Borges*, 10 (2000), 79–95 (p. 82).

identity is achieved through a variety of political, artistic and media discourses, among others. The combination of artistic expression and the mass media in particular creates meanings which have a powerful impact on the general public. It is the case of comics, a medium that is defined by Randy Duncan and Matthew Smith as an art form whose social reality implies their mass circulation and their function as economic commodity.[2]

This chapter comprises two parts: it begins by exploring the changing relationship of the so-called 'progre' generation of intellectuals — particularly active during the 1960s and 1970s as intensely politically engaged critics, writers and artists — with Borges. The second part constitutes a case-study which aims to demonstrate how this change was manifested in a selection of Argentine comic strips published in the 1980s. Therefore, what binds both parts together is the belief, following Duncan and Smith, that 'comics are a viable means for shining the light of inspection upon the presumptions and practices of the dominant ideology' (p. 267). This wide-ranging medium includes cartoons and comic strips. Cartoons are uderstood as single drawings with no accompanying text which — in much the same way as painted or photographic portraits — concentrate their meanings enthymematically.[3] Comic strips are, by definition, sequential narrations through a juxtaposition of drawings and text. Reference is made to a few cartoons of Borges to illustrate the construction of the author in the convergence of politics and popular art. However, the primary focus of the chapter is on comic strips.

'Pictureness', 'Verbalness' and Comic-strip Conventions

The potential for impact of comics lies primarily in their popularity, accessibility and ease of reading.[4] But it is these factors combined with their aesthetic potential to convey maximum meaning in minimal space that lends them their particular 'power to provoke' (Rubenstein). As Martin Barker explains, the wide ranging representational ability of still frames is achieved by means of a series of conventions whereby readers apply a set of comic-reading skills in order to make sense of the narrative that the frames present.[5] These conventions — which enable

---

[2] Randy Duncan and Matthew Smith, *The Power of Comics: History, Form & Culture* (New York and London: Continuum, 2009). Duncan and Smith refer to the comic as an art form because it 'can accommodate content as profound, moving and enduring as that found in any of the most celebrated vehicles for human expression', pp. 1–2.

[3] Mario Saraceni compares cartoons to single sentences, as in order for their meaning to be understood, the viewer needs pre-existent contextual information. Mario Saraceni, *The Language of Comics* (London and New York: Routledge, 2003), p. 36.

[4] Anne Rubenstein, *Language, Naked Ladies, & Other Threats to the Nation: A Political History of Comic Books in History* (Durham and London: Duke University Press, 1998), p. 7.

[5] Martin Barker, *Comics: Ideology, Power and the Critics* (Manchester and New York: Manchester University Press, 1990), p. 6.

the effective juxtaposition of text and image — concern both narrative structure and graphic layout. Thus, apart from predictability and repetitiousness of setting, character and plot, the most distinctive graphic conventions are the speech balloon and the frame. The speech balloon achieves a strong condensation of meaning through the interaction between its 'pictureness' and its 'verbalness' which produces 'the meaning of sound' (p. 11). Most significantly, as Barker points out, the speech balloon 'itself conditions the meaning' (p. 11). Similarly, as it delineates the boundary of the picture, the frame determines how we relate to the world being presented. Barker concludes that beyond transmitting meanings, comic conventions 'condense social relationships,' as they 'make reading a social relationship between us and the text' (p. 11).

The analysis of comic strips in the second part of this chapter is based on the social nature of the dialogue that this unique coalescence of elements establishes with readers. It is consistent with Barker's own dialogical approach to the study of comics, which is in turn based on the work of early twentieth-century Russian theorist Vladimir Propp. From Propp, who famously studied the form of folk tales, Barker takes the practice of deducing from the 'structure and transformations' of the stories in comics 'the typified social relations which are sedimented in them' (p. 275). Barker's study is thus based on the assumption that 'understanding involves placing ourselves socially in relation to the utterer' (p. 264).

As, in most cases, the creation of comic strips is a collaborative process, the 'utterer' generally refers to a team comprising writers, artists and technicians such as letterers, pencillers and colourists. As the epigraph to Duncan and Smith's chapter on comics and ideology highlights, 'the people who make comics have never existed in a vacuum. They instead live within a surrounding culture, a culture that is naturally reflected in their work.'[6] It can be argued, in this sense, that the ideological content of a strip originates in the ideas and preconceptions that the team brings to the creative process. Thus, the analysis of a selection of Argentine comic strips of the 1980s later in this chapter will illustrate Rubenstein's view of the development of *historietas* as a window into political and cultural processes.[7] The extended analysis of the changing relationship of politically engaged intellectuals with the figure of Borges in the first part of the chapter is thus necessary to establish the ideological background that is reflected in the creation, circulation and consumption of the comics analysed later.

After the first modern comics appeared in the late nineteenth century in magazines of political satire and in newspapers, they developed differently,

---

[6] Quoted from Fredrik Strömberg's *Black Images in the Comics: A Visual History* (Korea: Fantagraphic Books, 2003), page number not provided, in Duncan and Smith, *The Power of Comics*, p. 246.
[7] Rubenstein, *Language, Naked Ladies & Other Threats to the Nation*, p. 6.

according to Rubenstein, in 'the cultural ecologies of every region where they are found, and they rarely translate well' (p. 7). This serves as an indication of the medium's strong links with idiosyncrasy and context. Studies of comics and ideology have focused on cases from the U.S.A. In addition, representations of history and politics and the impact of comics on public opinion have been studied in Francophone *bandes desinées*, Japanese *manga* and Mexican *historietas*.[8] Argentina's own tradition of comics with a significant function of political and social commentary dates back to the appearance of *Caras y Caretas* magazine in 1894. The first decades of the twentieth century saw a proliferation of strips in a variety of publications, with the first comic book, *El Tony*, appearing in 1928 and continuing publication for over 70 years.[9] A long list of outstanding Argentine *historietistas* were to follow: Lino Palacio, Raúl Roux, Hector Germán Oesterheld and Alberto Breccia to name but a few who were also contemporaries of Borges. This is testimony to the profound bond between comics and their context of production. With this in mind, this chapter pivots on the belief that it is imperative to read these images not only as documents of an era but also 'como interés específico de una transformación estética y política,' as 'Viñetas Serias', the first international conference dedicated to comics held in Buenos Aires, sought to highlight.[10]

Cartoons, Politics and Borges

Several cartoon depictions of Borges appeared in the press in the Southern Cone, the earliest one of which is thought to be in Buenos Aires's magazine *Caras y Caretas* in the 1920s. But it was only in the 1970s that both Montevideo and Buenos Aires began to see more frequent drawings of the now world-famous author in their pages. In 1973, for example, Argentine newspaper *La Opinión*, which was considered 'mandarín absoluto del mundo cultural' of the city of Buenos Aires,[11] published a cartoon which shows a resigned Borges holding an

---

[8] Consider, for example, Mark McKinney's *History and Politics in French-Language Comics and Graphic Novels* (Jackson: University Press of Mississipi, 2008), Frederik Schodt's *Dreamland Japan: Writings on Modern Manga* (Berkeley: Stone Bridge Press, 1996), and Anne Rubenstein's *Language, Naked Ladies & Other Threats to the Nation*.
[9] Gociol and Rosemberg's 2003 chronology of Argentine strips includes more than 300 titles, in Judith Gociol and Diego Rosemberg, *La historieta argentina: una historia* (Buenos Aires: Ediciones de la Flor, 2003).
[10] '1er Congreso internacional de historietas Viñetas Serias (Buenos Aires, Argentina)', *Imaginaria*, 276 (2010), online at www.imaginaria.com.ar/?p=6889 [last accessed 27 September 2013].
[11] Mario Diament, 'Prólogo', in Fernando Ruiz, *Las palabras son acciones. Historia política y profesional de* La Opinión *de Jacobo Timerman (1971–1977)* (Buenos Aires: Perfil, 2001), p. 10.

umbrella to shelter from adverse criticism represented as raining words.[12] It is an accurate depiction of the writer's position at the centre of fundamental debates taking place on both sides of the Río de la Plata. Headed by Uruguayan critics Angel Rama and Emir Rodríguez Monegal, these debates concerned the place and responsibilities of literary production in the socio-political configuration of Latin America.

It was also in *La Opinión* that renowned Uruguayan-Argentine cartoonist Hermenegildo Sábat published many of his own drawings of Borges.[13] Sábat, whose artistic and journalistic trajectory spans five decades, is a great admirer of Borges, whom he has drawn and painted many times. One of his colour cartoons of the writer holding his walking stick and looking to the left was made into a commemorative stamp by the Argentine postal service in 2000 (Fig. 19). During his time at *La Opinión*, Sábat published a few cartoons of the author, amongst which is an extraordinary one of a hippie Borges, smoking marihuana (Fig. 20). This particular drawing subverts the classic image of the canonical writer, as all the elements which are characteristic of the traditional Borges are absent: there is no walking-stick, his hair is in a mess and the suit and tie have been replaced by a tunic and jeans. All this, together with the fact that his toes can be seen peeping out of a pair of rustic sandals, make Borges not only young but also, an 'ordinary' human being. It is the fact that the expected image is one of solemnity and tradition that makes this subversion shocking.

Founded by Jacobo Timerman in 1971, *La Opinión* was aimed, according to Fernando Ruiz, author of a history of the newspaper, at a young intellectual readership which had gained strength in the 1960s and was now in transition from culture into politics.[14] *La Opinión*, which therefore represented that transition, has remained a veritable referent and conveyor of recent Argentine history (p. 16). It may be considered to be broadly centre-left, even though its political allegiances are complex and at times contradictory. Its persistent denunciation of human rights violations resulted in editor Timerman's imprisonment and torture for two years and the newspaper's expropriation by the military regime in 1977. The coexistence of Borges and Sábat in this publication places them both at the core of the Argentine cultural scene of the 1970s.

In 1973, the culture section of *La Opinión* carried an article about Surrealism in Argentine literature, which was illustrated by Sábat. Four of these illustrations were drawings of Borges which later became part of the book *Georgie Dear* (1974). The book consists of twenty drawings, each accompanied by very brief dialogue

---

[12] The drawing by Ribeiro was published in *La Opinión* on 19 August 1973, and it is reproduced in Asociación Borgesiana de Buenos Aires, *Borges: 1001 Imágenes* (Buenos Aires: Fundación Banco Ciudad, 2003), p. 25.
[13] Hermenegildo Sábat is currently a cartoonist for *Clarín* newspaper (September 2013).
[14] Fernando Ruiz, *Las palabras son acciones*, pp. 43–44.

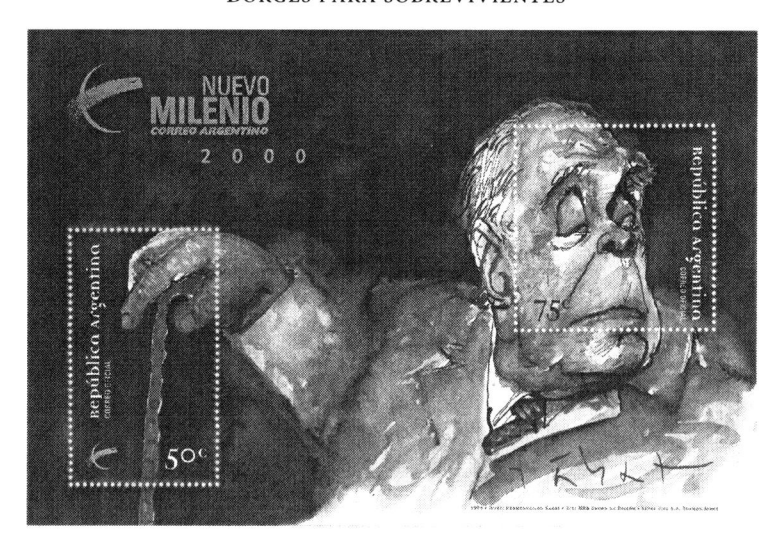

FIGURE 19. Hermenegildo Sábat, Commemorative stamp, *Correo Argentino*, 2000. Reproduced by permission of Hermenegildo Sábat.

FIGURE 20. Hermenegildo Sábat, *La Opinión*, 4 February 1973, reproduced in *Borges: 1001 Imágenes*, p. 26. Reproduced by permission of Hermenegildo Sábat.

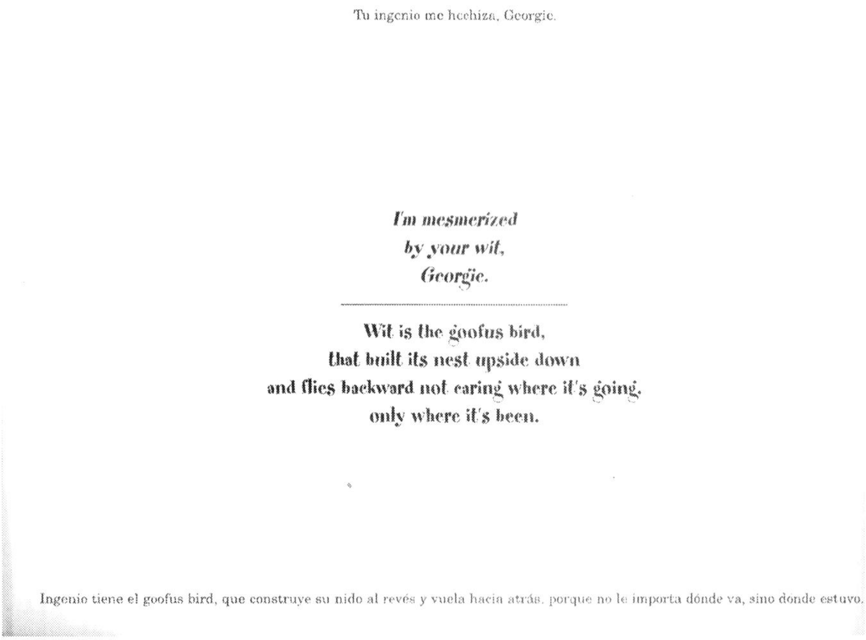

Tu ingenio me hechiza, Georgie.

I'm mesmerized
by your wit,
Georgie.

Wit is the goofus bird,
that built its nest upside down
and flies backward not caring where it's going,
only where it's been.

Ingenio tiene el goofus bird, que construye su nido al revés y vuela hacia atrás, porque no le importa dónde va, sino donde estuvo.

FIGURE 21. Text corresponding to the 8th drawing. Hermenegildo Sábat, *Georgie Dear*, 2nd edn (Nuevos Tiempos and Biblioteca Nacional, 1999), pages unnumbered. Reproduced with permission of Hermenegildo Sábat.

in English with rather distorted Spanish translations in the manner of film subtitles (Fig. 21). It shows 'Georgie' and the Argentine Republic in conversation. Borges's family nickname, which points to his English ancestry, is here used in a mocking tone. The reference to the Republic anchors the situation described to the world of politics. However, the quirky, surreal tone and content of the dialogue, together with the white background against which the drawings are set, give an impression of almost total detachment from the real world. Borges's bookish references to foreign writers and philosophers, and the fact that the conversation is held in English, not only show him in association with a foreign culture, but also create the illusion that whatever he is saying is obscure and unavailable to the 'ordinary' Argentine. In a similar playful style, Sábat recalls that 'el "chiste" era un diálogo en inglés y una traducción deliberadamente arbitraria, la suma de ambas cosas resultó *a lot of fun*.'[15] It is a remarkable exchange in which a flirtatious 'Republic' is personified by a Phrygian cap-wearing woman, in accordance with the national symbols (borrowed from those of the French Republic) that all Argentines are taught to recognize and honour (Figs. 22 and 23).

---

[15] E-mail conversation with Hermenegildo Sábat, 21 October 2009.

FIGURE 22. 8th drawing, Hermenegildo Sábat, *Georgie Dear*, 2nd edn (Nuevos Tiempos and Biblioteca Nacional, 1999), pages unnumbered. Reproduced with permission of Hermenegildo Sábat.

FIGURE 23. Cover of the 1974 edition of Hermenegildo Sábat's Georgie Dear (Buenos Aires: Crisis). Reproduced with permission of Hermenegildo Sábat.

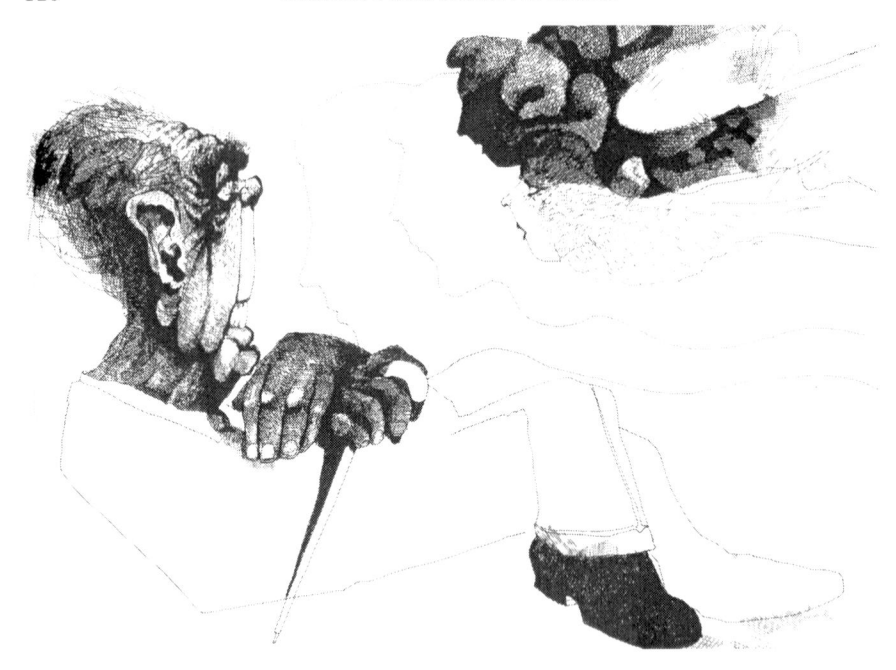

FIGURE 24. 'Isn't that a little bit of an understatement, Georgie?/No digas la mitad de lo que sabes, Georgie,' 2nd drawing, Sábat, *Georgie Dear*, 2nd edn, page unnumbered. Reproduced with permission of Hermenegildo Sábat.

The Republic appears demanding and insistent, as she asks Georgie to give a lecture on Borges. Interestingly, in some of the drawings her figure has been split into two or more layers (Fig. 24), whereas Borges remains one solid figure throughout, even though the dialogue suggests the existence of an alter ego. This depiction of the Republic interrogating the icon constitutes a fitting metaphor for the relationship between Borges and Argentina: the Republic is represented by a traditional symbol of liberty, which condenses the anxieties and expectations of the Argentine people. It has been repeatedly appropriated by so many groups purporting to defend it that it consequently suffers from a split identity. The Republic appears to seek the solidity and strength of the greatest mind amongst her subjects, and she chooses Georgie because the people of the nation have proclaimed him to be a monument to her culture: 'Tu ingenio me hechiza, Georgie,' sighs a smitten Republic.[16] Desperate to nourish her mind with Borges's wisdom, she flatters him, but he teases her, remaining noncommittal. When the Republic loses her patience, she confronts him with her real intentions and

---

[16] Hermenegildo Sábat, *Georgie Dear*, 2nd edn (Nuevos Tiempos and Biblioteca Nacional, 1999), the text accompanies the eighth drawing (pages not numbered), Figures 21 and 22.

FIGURE 25. 'I solemnly swear to respect the Constitution of my country', 21st (and last) drawing, Sábat, *Georgie Dear*, 2nd edn, page unnumbered. Reproduced with permission of Hermenegildo Sábat.

demands that he become president. Borges humbly accepts but not before he is able to choose English poet S.T. Coleridge as his vice-president. The dialogue ends as Georgie swears allegiance to 'his country'. The ambiguity of these last words is emphasized by the drawing that illustrates this last exchange, where the figures of Borges and the Republic appear separated by a cow divided up in marketable sections (Fig. 25). This image associates Borges with the landowning, cattle-breeding Argentine oligarchy, placing the future of the Republic in the hands of an elitist and culturally imperialistic Borges. Borges emerges as powerful and the Republic as weak and available to the highest bidder. Sábat claims that *Georgie Dear* was very tongue-in-cheek. His mockery of Borges's vilification illustrates his perception of Argentina as a politically weak country incapable of dealing with exceptional greatness.[17]

Sábat's ironic portrayal of Borges in *Georgie Dear* epitomizes the perception of the author that was common currency in the Argentina of the 1960s and 1970s.

---

[17] Sábat begins his e-mail of 21st October 2009 by saying: 'Mi relación con Borges comenzó con la lectura de su obra. Las envidias y los celos que sigue padeciendo Borges son la prueba de que somos un pequeño pueblo del interior que no tolera gente de excepcional inteligencia.'

In this period, the country's greatest man of letters was internationally acclaimed but denounced and vilified at home by the influential intellectuals of the younger generation. Broadly referred to as 'progresistas', this generation has played a central role in the development of Argentine culture in the latter part of the twentieth century and the beginning of the twenty-first. Given the importance of the reception of Borges in relation to politics, this chapter devotes considerable space to examining the evolution of this relationship. An appraisal of the intersections of Borges's literary production with the milieus of popular culture will be followed by an overview of the evolution of Argentine Borgesian criticism in its political context, which describes an ideological arc from the mid-1950s to the late 1990s.

In a discussion of mass culture in literature, Jean Franco considers 'the violent rejection of mass culture as anti-art' as 'only the initial stage in a long and intricate relationship marked by denunciation, appropriation, and, finally, celebration.'[18] As this analysis deals with the intersections of literature, politics and mass culture, it appears pertinent to apply the terms of Franco's description to the relationship between the figure of Borges and the younger generations throughout the second half of the twentieth century in Argentina. This 'ideological arc' begins with rejection and denunciation — which sometimes coexists with, and is indeed followed by, appropriation — and culminates in celebration. This changing assessment of Borges is here examined following the development suggested by Martín Lafforgue in *Antiborges* (1999), with a focus on the stage of 'appropriation'. This stage coincides, in the second half of the 1980s, with the period of transition to democracy following the 1976–1983 dictatorship.

I will provide an analysis of two comic strips that appeared in *Fierro* magazine between 1984 and 1986. I will first refer to 'Historia del guerrero y de la cautiva', a comic strip adaptation of Borges's story by the same title by Alfredo Flores and Norberto Buscaglia (later published in Ricardo Piglia's *La Argentina en pedazos* in 1993). Then, I will consider excerpts from the comic strip *Perramus*, by Alberto Breccia and Juan Sasturain. The chapter concludes with a brief examination of the comic strip version of another of Borges's stories, 'El Fin', also by Breccia and Sasturain, published in 1984 in *Crisis* magazine (later published in a collection of adaptations of literary works under the title *Versiones*, also in 1993). Although its circulation was significantly lower than that of the strips published in *Fierro*, this adaptation provides a fitting metaphor for the closure of an era in Borgesian criticism and the advent of a new one.

---

[18] Jean Franco, 'Comic Stripping: Cortázar in the Age of Mechanical Reproduction'(1997), in *Critical Passions: Selected Essays*, ed. Mary Louise Pratt and Kathleen Newman (Durham and London: Duke University Press, 1999), pp. 405–25 (p. 406).

'Entre la alta cultura y las ilustraciones populares'[19]

With unapologetic irreverence, cartoon depictions position the figure of Borges in the world of popular culture, bringing the image of the writer closer to the general public. Surprising as it may seem, this was not a milieu that Borges was unfamiliar with. A young Borges surreptitiously gluing the single sheet of the mural magazine *Prisma* onto the walls of Santa Fé street is perhaps not an image that readily comes to mind when thinking of the author of *Ficciones*. However, this is a well documented fact that points to a young author with a democratic view of literature.[20] Indeed, Borges's early trajectory in the popular media is varied and substantial: his regular contributions to *El Hogar* magazine and his role as literary editor of *Revista Multicolor de los sábados*, a section of popular newspaper *Crítica*, for example, have been well documented.[21] In *Borges: Una biografía literaria* Rodríguez Monegal enumerates the important texts published by Borges in this magazine and underlines his role in bringing a variety of authors to its pages and thus to the general public. Discussed under the title 'La prensa literaria de escándalo', Monegal defines *Crítica* as a tabloid which was, at the same time, highbrow.[22] The positive value and significance of these contributions, however, only began to be highlighted in the late 1990s, a point which Alan Pauls makes in 'Cartón pintado y metafísica' (2000):

> Recién ahora, tarde pero seguro, empieza a reconocerse que gran parte de la obra de Borges fue originalmente escrita y publicada en medios gráficos (diarios, suplementos culturales, revistas de interés general, publicaciones literarias), en un contexto de fugacidad, de normas y convenciones socioculturales que tenían muy poco que ver con ese limbo idílico llamado 'libro'.[23]

Borges contributed to these publications as a means of subsistence and what he wrote for them would have been determined by the long hours and tight deadlines involved. His employment in the popular press lasted until the late 1930s, when he took up a full-time position in the Miguel Cané Library; from here he went on to become director of the Biblioteca Nacional and he also held various teaching positions. The image of a working Borges, not to mention that of him as a trade unionist (as Lafforgue points out, he was president of the

---

[19] Alan Pauls, 'Cartón pintado y metafísica', in *El factor Borges*, pp. 125–40 (p. 139).
[20] Jorge Luis Borges, *Cartas del fervor: Correspondencia con Maurice Abramowicz y Jacobo Sureda (1919–1928)*, ed. by Cristóbal Pera (Barcelona: Galaxia Gutenberg-Círculo de Lectores de Emecé, 1999), pp. 206–10.
[21] These contributions were collected and published posthumously by Emecé in *Textos recobrados 1919–1929* (1997), *Borges en El Hogar* (2000), *Textos recobrados 1931–1955* (2001) and *Textos recobrados 1956–1986* (2003).
[22] Emir Rodríguez Monegal, *Borges:Una biografía literaria*, p. 227.
[23] Alan Pauls, 'Cartón pintado y metafísica', p. 128.

Argentine writers' guild S.A.D.E. for three years),[24] is somewhat in opposition to that of the artist in an ivory tower as depicted in some early biographies and denounced by many critics between the 1950s and the 1970s. Quite the contrary, as Pauls underlines, the texts of that same Borges who was considered an elitist writer in the 1970s 'compartían la misma página de revista con un aviso de corpiños o de dentífrico y con artículos para esclarecer a las amas de casa.'[25] Speaking from the pages of a 'sensationalist' publication, these texts allow him to weave his way across the world of the popular and that of so-called 'high literature'. These two realms should not therefore be considered separate in the case of Borges.

Pauls points out that these two sides to the Borgesian production — one which is 'culta, hermética, "intelectual", dirigida a un cenáculo de amigos e iniciados;' and another one which is 'popular, accesible, ligera, atenta a las apetencias de un público masivo y anónimo' (p. 134) — 'entran en una relación de reciprocidad' (p. 135). This reciprocity is brought to the fore by the context of the popular press. The title of the essay in which Pauls discusses this is borrowed from Borges's 1928 piece 'El truco', which illustrates the intersection of the realms of the popular and 'high' literature that is so typical of Borges's literary production (p. 135).[26] The fact that Borges's essay was published in *La prensa* accompanied by a caricature by famous cartoonist Lino Palacio, drives this point home.[27]

The combination of text and illustration is testimony to the coexistence of different spheres of cultural production and consumption, and it brings to mind a certain pictorial quality that is also present in the work of Borges. Although his work is very seldom published with illustrations, his narratives are visually evocative — particularly the visualization of space, illustrated by images which are central to his literature: the iconic labyrinth; the intricate designs and symmetries of gardens and libraries; the geometrical precision of the events in detective stories such as 'La muerte y la brújula'; the ever present colours yellow and red; bars, crevices and windows through which the main events of a story are seen to take place; the exploration of the boundaries of the real through the image of the mirrors; the fantastical creatures of *El libro de seres imaginarios*, and his study of the visual itself, 'El Aleph'. Franco observes that amongst other manifestations of popular culture, 'comic strips provided new media for narrative, altering, by the very method of production, received notions of author (there is often no single author), reception and originality.'[28] It could be argued that the

---

[24] Lafforgue, *Antiborges*, p. 123.
[25] Pauls, 'Cartón pintado y metafísica', p. 128.
[26] "Así,' termina Borges, 'desde los laberintos de cartón pintado del truco, nos hemos acercado a la metafísica." Alan Pauls cites Borges's 'El truco' in 'Cartón pintado y metafísica', p. 135.
[27] Jorge Luis Borges, 'El truco', *La Prensa*, 1 January 1928, illustrated by Lino Palacio, in Pauls, *El factor Borges*, p. 138.
[28] Franco, 'Comic Stripping', p. 405.

crossing of boundaries of genre, language, format, narrative technique, and the problematization of the notion of authorship, are as essential to comic strips as they are to Borges's work.

As we shall see, certain elements of the image of Borges have been appropriated by the popular genre of the comic strip. Here, the coexistence of graphics and printed text, of narration and dialogue, and the predominantly fragmentary nature of the medium, also call to mind the main elements of Borges's narrative style. It is crucial, at this point, however, to consider the politically motivated vilification of Borges on the part of the younger generation of intellectuals of the 1950s, 1960s and 1970s, and how this evolved into a period of reassessment in the mid-1980s. Thus, the next three sections will set the scene for the analysis of the significance of the presence of Borges in comic strips of the post-dictatorship period, which follows immediately after.

Argentine 'New Generations' and Borges: From Patricide to Restoration

The history of the relationship between Borges and Argentine critics is complex and at times, contradictory. However, it is possible to identify certain shifts which have accompanied different periods in Argentina's cultural history. The centrality of the figure of Borges within these debates speaks of his role as representative of a 'national' literature and, as we shall see, as a kind of cultural father-figure.

In 'Crónica de relación con Dios/Borges'(1992),[29] Argentine poet and former director of the Biblioteca Nacional Héctor Yánover descibes Borges as 'un monstruo que ha preñado a millones' (p. 172) who inspires extreme passions such as fear and hatred. This rather emotive image of insemination suggests Borges as a father-figure, whose children reject him because, according to Yánover's interpretation, 'se odia más a quien más nos ha dado' (p. 172). This image of Borges as god-the-father has its origins in the first generation of Borgesian criticism, dubbed 'the Patricides' by Emir Rodríguez Monegal, who in the mid-1950s rejected Borges based primarily on politics.[30] Yánover uses religious imagery to describe the passionate nature of this relationship: 'Borges se salvó de que lo crucificaran pero estuvo al borde mismo' (p. 173). At the same time, he points out that, beyond the intellectual arena, critics on the two sides of the political divide were equally incensed by Borges: 'Desde la izquierda, que proclamó distintas veces la necesidad de fusilarlo en Plaza de Mayo, a la derecha, militar o no, que miraba de reojo y con odio cuando sonaba su nombre' (p. 173).

---

[29] Héctor Yánover, 'Crónica de relación con Dios/Borges', *Cuadernos Hispanoamericanos*, 505–07 (1992), 171–6.
[30] Emir Rodríguez Monegal, *El juicio de los parricidas: la nueva generación argentina y sus maestros* (Buenos Aires: Deucalión, 1956).

The changing relationship of the main intellectual actors of Argentine culture with Borges has been a sign of the times, which Beatriz Sarlo refers to as 'the cycle of ideological, political and cultural transformations begun in 1956.'[31] There are, of course, many nuances. However, the following three decades can be broadly divided into two main moments: one of denunciation, in the two decades prior to the last dictatorship in 1976; and another of reclamation, which started in the transition to democracy after 1983. As Sarlo points out, the dictatorship years were a time when 'algunas cuestiones no podían ser pensadas a fondo, se las revisaba con cautela o se las soslayaba a la espera de que cambiaran las condiciones políticas.'[32] Therefore, although I will refer briefly to this period, I will concentrate on comparing the moments before and after it in order to underline its impact.

The time when the first phase, of vilification and denunciation of Borges, occurred is described by Sarlo as one when politics was taken as 'the criterion of truth and assured a unique foundation for all practices.'[33] The world was seen by politicized intellectuals in strict categories and a search for certainties was predominant. This, she continues, 'determined appropriate loci for culture and the arts' where the 'interlocutors, whether classified as "allies" or as "enemies," were assigned permanent positions in rigid relationships' (p. 255). Conversely, compared to the homogenizing 1960s and 1970s, it can be said that the post-dictatorship 1980s were characterized by a 'shattering of meanings'. Therefore, the second phase, of reclamation, occurs in the context of a more fragmented zeitgeist, in which the erosion of old certainties gave way to the possibility of diversity and coexistence.

The denunciation of Borges in the period between the mid-1950s and the late 1970s pivots on the relationship between literature and politics. In one of his lectures in 1985, Enrique Pezzoni identified this sector in relation to Borges as 'cierto tipo de izquierda que todavía no se ha resignado a ver la subversión en ciertos órdenes del sujeto Borges y no en otros.'[34] This period was characterized by unprecedented political activity among Argentine students in particular and intellectuals in general,

---

[31] Beatriz Sarlo, 'Intellectuals: Scission or Mimesis' (originally published as 'Intelectuales: ¿Escisión o mímesis?' in *Punto de Vista* 25 (1985)), trans. by Ana del Sarto, Abril Trigo and Alicia Ríos, in *The Latin American Cultural Studies Reader*, ed. by Ana del Sarto, Alicia Ríos, and Abril Trigo (Durham and London: Duke University Press, 2004), pp. 250–61 (p. 251). In 'Intérpretes culturales y democracia simbólica', Horacio Machín assesses the rethinking of the position of the leftist intellectual in the context of the 'Alfonsinista' years 1983–1989. In *Nuevas perspectivas desde/sobre América Latina: el desafío de los estudios culturales*, ed. by Mabel Moraña (Providencia, Santiago: Cuarto propio/Instituto Internacional de Literatura Iberoamericana, 2000), pp. 335–50.

[32] Beatriz Sarlo, *Tiempo pasado. Cultura de la memoria y primera persona* (Buenos Aires: Siglo XXI, 2005), p. 23.

[33] Sarlo, 'Intellectuals', p. 255.

[34] Transcripts of the recordings of some of Pezzoni's lectures on Borges at the Facultad de Filosofía y Letras of the Universidad de Buenos Aires were published in *Enrique Pezzoni, lector de Borges. Lecciones de literatura 1984–1988*, ed. by Annick Louis (Buenos Aires: Sudamericana, 1999), p. 123.

a moment when, as Sarlo puts it, 'intellectual activity and the task of producing new political perspectives had come together.'[35] It was in this context that the figure of the 'intelectual comprometido' emerged with particular force. The brutal response to this intense intellectual political activity, which was perceived as subversive by the military dictatorship (1976–1983) and its Proceso de Reorganización Nacional, achieved a devastating repression of anything that was perceived to be critical. This is summarized in a 2009 article in *Clarín*'s *Revista Ñ*:

> Dentro del amplio abanico de calamidades que dejó como legado la última dictadura militar se halla la de haber cercenado de forma brutal a la escena cultural argentina. En los campos de concentración de la década del 70 desaparecieron escritores, poetas, músicos, y artistas plásticos — algunos de ellos ya consagrados, otros en vías de lograrlo — quienes, junto con aquellos que tomaron la ruta del exilio, conforman una especie de generación ausente, un eslabón roto en la cadena de la identidad cultural de este país.[36]

This extermination of the 'intelectual comprometido' was both figurative and literal, as many were murdered, as Marinelli states above, and most were intimidated into silence.[37] This resulted in a sense of defeat and disorientation that characterized the years immediately following the return to democracy in 1983. This period in Argentina's history saw the reconsideration, in a new context and in a new light, of the categories that had so strongly defined the cultural political activity before the 'Proceso'. The relationship between Argentine leftist intellectuals[38] and the figure of Borges is one of the elements that was revised at this time of uncertainty, and it is the redefinition of this relationship that comic strips of the mid-1980s convey. Against the background of such turmoil, Borges appears to be a constant in Argentine culture: even when denounced and denied the Nobel Prize for his alleged support of totalitarian regimes, as we shall see, he is still perceived to be Argentina's greatest writer.[39] The quest for a national identity for Argentina through Borges lies at the core of this perception.

---

[35] Sarlo, 'Intellectuals', p. 251.
[36] Diego Marinelli, 'El sueño del Eternauta: el proyecto inconcluso de Oesterheld', *Revista Ñ*, 21 November 2009, online at www.revistaenie.clarin.com/notas/2009/11/21/_-02045193.htm [last accessed 27 September 2013].
[37] See Vicente Muleiro, 'Listas negras y escritores desaparecidos', *Clarín*, 24 March 2006, online at www.clarin.com/suplementos/especiales/2006/03/24/l-01164155.htm [last accessed 27 September 2013].
[38] I use this denomination in full awareness, as Sarlo wisely underlines, of 'all the ambiguity and indeterminacy that the adjective ['leftist'] implies.' Sarlo, 'Intellectuals', p. 260.
[39] This is corroborated by Volodia Teitelboim's account of a private conversation with one of the most influential members of the Swedish Academy, Arthur Lundkvist, in which he said: 'Soy y seré un tenaz opositor a la concesión del Premio Nobel de Literatura a Borges por su apoyo a la dictadura de Pinochet, que ha sido usado por la propaganda de la tiranía para intentar una operación cosmética', in *Los dos Borges: vida, sueños, enigmas* (1996), cited in Lafforgue, *Antiborges*, pp. 253–54.

The first book of Borgesian criticism was inspired by the emergence of the Sartrean idea of the *engagé* writer in the 1950s: Adolfo Prieto's *Borges y la nueva generación* (1954) gathers the views of a group of Marxist existentialists who had founded literary magazine *Contorno*. Amongst these were influential intellectuals who would play a vital role in Argentine cultural life in the following six decades: writer and academic David Viñas; writer, critic and academic Noé Jitrik; sociologist, critic and historian Juan José Sebreli and philosopher and academic León Rozitchner.[40] In *El juicio de los parricidas* (1956), Rodríguez Monegal was already aware of the potential extent of the influence of this generation: 'entre 1945 y 1955, estos jóvenes harán pesar cada vez más su opinión, proyectarán cada vez más lejos su palabra, hasta hacerse oír de los mismos a quienes comentan o atacan.'[41] He identifies a certain duality in their attitude and concludes that the young intellectuals 'atacan-veneran' the most prestigious literary figures of the previous generation with a certain 'salubrious violence' (p. 4). In the case of Borges, Monegal identifies 'el borgismo y el antiborgismo' (p. 4) which, he concludes, are two sides of the same coin. This is seen as a continuation of the controversy surrounding Borges's figure which dates back to a debate in *Megáfono* magazine from 1933, where the dichotomous nature of Borgesian criticism arises: 'aceptación y rechazo, igualmente fervientes, igualmente apasionados' (p. 20).[42] Monegal rightly highlights that the difference between the polemic of the 1930s and that of two decades later lies in the change in the historical context of Argentina. This will hold true for the remainder of the century, as violent upheaval marks the country for the next three decades and the construction of the Borges figure fluctuates alongside these social, cultural and political changes.

Rodríguez Monegal sees both defence and criticism of Borges as two forms of admiration, invoking envy or resentment as the sole reason why anybody would reject the 'Maestro': 'Tanto o más borgistas son quienes lo atacan que quienes lo defienden. Porque esa larga sombra de resentimiento que provoca su obra es también hechura o proyección del borgismo' (p. 21). He also considers the 'rebels' of the new generation as unruly adolescents going through a stage of rejection of the parent. True to the trend of the time, Monegal, in turn, has a dualist view of the critics' relationship with Borges, referring to Prieto as a 'Borgiano negativo o de sombra' (p. 25), who uses typical Borgesian words in his denial of Borges. Followers and admirers of Borges writing at the same time, such as Néstor Ibarra, are seen, conversely, as 'Borgistas de luz' (p. 25).

A separate type of 'parricida' of distinct nationalistic orientation emerged alongside the *Contorno* group. These 'Nacional Popular' intellectuals (Lafforgue)

---

[40] David Viñas died in March 2011.
[41] Rodríguez Monegal, *El juicio*, p. 3.
[42] Lafforgue offers an extract of this debate in *Antiborges*, pp. 27–30.

had Peronist sympathies which set them aside from those on the existentialist left. Characterized by a strong anti-oligarchic and anti-imperialistic stance, this group glorified the working class and denounced Borges as elitist, foreign-loving and anti-Argentine, detached from the plight of the 'pueblo'. In 1954, their most vocal advocate, Jorge Abelardo Ramos, wrote: 'El odio contra los de abajo es en Borges incontenible.'[43] This extremely agressive position outlined in his widely read book *Crisis y Resurrección de la literatura argentina* greatly influenced the perception of Borges as an enemy of the people. Although comparatively less fervent, it is a view still held by many today.

The early 1960s saw the rise of the 'nueva izquierda intelectual' in Argentina, inspired, like many other Latin American groups of intellectuals, by the ideals of the Cuban Revolution. Subsequently, 'los campos se delimitaron; el espacio para la duda, la ambigüedad o aun la indiferencia se pulverizó,' explains Martín Lafforgue.[44] Even though Lafforgue hastens to relativize the extent of the vilification of Borges on the part of the intellectual left, he does consider this group hegemonic within the Argentine cultural arena for a considerable period of time (p. 193). The fact that they are thought of as vehement Borges detractors leads to the inevitable conclusion that this position would have been heard in lectures, read in literary magazines and newspapers and published in books and, consequently, shared by many.[45]

In 1969, Blas Matamoro wrote: 'La cultura y la sociedad son, para Borges, escindidas e incomunicables,'[46] and then he proceeds to assess Borges's responsibilities in the world. He reaches the conclusion, after a detailed analysis of his philosophical and aesthetic stance, that Borges has always been a right-wing thinker, 'al servicio de la factorización inglesa del país, individualista y conservador, defensor del régimen y del orden' (p. 231). Furthermore, Matamoro denounces the confusion of ethics with aesthetics that he blames Borges for disseminating among what he terms 'the fallacious left'. He indignantly protests that 'no puede ser sino humillante para los argentinos que un escritor como Borges sea tomado por el paradigma intelectual argentino en el exterior' (p. 249). Matamoro questions Borges's position as 'jirafa sagrada, un gran escritor de derecha que ha hecho un aporte escencial a la cultura y, por lo mismo, a la historia del hombre, por lo que será reivindicado por revoluciones futuras' (p. 245). He considers that this elevating of Borges to the category of great writer regardless

---

[43] Jorge Abelardo Ramos, 'Borges, bibliotecario de Alejandría', *Crisis y Resurreción de la literatura Argentina* (Buenos Aires: Coyoacán, 1954), in *Antiborges*, pp. 127-40 (p. 135).
[44] Lafforgue, *Antiborges*, p. 196.
[45] Most of the intellectuals of the Nueva Izquierda writing at the time had links with the Universidad de Buenos Aires, in particular the Facultad de Filosofía y Letras, where they had academic responsibilities. Since then, this has been a space for intense political activity.
[46] Blas Matamoro, 'Detrás de la penumbra está Inglaterra', *Borges o El juego trascendente* (Buenos Aires: Peña Lillo, 1971), in *Antiborges*, pp. 193-250 (p. 201).

of his political views lies at the core of the myth of the left, and complaining about the inability of the left to judge the greatness of a literature beyond its formal or stylistic perfection. Matamoro equates the glorification of Borges with acquiescence to foreign domination and a generally weak nation. This exaltation of Borges by the left which Matamoro finds inexcusably paradoxical is exemplified by the position taken by influential literary magazine *El escarabajo de oro*. Founded by writers Abelardo Castillo and Liliana Heker in 1961, their left-wing existentialism did not prevent them from praising the qualities of Borges's oeuvre, which exemplifies the complexity within the left itself of its relationship with Borges.

Borges's perceived political leanings to the right and his support of the military governments of Chile and Argentina in the late 1970s are said to have cost him the Nobel Prize, as mentioned before.[47] By contrast, the fact that it was the Chilean communist poet Pablo Neruda who was awarded it instead in 1971, sealed Borges's image as a conservative writer in the public eye.[48] The next section examines this in further detail.

'Ochenta y dos disfrazados':[49] Borges's Relationship with the Videla Regime

As the 'Proceso de Reorganización Nacional' entered its period of greatest brutality in the transition from the 1970s to the 1980s, Borges received the greatest media exposure. He was, by then, very well-known abroad, and the military government had to choose between condemnation and recruitment. In line with their propagandist publicizing of anything that showed Argentina positively, the regime made sure that Borges's fame and recognition abroad occupied its rightful place in the national press, which was also full of reports of outstanding sporting achievements, for example.[50] This proves what Matamoro had predicted as he referred to a previous dictatorship: 'la industria publicitaria del régimen se encargará de hacernos creer que los galardones [Borges's] se prenderán en el pecho de la Argentina.'[51] Thus, the junta appropriated the figure

---

[47] Lafforgue provides a brief discussion of the possible reasons for this in *Antiborges*, pp. 253–54.
[48] Williamson provides a detailed analysis of Borges's relationship with the dictatorships of Chile and Argentina in the mid-70s in *Borges*, pp. 416–27.
[49] Borges refers to Argentina's suffering, or 'adolescence', of eighty-two generals throughout its history, in Osvaldo Ferrari, *Jorge Luis Borges-Osvaldo Ferrari. Reencuentro: Diálogos Inéditos* (Buenos Aires: Sudamericana, 1999), p. 60.
[50] A 1979 advertisement in popular sports magazine *El Gráfico* shows the triumphalist juxtaposition of two Argentine success stories: Borges and football. Argentina had hosted and won the World Cup in 1978. This brought media attention to Argentina, which led to alerting the world to the abuses of the regime. The government needed to keep the public at home focused on the country's sporting success. The image is reproduced in *Borges: 1001 Imágenes*, p. 55.
[51] Matamoro, 'Detrás de la penumbra está Inglaterra', p. 249.

of Borges as a representative of Argentine culture, which resulted in Borges being perceived as a legitimising force for the atrocities committed during the 1976–1983 dictatorship. This is corroborated by Argentine writer Pedro Orgambide, writing in 1977 from his exile in Mexico: 'la imagen internacional de Borges es aprovechada por la dictadura que encuentra en él a un vocero prestigioso.'[52] The same year, an article by Katherine Singer Kovacs in the *Boston Review* further confirms the efficacy of this appropriation.[53]

Two widely publicized instances of Borges's association with the regime made a lasting impression in the minds of the Argentine public: one was a lunch at the Casa Rosada with General Videla, the then newly appointed president of the junta, on 19th May, 1976, which Borges and three other writers attended. This event made the front page of *La Nación* the following morning and *La Prensa* quotes Borges as having thanked Videla for 'el golpe de Estado del 24 de marzo que salvó al país de la ignominia.'[54] The other is the censoring of a very popular television program called *Operación Ja-Ja*, on 3rd July, 1981. This was motivated by an impression of Borges made by one of the country's best known comedians in the show. The airing of the sketch was prohibited and an article in *Clarín* the following day quoted the general in charge of the censoring body as saying that the imitation constituted 'un atentado al patrimonio cultural de la Argentina.'[55]

Borges's ill-advised remarks about three of the most notorious dictatorships of the twentieth century, namely that of his own country, General Pinochet's in Chile and General Franco's in Spain, also circulated in the domestic and international media. This seriously aggravated the already vehement denunciation of the leftist intellectuals in the 1960s, and fed into the appropriation of the figure on the part of the Videla regime in particular. The balance was not fully redressed until after Borges's death in 1986. Orgambide could see through this and had forecast that the Argentine people 'asumirá […] el ejercicio del criterio,'[56] although Borges's image as a supporter of totalitarianisms was very difficult indeed to shake. For many years, the photograph of Borges after the lunch with General Videla — accompanied by the now infamous words of thanks — was better known than Borges's support for the Human Rights group 'Madres de Plaza de Mayo': the fact that Borges signed their 'solicitada' demanding the

---

[52] Pedro Orgambide, 'Borges y su pensamiento político' (México: Comité de Solidaridad con el Pueblo Argentino, 1978), in *Antiborges*, pp. 257–331 (p. 327).
[53] Katherine Singer Kovacs, 'Borges on the Right', *Boston Review*, Fall 1977, online at http://bostonreview.net/kovacs-borges-on-the-right [last accessed 27 September 2013].
[54] Eduardo Blaustein and Martín Zubieta, *Decíamos ayer: La prensa argentina bajo el Proceso* (Buenos Aires: Colihue, 1998), pp. 125–6.
[55] Alberto L. Carbone, 'Fue prohibida la emisión de un sketch sobre Borges', *Clarín*, 4 July 1981.
[56] Orgambide, 'Borges y su pensamiento político', p. 330.

freedom of their 'disappeared' relatives in October 1980 is well documented.[57] Curiously, the fact that Ernesto Sábato, a communist writer and editor of the *Nunca Más* document,[58] was also present at the notorious lunch of 1976 is still today seldom publicized. Sábato was reported to have said about Videla: 'Excelente. Se trata de un hombre culto, modesto e inteligente. Es un general con civismo [...] Me impresionó la amplitud de criterio y la cultura del Presidente.'[59] Indeed, another crucial point that is seldom talked about is that the writers' main objective for the meeting was to bring up the issue of the recent 'disappearance' of fellow writer Haroldo Conti, as well as that of sixteen other colleagues.[60]

The power of the construction of Borges as legitimising the atrocities of the dictatorship by association demonstrates the crucial role played by the political discourses prevalent at the time: both that of the left which had denounced the author as conservative, and that of the military right who now appropriated that image to its own advantage. The advent of democracy brought about a reassessment of Borges which the following section examines.

The Beginning of the Restoration

The question of whether Borges should be loved or hated was approached differently towards the end of the century. As criticism itself moved with the times, the complexity of the sometimes contradictory nature of his aesthetic and philosophical disquisitions was embraced rather than dissected. 'Los años han mitigado las pasiones' and 'los tiempos del Borges de luz y sombra [...] han sido

---

[57] Blaustein and Zubieta, *Decíamos ayer*, p. 366. Williamson provides a detailed account of how this letter came about, as well as an overview of Borges's disgust for the atrocities of the dictatorship in *Borges*, pp. 454–62.

[58] *Nunca Más* is the report compiled by the *Comisión Nacional Sobre la Desaparición de Personas* (CONADEP). Even though the document only records some 6,800 of the estimated 30,000 cases of 'disappearances' during the 1976–1983 dictatorship, it made the general Argentine public acutely aware of the scale of human rights abuses and violations of their recent history, as it provided evidence for what up to then had only been rumours.

[59] 'Habló con escritores el presidente de La Nación', *La Nación*, 20 May 1976, reproduced in Blaustein and Zubieta, *Decíamos ayer*, pp. 125–6. Hugo Montero offers a well documented 'recorrida por el mapa de [...] hipocresías del escritor Ernesto Sábato durante los años más oscuros de nuestro país [...] un intelectual funcional a la dictadura militar en los años setenta y, años después, erigido como prócer de la democracia y los derechos humanos' in 'Ernesto Sábato: mejor no hablar de ciertas cosas', *Revista Sudestada* 27 (2004), online at www.revistasudestada.co m.ar/web06/article.php3?id_article=124 [last accessed 27 September 2013].

[60] See María Moreno's interview with Marxist historian Horacio Tarcus, 'Era insoportable saber, pero sabíamos', where Tarcus compares Borges's attitude towards the military dictatorship with Sábato's, in 'Radar Libros', *Página/12*, 25 March 2001, online at www.pagina12.com.ar/2001/suple/Libros/01-03/01-03-25/nota2.htm [last accessed 27 September 2013].

desplazados por otros intereses,' wrote Saúl Sosnowski in reference to the state of affairs of Borgesian criticism at the end of the twentieth century.[61] The need to affiliate Borges to one particular way of doing literatutre and politics began to give way, in the mid 1980s, to a different perspective. This enabled many of the most earnest detractors to assume a different, more balanced perspective in respect of Borges. This change was heralded, as we shall see, by the appropriation of his image in comic strips, but it was only in the 1990s that this change of attitude started to become more noticeable in the written press and in academic writing. It was also during this period of transition, in 1986, that Borges died. The author's 'entering into immortality'[62] allowed for the beginning of the consolidation of his iconic image: rather than having all his movements scrutinised by the media, Borges had become a historical figure who could now be revised, and constructed in retrospect. The significance of the circumstances surrounding the writer's death in Geneva, as was his choice, cannot be underestimated. This, as Chapter 4 discusses in more detail, was the last controversy surrounding Borges, whose repercussions echoed the attitudes towards him that had been prevalent throughout his life.

In 1993, Argentine poet and journalist Juan Gelman, an influential intellectual of the Peronist Left, wrote an article in *Página/12* about Borges's words of support for dictatorships. Gelman admires Borges's courage in admitting that he had been wrong to express this support for such regimes, which he said had been due to plain ignorance. He quotes an interview in which Borges sadly recognized: 'Al ser ciego y no leer los diarios, yo era muy ignorante [...] pero ahora esas cosas no pueden ser ignoradas.'[63] Borges is said to have been unable to cope with hearing of the accounts of torture and other human rights abuses in the 'Juicio a las Juntas' of 1985.[64] Gelman ends by referring to Borges as great and courageous, which would have been unthinkable during Gelman's days at *La Opinión* or during his most active years as a member of the Peronist Left.

---

[61] Sosnowski, 'Memorias de Borges', p. 80.

[62] Such had been the phrase used to refer to Eva Perón's passing. It was repeated on national radio, for example, every evening at 20.25, when the presenter would remind the audience that 'Son las 20.25, hora en la que Eva Perón entró en la inmortalidad', which in Evita's case, first accompanied the creation of, and later perpetuated, her iconicity. See, for example, Hugo Gambini, *Historia del peronismo: El poder total (1943-1951)* (Buenos Aires: Planeta, 1999), p. 411. The fundamental significance of death in the iconization of Argentina's Eva Perón, Carlos Gardel and Che Guevara is somewhat different from that of Borges, as the first three died at a young age and are therefore considered 'fixed in time' or immortal, as it were, in their prime. Unfortunately, an in-depth comparative analysis of this subject exceeds the scope of this thesis.

[63] Juan Gelman, 'Borges o El valor', *Página/12*, 28 October 1993, reproduced in *Antiborges*, p. 335.

[64] Williamson, *Borges*, p. 474.

Another clear example of this shift is Juan José Sebreli's 1996 revisiting of early anti-Borgesian criticism in his article 'Borges: el nihilismo débil'.[65] Here, Sebreli discusses the impassioned opposition to Borges between the 1950s and 1970s, which was motivated by his perceived lack of engagement with the political reality of Argentina. Borges had been seen as decadent by the Sartrean new generation, and vilified as imperialistic and oligarchic by the Marxists of the New Left; they all considered Borges to have wrongly subordinated 'lo verdadero, lo bueno y lo justo' (p. 339) to the aesthetic. Sebreli then offers a revision of Borges as 'uno de los primeros y raros intelectuales en valorar ciertas expresiones de la cultura de masas' (p. 343) and he praises his capacity to 'mantenerse inmune al contagio de [...] esos delirios colectivos de unanimidad que suelen atacar a los argentinos en ciertas circunstancias de su turbulenta historia contemporánea' (p. 341). This is a significant statement from a highly influential intellectual with a six-decade-long trajectory.[66]

Sebreli's re-evaluation of Borges as a boundary-crossing figure uncovers him as a writer whose contact with the reality of his country is expressed in the complexity and multilayered nature of his work. This Borges, who resists simplistic labelling and pigeonholing, is the one that comes across in comic strips of the 1980s. The next section examines the particluar scene in which this appropriation took place.

'Historietas para sobrevivientes'

Published by Ediciones de la Urraca, *Fierro* magazine first appeared in September 1984, almost a year after the democratic elections of October 1983 which marked the end of the military regime. It was also the same year as the publication of CONADEP's report, *Nunca Más*, on the atrocities and human rights abuses that had been committed under the dictatorship. There were one hundred issues of *Fierro*, which ceased publication as a separate magazine in 1992 (a 'second era' started in 2007, as *Fierro* began to be published as part of *Página/12*). Its full title, *Fierro a Fierro*, was taken from a strip in Raúl Roux's 1930s historical and idiosyncratic comic *Patoruzito*. Even though it was not an original idea, the choice of the subtitle 'Historietas para sobrevivientes' clearly imagined an audience of young adults who had recently emerged from the dark years of the 'Proceso'. 'Sobrevivientes' had a wide appeal, as it encompassed not only the survivors of the Malvinas conflict, but also those of the brutal years of repression during which there had been so many disappearances; and the exiles. It referred, as well, to a

---

[65] Juan José Sebreli, 'Borges: El nihilismo débil', in *Escritos sobre escritos, ciudades bajo ciudades* (Buenos Aires: Sudamericana, 1997), in *Antiborges*, pp. 337–83.
[66] Lafforgue refers to Sebreli as 'animador permanente del debate intelectual argentino mediante una profusa y siempre polémica producción' in *Antiborges*, p. 383.

new generation of young adults who had grown up during the dictatorship, and who were confronted with the need to learn how to 'survive' in a democracy.

The covers of the first two issues of *Fierro* (September and October 1984) illustrate the general mood of darkness and confusion, but they also offer a glimpse of hope, albeit cautious, for the future.[67] In both, the centrality of the human figure facing the reader suggests a sense of protagonism and empowerment amidst the general murkiness and uncertainty that the use of very dark colours conveys (The colour scheme of subsequent covers becomes progressively lighter). The aggressive, highly sexualized portrayal of the female figure on the first cover is consistent with the fact that words such as 'patria', 'república' and 'Argentina' are feminine in Spanish. These words have been personified by the female figure in the official iconography and especially exploited by the extreme chauvinism of nationalistic and military governments. It also taps into the sexist side of *Fierro*'s predominantly male readership, of course. The female figure on this particular cover appears trapped in the claws of heavy machinery, in such a way that it can be interpreted as being about to be crushed. It could also be interpreted as offering an — albeit faint — glimmer of hope to defeat the mechanism and achieve freedom from it. It is a striking metaphor for the sense of challenge which the newly-found freedom posed to the youth of the time. The bright light shone on the figure's genital area suggests, crudely but effectively, the birth of a new era. The image of a young soldier stepping out of an army truck onto a sea of blood on the second cover achieves a similar effect: freed from the oppression of the regime and its senseless war, the challenge now is to pick up the pieces in order to rebuild the nation's identity.

In this second issue of *Fierro*, Martín García explores the work of H.G. Oesterheld, creator of iconic strip *El Eternauta*, himself a victim of the dictatorship's repression. García refers to the general mood of the time, a mixture of hope and uncertainty, and to the alternating of dictatorship and democracy characteristic of much of twentieth-century Argentine history:

> La vida constitucional y democrática ha vuelto a la Argentina desde 1983 [...] Con el ejercicio de las libertades constitucionales y el de la opinión crítica volveremos a creer en una realidad favorable a los intereses de la nación. La realidad posterior dirá si hemos llegado a transitar el camino de una verdadera zona liberada o [...] una nueva zona de exclusión-trampa adonde acudimos de buena fe para ser nuevamente destruidos [...] Quienes han transitado la historia de los últimos años están magullados, doloridos, descreídos.[68]

---

[67] Although they are subject to Copyright, these memorable covers designed by Oscar Chichoni circulate on the internet. See, for example: http://www.historieteca.com.ar/Revistas/fierro.htm and http://www.historieteca.com.ar/Especiales/malvinas.htm [last accessed 27 September 2013].
[68] Martín García, 'Oesterheld releído: El eternauta, la zona de exclusión y la democracia', *Fierro* I, 2, (October, 1984), p. 36.

The article ends with two thoughts, one of which is quoted from a character in *El Eternauta*: 'no creo que tengamos la más remota esperanza de vencer. Pero no digas a nadie lo que pienso, será más fácil sucumbir si lo hacemos peleando' (p. 36); the other quotation is attributed to Borges: 'Dios, se está haciendo' (p. 36). The presence of the comma makes the latter sentence ambiguous. However, the very fitting juxtaposition of science fiction, comic-strip character and iconic writer represents the idea of a new zeitgeist, one in which these combinations are possible. The final words leave the reader with a taste of things to come, as the path to a future, uncertain ('no creo que tengamos la más remota esperanza de vencer'), democratic Argentina, unravels as it is tread upon ('se está haciendo').

The view of history as the weaving of a fiction, which Sosnowski concludes is Borges's perspective,[69] is echoed in the words of Alberto Breccia and Juan Sasturain's cartoon 'Borges' in comic strip *Perramus*: 'La realidad **es** un invento fantástico, la **historia** misma lo es,' to which the famously nameless main character, Perramus, replies: 'Sin embargo, usted se mete en esa ficción; actúa, toma partido, pretende modificarla.'[70] Thus, as we shall see, 'Borges' seamlessly moves across fiction and action, constructing history. This 'Borges' is in stark contrast with the Borges of the previous thirty years. Sosnowski concludes that both history and literature aim to construct memory, which in itself is 'historia tamizada de deseo, de mitos y de ambiciones individuales y comunitarias,' as new versions that respond to national needs are woven from selected fragments of history.[71] It is the exploration of this conception of a history that is constructed, fragment by fragment, through a complex process that involves individual and collective myths and expectations, and in which Borges plays an active part, that enabled the production of many of the comic strips published in *Fierro*.

The Argentine term for 'comic strip', 'historieta', suggests that the genre constitutes a more relaxed, less serious, and most importantly, less 'official' version of history. In the informal register appropriate to its context, editor Juan Sasturain defines it in the second issue of *Fierro*, as he marks a new, more mature era for the genre in Argentina:

> Entre nosotros la denominación adoptada — **historieta** — tiene la singularidad y el oscuro privilegio de inaugurar un concepto: la simpática desvalorización.
> Esa terminación entre diminutiva y cariñosa, casi paternalista, hace de la historieta algo menor y no demasiado importante, cosa de pibes [...] Sin

---

[69] Sosnowski, 'Memorias de Borges', p. 82.
[70] Alberto Breccia and Juan Sasturain, '*Perramus*: No saber y saber', *Fierro* II, 18 (February, 1986), p. 60 (bold type in the original).
[71] Sosnowski, 'Memorias de Borges', p. 93.

embargo, las relaciones entre historia-madre e historieta-hija suelen ser mucho más complejas. En algunos casos, como en la actualidad, la piba debe apurar el paso para emular las violentas hazañas cotidianas de la madre. [...] Tal vez se trate [...] de darle a la historieta [...] definitiva carta de adultez. Que la piba haga su vida.[72]

The 'pibes' who were now living their own lives included many intellectuals who were also re-thinking the cultural configuration of their newly-democratic environment, while at the same time, re-evaluating ways of questioning old hierarchies. The question of the intersections of high- and low-brow art was revisited, this time from a less rigid perspective. Sarlo considers that there is no direct ('mimetic') correspondence between culture and politics, but, rather, that 'there are different sets of relationships among always heterogeneous elements.'[73] This, she believes, 'would also be, in itself, a theoretical resource for building relational networks between the culture of the intellectuals and popular culture' (p. 260). As understood by Jean Franco, the aim was not to dethrone what is perceived as high art, but to consider it in a new light, reformulating it as a commodity.[74] These intersections, which Borges had already explored in the 1930s, were embraced by the genre of the comic strip in the 1980s, as magazines such as *Fierro* created its readership, as Carlos Scolari explains in *Historietas para sobrevivientes: Comic y cultura de masas en los años 80* (1999):

> El comic argentino de los años '80 también creó su público, lectores con una concepción adulta de la historieta y con renovadas exigencias narrativas y gráficas. Fierro inventó a los lectores sobrevivientes [...] No sería justo sostener que este lector *exigente* y atento a la experimentación haya nacido en los años '80; ya en los años '60 los intelectuales [...] se habían acercado al lenguaje de la historieta [...] 20 años más tarde este tipo de lector modelo — ahora extendido a los jóvenes sin una específica formación teórica — consolidará su presencia dentro del sistema historietístico argentino. Será Fierro [...] la encargada de satisfacer esta demanda de historietas *high brow* que había contribuido a crear.[75]

This particular juncture at which Argentine comic strips of the 1980s found themselves appears to be a propitious milieu for the appropriation of a transgressive Borges. This is examined in the next section in the comic strip adaptation of a Borges story.

---

[72] Juan Sasturain, 'Editorial', *Fierro*, I, 2 (October, 1984), bold type in the original.
[73] Sarlo, 'Intellectuals', p. 260.
[74] Jean Franco, 'Comic Stripping', pp. 405–06.
[75] Carlos Scolari, *Historietas para sobrevivientes: Comic y cultura de masas en los años 80* (Buenos Aires: Colihue, 1999), pp. 271–73, italics in the original.

'Cruce y condensación': 'Historia del guerrero y de la cautiva' in La Argentina en pedazos

In 'Comic Stripping' (1997), Franco tackles the relationship between well-known Latin American writers and popular culture, arguing that their 'overtures' to the emergence of new, popular media were motivated by a 'need to hold on to the slipping hegemony of the intelligentsia.'[76] Franco was thinking in particular about Ricardo Piglia's original piece of 'comic strip criticism' (p. 405), *La Argentina en pedazos*, as marking the moment when 'the book itself has become an adaptable and transient commodity' (p. 405). Published in 1993, Piglia's volume is a collection, in book form, of pieces first published during *Fierro*'s first year.

Adding further nuances to Alvaro Alemán's term 'paraliterature',[77] Piglia's original experiment consists of comic strip adaptations of well-known Argentine texts (most of them are literary texts), each accompanied by an introduction written by Piglia himself. The title, *La Argentina en pedazos*, echoes, simultaneously, the fragmentation and variety characteristic of the genre of the comic strip, and the montage-style design of this particular compilation of snippets of literary criticism, comic strips and illustrated tango lyrics. The volume is difficult to classify because of its richness: its distinct 'cambalache' nature reinforced by the juxtaposition of works by writers as diametrically opposed as Viñas and Borges, or genres as dissimilar as the short story and the tango lyric. 'En pedazos' also brings to mind Argentina's predominant sense of fragmentation mentioned before. The work of iconic Argentine writers as Borges and Arlt, through the predominantly popular Puig and the eccentric Quiroga have all been adapted and drawn by different comic-strip artists. The juxtaposition of illustration and minimal text, the selection of fragments of original text included in speech bubbles or in boxes — either as dialogue, narration or commentary, the choice of perspective and other visual elements, manage to achieve a myriad of meanings which enhance the experience of the original story from a different perspective, as we shall see.

Borges's 'Historia del guerrero y de la cautiva' is one of the stories in *La Argentina en pedazos*. It was adapted by comic-strip writer Norberto Buscaglia, who had already worked on other adaptations of literary works (notably a series of stories by H.P. Lovecraft in collaboration with Alberto Breccia).[78] The drawings are by Alfredo Flores. First published in 1949 in *Sur* and later included in *El Aleph*, 'Historia del guerrero y de la cautiva' is a story of bravery, exile, and most

---

[76] Franco, 'Comic Stripping', p. 405.
[77] Comic-strip theorist Alvaro Alemán refers to forms of narrative other than conventional literary texts, and whose popular consumption contains a 'ludic' element, as 'paraliterature', in 'Paraliterary Immersion and the Puzzleform: An Essay in Social Restitution', *ImageTexT:Interdisciplinary Comics Studies*. 2.1 (2005), online at www.english.ufl.edu/imagetext/archives/v2_1/aleman/ [last accessed 27 September 2013].
[78] Juan Sasturain, *El domicilio de la aventura* (Buenos Aires: Colihue, 1995), p. 35.

importantly, of boundary-crossing. Piglia chooses to concentrate on this point in his prefatory text, 'Borges y los dos linajes'. Here, the story is described as a fragmented tale, 'un lugar de cruce y de condensación,'[79] in which, Piglia argues, Borges locates the roots of his literature. These imaginary properties where writing springs from, he suggests, are memory and the library:

> Heredero contradictorio de una doble estirpe, esas dos ramas dividen formalmente su obra: son dos sistemas de relato, dos modos distintos de manejar la ficción. Por un lado aparece una serie de textos, afirmados en el relato oral, en la voz, en la memoria [...] por otro lado, una serie de textos afirmados en la lectura, en la traducción, en la cita, en la biblioteca, en el culto a los libros. (pp. 103–04)

It is fitting, then, that this story appears as a comic strip, whose format offers the immediacy of dialogue, emphasizing that sense of oral narrative that Piglia mentions. The subject of the story itself is historically at the core of one of the most relevant debates of the previous decades, as it relates to the construction of Argentine identity: civilization versus barbarism. In this sense, Piglia highlights the importance of Borges's fictionalisation of his double heritage, as he considers that 'le permite integrar y manejar como internos a su propia familia los grandes ejes antagónicos que han dividido nuestra historia desde su origen' (p. 103).

Reinterpreted as the irreconcilable opposition between the rule of the elite or the oligarchy versus the masses, this debate is present in many of the most politically impassioned texts of the 1960s. In 1965, for example, Arturo Jauretche, the epitome of the 'intelectual nacional y popular,'[80] interpreted the moral of this story as Borges's justification for someone who 'se da vuelta de su nación para pasarse a la otra, explicándolo por la cultura.'[81] On this occasion, as on many others, Borges is called a 'cipayo' ('traitor'), the staple 'insult' periodically uttered in relation to the author by his detractors at the time.[82] Twenty years later, the words 'No fue un traidor (los traidores no suelen inspirar epitafios piadosos); fue un iluminado, un converso' are given the prominent space of a single frame in Flores and Buscaglia's comic strip version of 'Historia del guerrero y de la cautiva'.[83]

---

[79] Ricardo Piglia, 'Borges y los dos linajes', *La Argentina en pedazos* (Buenos Aires: Ediciones de la Urraca, 1993), pp. 102–04 (p. 102).
[80] Lafforgue, *Antiborges*, p. 177.
[81] Arturo Jauretche, 'Moraleja de Borges: su "guerrero y su cautiva"', originally published in *Marcha*, 1259 (1965), in *Antiborges*, pp. 169–76 (p. 169).
[82] 'Cipayo: soldado indio en una unidad militar al servicio de una potencia europea', María Moliner, *Diccionario del uso del Español* (Madrid: Gredos, 2000).
[83] Jorge Luis Borges, 'Historia del guerrero y de la cautiva', *OCI*, p. 558. In Flores and Buscaglia's version, 'los traidores no suelen inspirar epitafios piadosos' appears in bold type. Alfredo Flores and Norberto Buscaglia, 'Historia del guerrero y de la cautiva', in Ricardo Piglia, *La Argentina en pedazos*, pp. 106–13 (p. 108).

This emphasizes the irony of Borges's foresight, as he had a positive vision of multiculturalism that Jauretche's ideological blinkers did not allow him to share, but which the complex changes of the 1980s made it possible to embrace.

To emphasize the coexistence of different realms (historical eras, fiction and reality), Borges's renowned self-referentiality is expressed and given prominence in Flores and Buscaglia's version through two frames — which appear as windows — each devoted solely to the figure of the writer.[84] Through these, the reader is given the impression of the possibility of actually being invited into the story by a very expressive 'Borges' whose intent direct gaze seems to insist on this interaction (p. 108). An exaggerated close-up reinforces this irruption which brings together character and reader. This depiction is very far from the image of Borges as detached from the reality of his country and the common man that had circulated in the previous three decades.

The last frame (p. 113) shows the character/writer 'Borges' speaking the very last words of the story, as he summarizes the coexistence of the strands of his mixed heritage. This emphasizes the fact that comic strip and literary text have become two sides of one same weave. Here, Borges's physiognomy is easily recognizable and, interestingly, he has been drawn as the old man of the 1980s and not the middle-aged man he would have been at the time of writing the original story. This suggests the image of the writer known at the time: old and wise. However, apart from the presence of the walking-stick, any resemblance with the Borges known to all stops there: this 'Borges' appears dishevelled and barefoot in an untidy house, accompanied by a woman who is pouring 'mate'. Instead of the formal suit and tie that the real author would wear on most occasions, this 'Borges' appears wearing a string vest: the classic attire of the working-class man.[85] In the corner of the frame, on the floor, an angry cat gnaws at a discarded book, an image that is very different from that of the real Beppo, Borges's white cat. This image is in striking opposition to the type of image of the old sage described in Chapter 2, and which still circulates in photographs. Thus, the writer who had been perceived as elitist is brought closer to the everyday reality of the 'average' working-class Argentine. This construction of Borges would have been unthinkable in the 1960s and 1970s.

Comic strips like the one analysed in this section were significantly less widely circulated and therefore had less impact than photographic images, of course, which is why the meanings condensed in the latter are still generally prevalent. However, the contrast between the different depictions of Borges shows that the genre of the comic strip is a very powerful space of 'cruce y condensación', as Piglia suggests Borges's story to be. Through it, the image of the writer as an

---

[84] Flores and Buscaglia, 'Historia del guerrero y de la cautiva', p. 108.
[85] Hence the term 'descamisados' coined at the time of Eva Perón.

untouchable monument to high Argentine culture was able to be challenged and re-appropriated in a more democratic way.

Perramus: 'Borges' *guerrillero*

The bifurcating and entwining of history, memory, loyalty and identity mentioned by Piglia in 'Borges y los dos linajes' is taken up in *Perramus*. Drawn by Alberto Breccia and written by Juan Sasturain, this is a comic strip series in which there is a character called 'Borges'. First published in French magazine *Circus* in 1982, it also appeared in Italy, Spain, Sweden, Holland, Germany and the United States, before it finally arrived in Argentina where it began to be published as a regular feature in *Fierro* in 1985. Only one of the four long stories that it comprises, which were later compiled in three separate books, appeared in *Fierro*. However, all four continue the original storyline and setting.

Nicknamed 'Maestro' or 'El viejo', Alberto Breccia was a celebrated and much loved comic strip illustrator and accomplished painter. He worked with H.G. Oesterheld, notably producing *La vida del Che* (1968), which was censored and destroyed by the 'Revolución Argentina' regime (1966–1973). They also collaborated on a remake of iconic futuristic comic strip *El eternauta*, set in a Buenos Aires devastated by a dictatorship. These two collaborations in particular were evidence of an explicit political commitment which resulted in Oesterheld's abduction and execution by the military in 1978.[86] The founder of *Fierro* magazine, Juan Sasturain is a prolific writer and journalist who also taught literature at the Universities of Rosario and Buenos Aires until he resigned in 1975 after receiving death threats from the Argentine Anticommunist Alliance (commonly known as 'Triple A'). He has also written for *La Opinión* and numerous other newspapers. These two politically committed intellectuals came together for the creation of an accessible, saleable product, and instead they ended up with over four hundred pages of a comic strip which Sasturain later described as 'complicada, hermética, presuntuosa, hiperintelectual, comprometida.'[87] One of the main characters in the stories shares the name, physiognomy and the general demeanour of Jorge Luis Borges.

The metonymic title of Breccia and Sasturain's strip ('Perramus' is a raincoat brand, like 'Mackintosh') is reminiscent of traditional detective fiction, and its comic strip relative, 'Dick Tracy', or to name an Argentine character who also inhabited the pages of *Fierro*, Solano Lopez's 'Evaristo'. 'Perramus' is an otherwise

---

[86] Oesterheld is thought to have been murdered in a detention camp in 1978. His four daughters had also been 'disappeared' in 1977.
[87] 'Juan Sasturain: cronología', *Audiovideoteca de Buenos Aires. Literatura*, online at http://www.buenosaires.gob.ar/areas/com_social/audiovideoteca/literatura/sasturain_bio2_es.php [last accessed 27 September 2013].

nameless character who loses his memory after escaping from the repression of the governing 'Mariscales' and leaving his comrades behind. The dockyard brothel where he loses his memory is called 'El Aleph'. The morning after his cowardly escape and his visit to the prostitute Margarita, who offers him oblivion as a way out of his anguish, he is recruited by the oppressors to dispose of the bodies of his own friends whom they have murdered. Tormented by his cowardice, and in search of his identity, Perramus later becomes a 'guerrillero', a revolutionary in the clandestine 'Vanguardia Voluntarista para la Victoria' movement conspiring against the oppressors. The involuntary collaboration with the regime, which makes a mockery of the protagonist's loyalty to his dissident friends at the beginning of 'El piloto del olvido' recalls Borges's perceived support of the junta. Perramus's redemption through rejoining the cause symbolizes the revision of Borges's 'parricidio' on the part of the intellectuals of the previous decades.

Perramus's character 'Borges' is a sleuth of sorts, a 'conspirador al servicio de la revolución,'[88] a character akin to Ford Coppola's the Godfather. He is a father-figure, a sort of fount of all knowledge, working on the margins of the law. A motley crew of younger conspirators, including Perramus, turn to 'Borges' when their missions become more challenging. As Gociol and Rosemberg point out, this 'Borges', who knows Oesterheld's *El eternauta*, is also a world-known writer, who carries out his secret missions whilst moving in the usual literary circles; he uses his ballpoint pen, for example, to send Perramus vital information in a coded message as he delivers a lecture about Quevedo.[89] He is also shown in his Maipú street apartment, where even 'Mrs. Borges', recognizable as Borges's second wife María Kodama, makes an appearance.[90] This is an old Borges, who revels in the unravelling of mysteries that need linguistic decoding, but who is, at the same time, passionate about the revolutionary cause.

Thus, in *Perramus* 'Borges' becomes what the 'progre' intellectuals of the previous decades had complained Borges was not: an 'intelectual comprometido'. However, *Perramus*'s 'Borges' is not, as it might appear, a completely inverted depiction of the writer: on the contrary, the most relevant traits of the character are based on Borgesian characteristics, both biographical and literary. One of the

---

[88] Pablo de Santis, '*Perramus*, la mítica historieta con Borges y Gardel como personajes', *Clarín*, 3 June 2006, online at www.clarin.com/diario/2006/06/03/sociedad/s-06401.htm [last accessed 27 September 2013].

[89] Gociol and Rosemberg, *La historieta argentina*, pp. 40 and 448. Interestingly, it has since become known that Oesterheld and Borges had shared many long conversations, and that the influence of their respective oeuvres might be seen in Hugo Santiago's 1969 film *Invasión*, for which Borges wrote the script in collaboration with Bioy Casares. Diego Marinelli, 'El sueño del Eternauta: el proyecto inconcluso de Oesterheld', *Revista Ñ*, 21 November 2009.

[90] Alberto Breccia and Juan Sasturain, '*Perramus*: No saber y saber', in *Fierro*, II, 18 (February, 1986), p. 60.

most relevant of these is the embracing of contradictions and a sense of 'subversion' present in the Borgesian oeuvre. As Enrique Pezzoni suggests, the Borgesian oeuvre is 'sempiternamente subversiva, ideológicamente subversiva respecto de los órdenes habituales.'[91] The exploration of what Pezzoni calls the 'gran problema que es la superposición del sujeto empírico y el sujeto textual [...] ese conflicto entre pensamiento y acción' (pp. 123–25) is made possible by the genre of the comic strip. It is highlighted in *Perramus* through the superimposition of 'action' which is depicted by the images and 'thought' which is conveyed by the text.

The creators of *Perramus* suggest that both its settings and characters are entirely fictional: 'nada en *Perramus* es o aspira a la verdad: Borges no sólo no ha muerto sino que ha ganado el Nobel.'[92] However, the strip was awarded the 1988 Amnesty International Human Rights Award for its portrayal of some of Argentina's darkest years. The city through which Borges and his co-conspirators wander, for example, is easily recognizable as Buenos Aires even though it is called Santa María (Buenos Aires was founded as Santa María de los Buenos Aires, its port referred to as Puerto de Santa María in colonial times). Breccia's particular style manages to convey the fragmentary nature of the story and its context, his layered texturing technique described in *Fierro*'s third issue as having been found by the subject in *Perramus*: 'el tema ha buscado la técnica hasta encontrarla: tintas y collages consiguen una textura de grises para dar el clima de opresión y pesadilla en que se desarrolla la aventura'.[93] Argentine novelist and comic strip writer Pablo de Santis claims that from *Perramus* onwards, 'el Maestro' Breccia 'explota el gris hasta arrancarle una paleta completa. Hay un gris que corresponde al amarillo, un gris que corresponde al rojo: Breccia ha investigado y los ha descubierto.'[94] In Breccia's own words: 'el Buenos Aires de la represión [...] se volvía gris, perdía su alma. Todo estaba gris por el miedo, por el silencio.'[95] This depiction of the city as menacing and oppressive in its eternal twilight is reminiscent of the first two covers of *Fierro* mentioned above and of many of the songs by Argentine rock bands popular at the time.[96]

The issues around which *Perramus* revolves: memory, history and the place of culture — of literature in this particular case — are vital for the reconstruction of a fragmented national identity. Carlos Scolari considers that Argentine comic

---

[91] Louis, *Enrique Pezzoni*, p. 123.
[92] Alberto Breccia and Juan Sasturain, *Perramus: Diente por diente* (Buenos Aires: Ediciones de la Flor, 2006), back cover.
[93] *Fierro* I, 3 (November 1984), central poster.
[94] Scolari, *Historietas para sobrevivientes*, p. 273.
[95] Sergio Ranieri and Pablo Marchetti, 'Breccia y Borges', *La Maga* (1993), in *Archivos Negros*, 1, (2006), 2–9 (p. 3).
[96] Notably, Soda Stereo's 'La ciudad de la furia' describes Buenos Aires as dark and deathly, an almost gothic city of fragmented identities. This song is considered emblematic of the time.

strips of the 1980s went beyond just reflecting the social or political history of their time: they fed back into it, 'aportando crítica y reflexión, ayudando a reconquistar espacios negados o acompañando estas otras historias desde las páginas de las revistas.'[97] Gociol and Rosemberg believe that two battles are fought in *Perramus*, 'una real, contra los represores, y otra simbólica, vinculada a la cultura. Ambas confluyen finalmente, porque la literatura […] se vuelve el camino redentorio.'[98] They also argue that the choice of Borges as a conveyor of the redemptive powers of culture is significant because 'la culpa, el olvido, el tiempo, la memoria' (p. 448) are all recognizable Borgesian tropes. It is precisely because these tropes are also deeply rooted in the construction of an Argentine identity that Borges is able to herald the nation into a new era. In the words of its artist: 'En *Perramus* siempre se echaron claves netamente argentinas.'[99] Juan Sasturain thinks of Borges as pervading and exceeding the strip: 'La imagen y la literatura de Borges no están antes, dentro o después de la historieta *Perramus*' and using religious imagery explains that 'como el Espíritu — dicen — a María […] Borges atraviesa *Perramus* y lo calienta, le da aliento, y lo revuelve, un ingrediente y un sabor a la vez.'[100] In 1993, Breccia expressed a similar view of Borges, this time as a cultural father-figure for the nation: 'En *Perramus* le atribuimos el considerarse el tutor intelectual de Argentina … El Maestro.'[101] It is unexpected, for someone of the 'progre' generation so politically committed in the 1960s and 1970s, to refer to Borges as being loved by 'gente sencilla' (p. 2). But Breccia explains, rather passionately, that 'Borges era querido por el pueblo' and those who criticized him and drove him to end his days in Geneva 'no pertenecían al pueblo. La presencia de Borges en *Perramus* se debe a todo esto' (p. 2).[102]

The last story in the *Perramus* saga, 'Diente por diente' (written and illustrated between 1988 and 1989) (Fig. 26) constitutes a good example of the exploration of Borges's role as Argentina's intellectual leader. The mystery around which it revolves touches the heart of one of the strongest myths of twentieth-century Argentina: the teeth of the iconic tango singer Carlos Gardel have been lost, and the challenge is not only to retrieve them, but, more importantly, to make it possible to reconstruct his paradigmatic smile. What moves the narrative forward is this quest that will ultimately result in the restoration of the 'Argentine Smile': 'Esta era una tarea simbólica, nos dijeron … Recuperar la plenitud perdida hace cincuenta años …,' says Perramus after the mission has been

---

[97] Scolari, *Historietas*, pp. 298–99.
[98] Gociol and Rosemberg, *La hisorieta argentina*, p. 448.
[99] Scolari quotes from a 1990 interview with Alberto Breccia, published in *Señales* 1, Buenos Aires, (1990), in *Historietas para sobrevivientes*, p. 281.
[100] Scolari, *Historietas para sobrevivientes*, p. 279.
[101] Ranieri and Marchetti, 'Breccia y Borges', p. 2.
[102] Borges's decision to die in Geneva is still controversial today. The polemic surrounding the writer's last resting place is discussed in Chapter 4.

FIGURE 26.   Alberto Breccia and Juan Sasturain, *Perramus: Diente por diente* (Buenos Aires: Ediciones de la Flor, 2006), front cover. © 2006 *by* Ediciones de la Flor S.R.L., Gorriti 3695, C1172ACE Buenos Aires, Argentina www.edicionesdelaflor.com.ar. Reproduced with permission of the copyright holder.

accomplished.[103] As María Cristina Pons explains in *Delirios de grandeza* (2005), the significance of myths lies in the fact that they reflect socio-historical issues which are at the core of identity:

> Si las dinámicas histórico-sociales y culturales se reflejan en los mitos es porque ellos forman parte del universo simbólico de una cultura [...] que en ciertos momentos históricos reconoce ejes unificadores [...] De esta manera, la cultura genera identidades, un sentido de pertenencia, de raíces, de origen y de destino, de pasado y de futuro.[104]

The figure of Gardel generates a sense of cohesion and cultural identity not dissimilar to that of Borges. In 'Diente por diente', this is taken for granted in the case of Gardel and shown 'through actions', as the narrative develops, in the case of Borges.

In the second part of the story, three rather large frames depict a scene which Sasturain refers to as 'fraguada'[105] (Fig. 27): Borges is giving a very well attended talk on the profound effect of the fifty years Argentina has had without the smile of Gardel. This would have been unthinkable in real life, as Borges is known to have said that he disliked Gardel because he had the same smile as Perón, whom he famously despised.[106] A tale of the way in which cultural icons are created and — in particular, popularly — appropriated, 'Diente por diente' illustrates the need of a society to project its anxieties and expectations of reassurance onto iconic figures. Gardel embodies the 'tangoesque' joys of being Argentine as much as Borges constitutes the seat of wisdom and paternal 'cultural reassurance'. Interestingly, the storyline also illustrates the construction of identity as an ongoing process, as 'Borges' says in one of the last few frames: 'Lo único que existe es el camino. No se llega nunca a ninguna parte. Nada termina, Perramus' (p. 169). The story ends with the question '¿Y ahora ...? ¿Dónde vamos?' and the two characters are seen walking away in the distance (p. 169) (Fig. 28).

It is not, however, only as a fictional character within a certain storyline that the figure of Borges has been appropriated by the world of the comic strip: the editorial of issue 18 of *Fierro* (February 1986) is in the shape of a comic strip frame, and the character speaking the words in the speech bubble is none other than Borges.[107] The drawing of Borges's face, taken from *Perramus*, 8 in the same

---

[103] Breccia and Sasturain, *Perramus: Diente por diente*, p. 168.
[104] Pons, 'El mito', p. 18.
[105] Juan Sasturain, 'La última vuelta', in Breccia and Sasturain, *Perramus: Diente por diente*, p. 6.
[106] Jorge Rufinelli starts his essay 'La sonrisa de Gardel' with the epigraphs: 'El día que aparezca un presidente con la sonrisa de Gardel, se mete al pueblo en el bolsillo. Juan Domingo Perón' and 'No me gusta Gardel porque tiene la misma sonrisa que Perón. Jorge Luis Borges', in *Delirios de grandeza*, ed. by Pons and Soria, pp. 73–100 (p. 73).
[107] 'Editorieta', *Fierro*, II, 18 (February 1986), p. 12.

FIGURE 27. Breccia and Sasturain, 'La sonrisa perdida', *Perramus. Diente por diente*, extract from p. 36 © 2006 by Ediciones de la Flor S.R.L., Gorriti 3695, C1172ACE Buenos Aires, Argentina www.edicionesdelaflor.com.ar. Reproduced with permission of the copyright holder.

issue, is reminiscent of a well-known type of photograph of the writer.[108] It is surrounded by a Warhol-style montage of a portrait of the 'real' Borges, reproduced six times with varying degrees of distortion. In this unusual editorial, the fictional author 'Borges' wonders how he has come to be a 'dibujo

---

[108] The drawing included in the 'Editorieta' is very similar to the photograph in Figure 5 and to Argentine photographer Pedro Luis Raota's portrait on the cover of *Borges and Europe Revisited* in Figure 6 (centre left).

FIGURE 28. Breccia and Sasturain, 'Epílogo', *Perramus. Diente por diente*, p. 169. © 2006 by Ediciones de la Flor S.R.L., Gorriti 3695, C1172ACE Buenos Aires, Argentina www.edicionesdelaflor.com.ar. Reproduced with permission of the copyright holder.

de Breccia que habla por tinta de otro' (p. 12). Its effectiveness lies in the imitation of the Borgesian style, including the mention of biographical details, citations, name-dropping and other such quirks.

The introduction of the figure of Borges in the particular context of the editorial, moving him out of the confines of the comic strip itself, reinforces his position not only as trusted leader of Argentine culture, but also, as just one more 'ordinary' Argentine. Thus, by the mid-1980s, Borges appears to have evolved from the conservative enemy of the common people, a man who inhabited a world removed from the everyday reality of his country, to a figure of action, who is prepared to move across boundaries to explore what it means to be Argentine.

The Beginning of Closure: 'El fin'

Another collaboration between Breccia and Sasturain was the adaptation of Borges's story 'El fin' in 1984.[109] A brief examination of this little-known cartoon version seems an adequate way to close this chapter, as it represents the end of an era: Borges ceases to be the enemy of the new generations in order to be reclaimed as a cohesive force in the reconstruction of Argentine culture. This time, not so much as the untouchable monument, but as a 'compañero'.

First published in *La Nación* in 1953, Borges's 'El fin' provides an ending to José Hernández's canonical gauchesque *Martín Fierro*.[110] A seemingly simple title, its first subversion lies in the fact that one would normally expect to find these words at the end of a text or film, not at the start. 'Fin' denotes the demise of the 'gaucho' Fierro, killed in the story by the Moreno, as well as providing an ending — in terms of closure — that José Hernandez's original poem did not have.[111] But this 'fin' also refers to the close of the gauchesque cycle in Argentine literary tradition, as the canonical status of the poem as the 'Bible of Argentine letters' is called into question.[112] Alfonso García Morales suggests that 'el *Martín Fierro* fue el eje en torno al que giró gran parte de su constante preocupación por la literatura y la identidad de su país.'[113] He also underlines that Borges was against the poem's classification as 'a classic' because of what this entails: 'por lo que este adjetivo reverencial tiene de institucionalización y neutralización literaria y hasta de instrumentalización ideológica' (p. 33). With this in mind, Breccia and Sasturain's choice acquires further significance, as Borges is celebrated as a literary

---

[109] Alberto Breccia and Juan Sasturain, 'El fin', in *Alberto Breccia, Obras Completas*, vol. 1 (Buenos Aires: Doedytores, 1994).
[110] Later added to the 1956 edition of *Ficciones*, *OCI*, pp. 518–20.
[111] Although in logical terms, this ending opens up the possibility of an infinite progression, as pointed out by Pedro Luis Barcia, cited in Alfonso García Morales, 'Jorge Luis Borges, autor del *Martín Fierro*', *Variaciones Borges*, 10 (2000), 29–64 (p. 61).
[112] See Sarlo, 'Tradición y conflictos', in *Borges, un escritor en las orillas*, pp. 59–68.
[113] García Morales, 'Jorge Luis Borges, autor del *Martín Fierro*', p. 33.

subversive. Thus, by adapting Borges's 'revolutionary' story to the popular genre of the comic, these two old 'progres' embraced Borges's transgressive nature, finally recognising him as 'one of us' rather than as a political outsider.

As in the original story, 'Había matado a un hombre' are the last words in the strip.[114] This last sentence represents Borges's subversion of traditional hierarchies, as Martín Fierro dies at his hands, thus putting a symbolic end to the gauchesque cycle, as mentioned above. At the same time, the cartoon version of 'El fin' also illustrates the end of the rejection of the old Borges and the beginning of a new construction of the author brought about by a re-evaluation of his work in a new light. It is testimony to the fact that the Borges in sharp defining lines has given way to that of hues and nuances.

Conclusion

Gociol and Rosemberg claim that Breccia and Sasturain 'no reconstruyeron el Borges que fue sino el que ellos — y muchos argentinos progresistas — hubieran deseado que fuera: una figura sin fisuras ideológicas.'[115] This ideological coherence is, I have argued, what the intellectuals of the left would have wanted Borges to have in the 1960s and 1970s: a figure who could be fully committed to their cause, a 'compañero' and not an enemy. The 'Borges' that Breccia and Sasturain created in *Perramus*, however, is one that transcends those old classifications and, instead, is embraced in all his contradictions and complexities. The most effective strategy of *Perramus* lies precisely in its interrogation of old hierarchies, consistent with the specific historical context in which the comic strip developed: the end of the 'Proceso' regime and the transition into early 'Alfonsinista'[116] democracy represented a huge challenge for Argentina. This was particularly the case for the younger generation, who were listening to song lyrics such as: 'estoy parado en la muralla que divide todo lo que fue de lo que será.'[117] It was also true of the older generations who had been so politically active during the previous two decades, and who had borne the brunt of the worst of the dictatorship. Together, they were faced with the challenge of learning a new way of expression and building a new future. The 'Borges' constructed in *Perramus* is the father-figure who will be able to guide them through this transition. But it is a subversive Borges, whose task is to lead them to an appreciation of the richness that lies in the in-between, in the exploration of diversity rather than in its erasure. In the face of the failure of the 'friend or foe' way of doing politics prevalent in

---

[114] Borges, 'El fin', *OCI*, p. 520.
[115] Gociol and Rosemberg, *La historieta argentina*, p. 448.
[116] Raúl Alfonsín was elected president in free democratic elections in 1983, marking the end of the dictatorship that had started in 1976. Alfonsín's presidency ended in 1989.
[117] Los enanitos verdes, 'La muralla verde' (1986).

the 1960s and 1970s, this Borges can offer a more consensual and diverse mode. It is not Borges that has changed: his work, as we have mentioned, had questioned the old hierarchies of authorship and had problematized the boundaries of fiction, proposing a revolutionary approach to writing. It was the way in which he was constructed that began to change in the 1980s, as the way in which Argentine cultural identity was constructed also began to be revised. At this crucial juncture, Argentines needed their icon to usher them into the future.

The inclusion of the figure of Borges in comic strips represents a clear example of the many ways in which the celebrated author has been appropriated in order to be constructed according to such complex set of motivations within Argentine society and culture of the 1980s. It was the purpose of this chapter to explore the ways in which the particular generation of young Argentines mentioned above, who had lived through rejection and denunciation of Borges based on political motivations, chose to reclaim him in order to count with the author on their side, not just the representative of national values and tradition, but also, as an agent of change. In Pablo de Santis's words, Borges was seen as a Tiresias, the blind guide who is able to show them the way to the future.[118]

This post-dictatorship, post-transition period is examined further in the next chapter through the construction of 'Borgesian spaces' in the city of Buenos Aires as a strategy for the promotion of cultural tourism in the context of a globalized world. As the final chapter in this study, Chapter 4 assesses the impact of the constructions of Borges throughout the twentieth century examined so far, and their evolution, in the political context of early twenty-first-century Buenos Aires.

---

[118] Pablo de Santis, *La historieta en la edad de la razón* (Buenos Aires: Paidós, 1998), no page number given, cited in Gociol and Rosemberg, *La historieta argentina*, p. 448.

CHAPTER 4

El desaforado caminador: Buenos Aires's 'Borgesian Spaces'

Introduction

> Yo estaba siempre (y estaré) en Buenos Aires
>
> J.L. Borges, 'Arrabal' (1923)

The now iconic love affair between Borges and Buenos Aires has many facets. Borges gives to and takes from the city: Buenos Aires is described, fictionalized and mythologized in Borges's work, and the figure of Borges is constructed and narrated in the life and spaces of the city. Argentine writer and journalist Carlos Alberto Zito notes that Buenos Aires 'cría (crea) a Borges, y Borges re-crea a Buenos Aires, hasta llegar a inventarle una nueva fundación, poética y excéntrica.'[1] Zito refers to the poetic founding of the city powerfully depicted in Borges's 'Fundación mítica de Buenos Aires', a poem with a rich and varied genesis of which various versions exist. 'Fundación mitológica de Buenos Aires' was first published in 1926 in *Nosotros* magazine (issue 204), and its last revision, where 'mitológica' in the title is replaced by 'mítica', was included in *Cuaderno de San Martín* in *Obras Completas I* (1974).[2] In it, Borges intimately ties the origin of the city to his own, as he sets the arrival of the founding ships within the area where he spent much of his childhood: 'Fue una manzana entera y en mi barrio: Palermo,' now known as 'manzana mítica.'[3] The poem conjugates mythological creatures ('sirenas y endriagos') with concrete twentieth-century features of the

---

[1] Carlos Alberto Zito, 'El Buenos Aires de Borges', *Variaciones Borges*, 8 (1999), 108–21 (p. 108).

[2] Curator Juan Insúa produced a version of the poem which includes all the known revisions and corrections for the exhibition *Cosmópolis. Borges y Buenos Aires* (Barcelona, October 2002). The poem, where the changes are highlighted by the use of varying fonts, is reproduced in the book *Cosmópolis. Borges y Buenos Aires* (Barcelona: Centre de Cultura Contemporánia, 2002), p. 18.

[3] Jorge Luis Borges, 'Fundación mítica de Buenos Aires', *OCI*, p. 81.

'arrabales' (marginal areas) of Buenos Aires ('almacén', 'truco', 'compadre'), as it suggests that its past is illusory and Borges comes to the conclusion that its foundation is a fiction: 'A mí se me hace cuento que empezó Buenos Aires / La juzgo tan eterna como el agua y el aire' (p. 81).

The relationship between Borges and Buenos Aires, however, is far from bilateral, as it intersects with other people's relationships with the writer and with the city, producing constant revisions and reconstructions. Following Henri Lefebvre, considered as 'social space,' the space of these intersections 'is not a thing among other things, nor a product among other products: rather, it subsumes things produced, and encompasses their interrelationships in their coexistence and simultaneity.'[4] This social space known as 'El Buenos Aires de Borges' (as depicted, for example, in Sara Facio's book by this title, and the 2002 exhibition 'Cosmópolis') 'cannot be reduced to the rank of a simple object,' as 'it is the outcome of a sequence and set of operations' (p. 73).

However, as we shall see, these spaces have been treated as homogeneous entities in order to be objectified and commodified to serve political and economic interests. This is what Lefebvre, commenting on Gramsci, refers to as the use of social space to maintain the dominance of a hegemonic class, by promoting certain cultural values spatially. Thus, the connection between knowledge and power is made manifest, revealing opposition between 'a knowledge which serves power and a form of knowing which refuses to acknowledge power' (p. 10). It is therefore the purpose of this final chapter to examine the strategies put in place for the creation of what I call 'Borgesian spaces' for the promotion of Buenos Aires as a 'literary city'. I will focus on the Macri administration of the City, currently in power,[5] particularly in the years surrounding Argentina's bicentenary in 2010. In this context, a 'Borgesian space' would be a space carved out in the urban landscape that bears biographical or literary associations with the author, and which is included in a tourist trajectory. The chapter centres on a variety of Borgesian spaces, including those that made up the 'Recorrido Jorge Luis Borges', a tour suggested by the 'Gobierno de la Ciudad de Buenos Aires', which was available on its official website approximately between 2007 and 2012 (Figs. 29 and 30).[6] In the broader context of the present study, the examination of 'Borgesian spaces' sheds further light on the multifaceted process of construction of the iconic figure of Borges as a step

---

[4] Henri Lefebvre, *The Production of Space*, trans. by Donald Nicholson-Smith (Oxford: Blackwell, 1991), originally published as *Production de l'espace* in 1974, p. 73.
[5] Mauricio Macri was reelected as Jefe de Gobierno in December 2011 until December 2015.
[6] The walking tour was available online at www.bue.gov.ar. The official website of the city has subsequently changed as new and varied tourist offers have emerged. This change reinforces the point this Chapter makes in relation to the motivations for the creation of Borgesian spaces, namely the promotion of the city as literary in the particular historical context of the nation's Bicentenary.

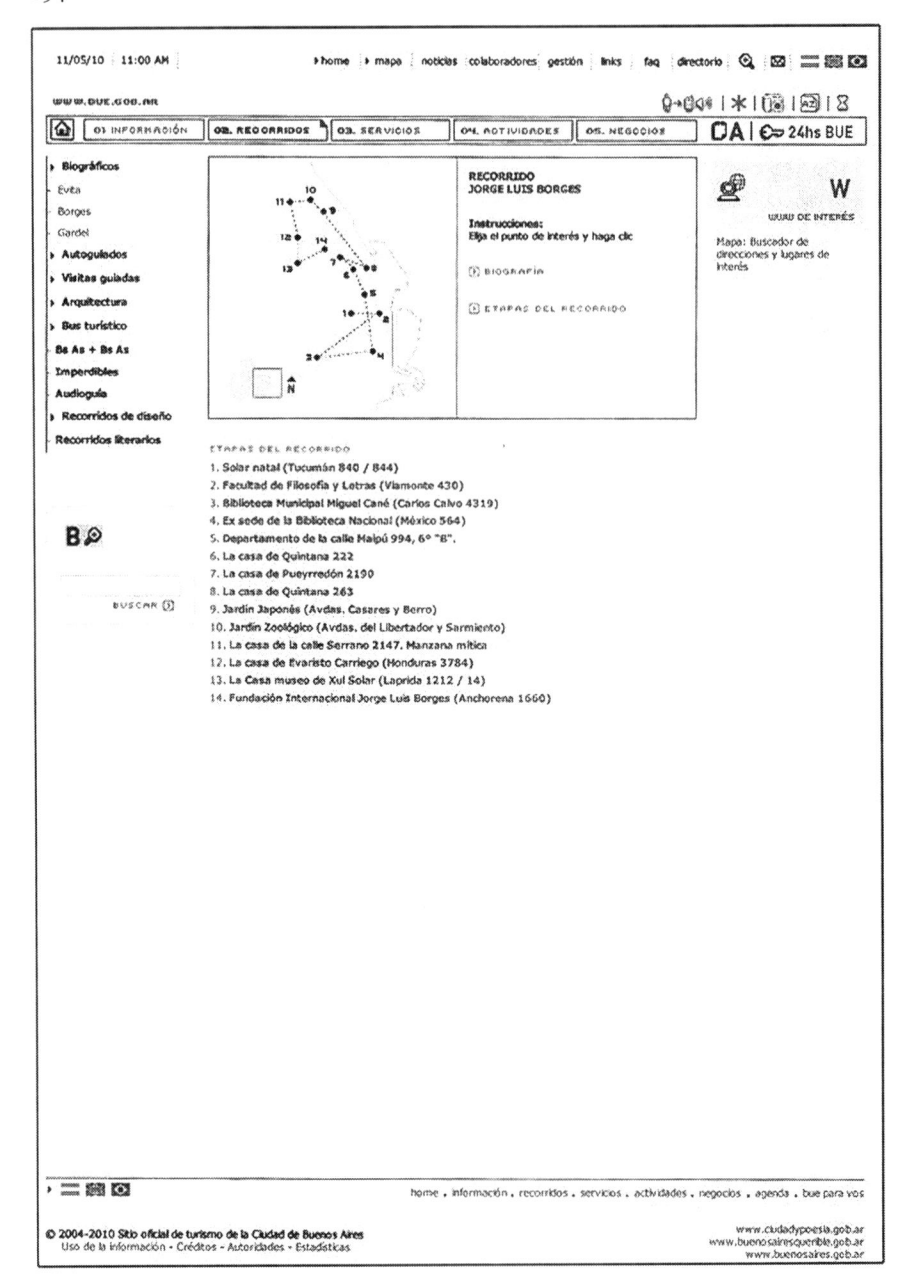

FIGURE 29.   Printout of the 'Recorrido biográfico "Jorge Luis Borges"', formerly online at www.bue.gov.ar/recorridos/index.php?menu_id=13&info=borges [last accessed 11 May 2010]. Current website http://www.turismo.buenosaires.gob.ar/es [last accessed 27 September 2013]. Reproduced with permission of the copyright holder.

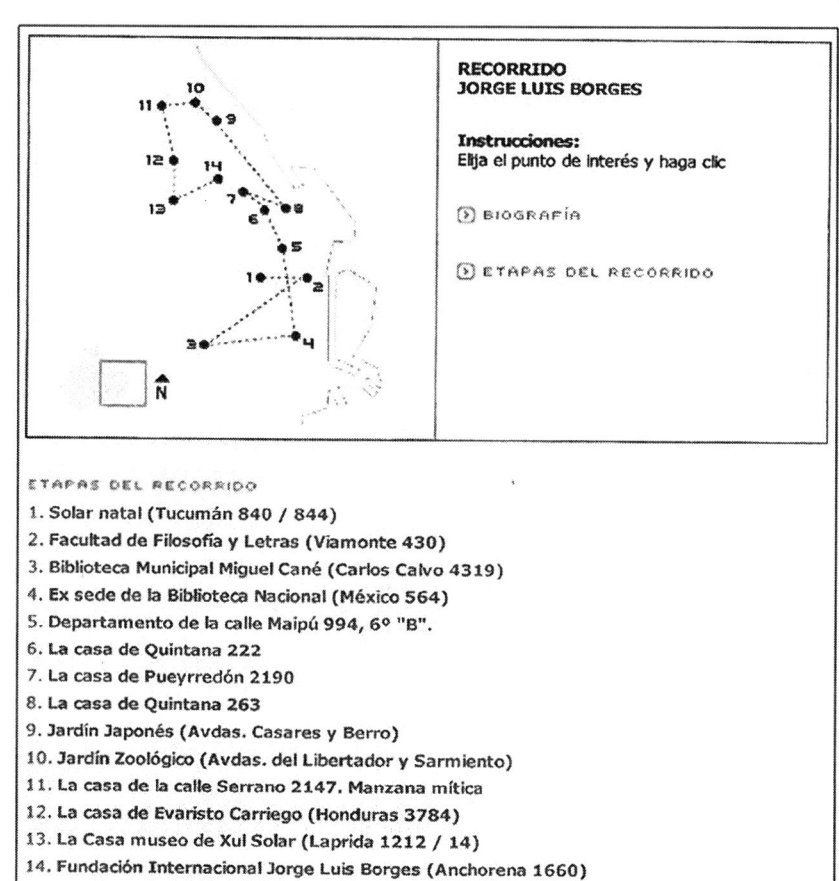

```
                    RECORRIDO
         10         JORGE LUIS BORGES
      11 ●···●
          ●9       Instrucciones:
    12●  14        Elija el punto de interés y haga clic
       ●7
    13●  ●●8        ▶ BIOGRAFÍA
        ●5
      1●··●         ▶ ETAPAS DEL RECORRIDO
           2
      3●···●4

      ▲
      N
```

ETAPAS DEL RECORRIDO
1. Solar natal (Tucumán 840 / 844)
2. Facultad de Filosofía y Letras (Viamonte 430)
3. Biblioteca Municipal Miguel Cané (Carlos Calvo 4319)
4. Ex sede de la Biblioteca Nacional (México 564)
5. Departamento de la calle Maipú 994, 6° "B".
6. La casa de Quintana 222
7. La casa de Pueyrredón 2190
8. La casa de Quintana 263
9. Jardín Japonés (Avdas. Casares y Berro)
10. Jardín Zoológico (Avdas. del Libertador y Sarmiento)
11. La casa de la calle Serrano 2147. Manzana mítica
12. La casa de Evaristo Carriego (Honduras 3784)
13. La Casa museo de Xul Solar (Laprida 1212 / 14)
14. Fundación Internacional Jorge Luis Borges (Anchorena 1660)

FIGURE 30.   Detail of Printout of the 'Recorrido biográfico "Jorge Luis Borges"', formerly online at www.bue.gov.ar/recorridos/index.php?menu_id=13&info=borges [last accessed 11 May 2010]. Current website http://www.turismo.buenosaires.gob.ar/es [last accessed 27 September 2013]. Reproduced with permission of the copyright holder.

towards a definition of an Argentine cultural identity. It also exposes the tension between the circulation of certain hegemonic perceptions of the writer and other, alternative constructions that oppose them. Thinking in terms of the 'polyvalence' of social space which is in constant production and consumption (Lefebvre) allows us to view the construction of a national cultural identity along similar lines: as a process. This, in turn, resembles Borges's notion of the aesthetic phenomenon as 'the imminence of a revelation that never occurs.'[7]

---

[7] Jorge Luis Borges, 'La muralla y los libros', *La Nación*, 22 OCtober 1950. Later published in *Otras Inquisiciones*, OCII, p. 13.

Considering the city as a multiplicity of spaces, a text that is continuously being written, as suggested by Michel de Certeau, the superimposition of Borgesian spaces on the part, mainly, of the government of the city, constitutes one of many ways of narrating the city, and in doing so, of narrating Borges.[8] This is in spite of the claim that such Borgesian spaces are capable of capturing and transmitting a certain essence, both of the city and of the writer, as we shall see later on. In addition to Lefebvre's notion of 'social space', on which I base my approach, I draw on Michel de Certeau's view of the city as speech act in *The Practice of Everyday Life* (1984). Kenny Cupers's 'Towards a Nomadic Geography' (2005), which problematizes the traditional concept of public space and dualist readings of the contemporary city (in terms of 'inside' and 'out', and consequently of exclusion), provides a basic framework, to my view, of the city as one of 'multiple spatialities' in constant evolution.[9] This is complemented by Andreas Huyssen's reading of urban space as palimpsest in *Present Pasts: Urban Palimpsests and the Politics of Memory* (2003). The work of Argentine critics Adrián Gorelik and Beatriz Sarlo provides a view of the development of the city of Buenos Aires and its 'barrios' throughout the twentieth century. A brief survey of the role of the city in Borges's work and his positioning as a *flâneur* will follow.

This will set the scene for the analysis of how this relationship is reversed as the city looks at Borges in search of its cultural identity through the creation of Borgesian spaces. The chapter will subsequently examine some of the stops of the 'Recorrido Jorge Luis Borges' in order to explore the mechanisms of their construction. Other instances of Borgesian spaces will be examined in order to illustrate the relationship between economic and political interests and the cultural icon. These are the creation of a Borges museum within the iconic Café Tortoni (which is a private enterprise) and the renaming of a street in Borges's honour (which was an initiative of the city council in 1996). To conclude, I will briefly consider the final objectification of the writer in the shape of the proposed repatriation of his remains from the cemetery of Plainpalais in Geneva to Buenos Aires's historical Recoleta cemetery on two separate occasions in 1988 and 2009. This is a significant example of the city's ultimate desire to 'possess' Borges. The fact that this chapter focuses on a period of fourteen years of recent history, from 1996 to 2010, provides a sense of appropriate closure and brings the present study up to date.

---

[8] Cf. Michel de Certeau, 'Walking in the City', *The Practice of Everyday Life*, trans. by Steven Rendall (Berkeley and Los Angeles: University of California Press, 1984), p. 93.
[9] Kenny Cupers, 'Towards a Nomadic Geography: Rethinking Space and Identity for the Potentials of Progressive Politics in the Contemporary City', *International Journal of Urban and Regional Research* vol. 29, No. 4 (2005), 729–39 (p. 737).

Spatialities and Identity Formation

The hegemonic nature of the urban imaginary in the cultural production of the River Plate is reaffirmed by Beatriz Sarlo in *Borges, un escritor en las orillas*, where she maintains that 'la lengua de la ficción rioplatense es la lengua de las ciudades.'[10] Sarlo refers to the city's various signifying practices for which the urban landscape constitutes the locus for both formal and mythological production, including politics, fashion and mass culture and claims that, as a backdrop against which literature is written, this cultural production invents and re-invents the city as 'un espacio imaginario que la literatura desea, inventa y ocupa' (p. 12). As suggested in previous chapters, the publication of Sarlo's book marked a change in Borgesian criticism, as it reconsiders Borges's positioning, both in terms of narrative technique, and also in relation to the literary establishment.[11] Apart from exploring his inhabiting of marginal textual spaces (his unique use of epigraphs, marginal notes and prologues are the most obvious examples), Sarlo especially tackles Borges's relationship with the edges of the city of Buenos Aires. The Spanish version of her title provides a more exact description of these edges in the context of Buenos Aires, as 'orillas' is the local word used to refer to the peripheral areas of the city and its cultural codes.[12] These edges provide a locus where many boundaries are blurred: between the rural and the urban, the local and the foreign, the criminal and the law-abiding. This complexity finds linguistic expression in 'lunfardo', a language born of the admixture of Spanish, Italian and other immigrant languages and dialects, but also of the surreptitiousness of criminal activity.

Urban historian Adrián Gorelik also considers the key role of Buenos Aires in twentieth-century Argentine literary production and underlines Borges's acute awareness of the need for an apocryphal past in the building of a modern culture in the city.[13] Borges's early work in the 1920s, he writes, was motivated by a desire

---

[10] Beatriz Sarlo, *Borges, un escritor en las orillas* (Madrid: Siglo XXI, 2007), pp. 13–14. Sarlo's *Borges, A Writer on the Edge* was originally published in London by Verso in 1993. In 1995, it was translated into Spanish and published in Buenos Aires by Ariel as *Borges, un escritor en las orillas*. In 2001, *Variaciones Borges* also published both versions online. Available at www.borges.pitt.edu/bsol/bsio.php and www.borges.pitt.edu/bsol/bseo.php [both last accessed 27 September 2013].

[11] The publication of an important number of Borges's early pieces not included in *Obras Completas*, as well as magazine and newspaper articles and reviews in *Textos Recobrados (1919-1929)* (1997) and *Textos Recobrados (1931-1955)* (2001); and the proliferation of publications exploring Borges's relationship with the city, including Sara Facio's *Borges en Buenos Aires* (2005) to name just one, go hand in hand with this phenomenon.

[12] Consider, for example, Borges's 'Hombre de la esquina rosada' where this word appears, *OCI*, pp. 331–6.

[13] Adrián Gorelik, 'El color del barrio', *Variaciones Borges*, 8 (1999), 36-68 (p. 51). A point which is illustrated by Borges's 'Fundación mítica de Buenos Aires', *OCI*, p. 81.

to create what Gorelik refers to as 'una epopeya para condensar los valores esenciales de la nacionalidad' (p. 51). Further echoing Sarlo, Gorelik positions Borges on the marginal space of the 'barrios': 'la novedad que introduce Borges es un cambio radical del escenario de esas búsquedas. [...] El barrio para Borges es [...] el lugar existencial de producción de la identidad social y cultural' (pp. 51-52).

Gorelik's interpretation of the 'barrio' as a social product and as 'a means of production'[14] echoes Lefebvre's *The Production of Space*. Lefebvre's view of space as socially produced rests, crucially, on the concept of space being 'non-Euclidean'. That is, space as non-linear, which takes account of the complexity of social relationships rather than 'an absolute or neutral "container" where humans or objects locate themselves.'[15] This is in opposition to 'Euclidean' space, which is abstract, homogeneous and institutional, serving 'those forces which make a *tabula rasa* of whatever stands in their way.'[16] The isotopic nature of Euclidean space makes it socially and politically useful and confers 'a redoubtable power upon it' (p. 285). In this sense, such linear, containable space is one which can be controlled. Further, Lefebvre particularly refers to how Euclidean space lends itself to 'the reduction of three-dimensional realities to two dimensions' (p. 258): thus, it undergoes a double abstraction when its already homogenized categorization is reduced to its two-dimensional representation on a map. The economic motivation for this strategy (as part of the development of urban cultural tourism) on the part of the city relies on the strong predominance and appeal of the visual. It does not, however, take into account that in order to include cartographic codes such as 'the map's legend, the conventional signs of map-making and map-reading,' and 'the objects represented, the lens through which they are viewed, and the scale used,' (pp. 85-86) an infinite number of maps would be needed.

Michel de Certeau picked up the concept of production of space in his exploration of consuming activity, *The Practice of Everyday Life* (1984), where he applied linguistic concepts to the study of urban spaces and compared the act of wandering through the city with the speech act. He argued that pedestrians relate to the city as text and that, as such, the city is constantly written and re-written.[17] In this context, and following Lefebvre, de Certeau points out that the notion of 'trajectory', as a two-dimensional representation, 'suggests a movement, but it also involves a plane projection, a flattening out. It is a transcription.'(p. xviii). As we shall see, this 'flattening out' of the urban landscape occurs alongside

---

[14] Lefebvre, *The Production of Space*, p. 85.
[15] Lúcia Sá, *Life in the Megalopolis. Mexico City and São Paulo* (London and New York: Routledge, 2007), p. 83.
[16] Lefebvre, *The Production of Space*, p. 285.
[17] de Certeau, *The Practice of Everyday Life*, p. 93.

artificial selection of relevant details that go into the design of maps and tourist itineraries such as the ones offered by the 'Gobierno de la Ciudad de Buenos Aires' mentioned above. This entails a simplification of the multi-layered reality of the city as experienced and therefore, as constructed, by its inhabitants and visitors. Such imposition of a fixed pattern on an ever-changing configuration is only possible as an assertion of hegemonic institutional power, as Lefebvre points out, and constitutes an example of what de Certeau terms 'strategy': 'the calculus of force-relationships which becomes possible when a subject of will and power (a proprietor, an enterprise, a city, a scientific institution) can be isolated from an "environment"' (p. xix). In this context, city dwellers, as well as visitors, carve out and signify spaces for themselves, away from the controlling gaze of such power.

Two decades after de Certeau, Kenny Cupers also takes up Lefebvre's refutation of Euclidean space and comes to the conclusion that the idea of a 'public sphere', traditionally 'envisioned as uncontested abstract space' on which institutional strategies are based, can 'be dismantled as an *ideological construct.*'[18] Cupers focuses on the fact that such a view of space relies on the repression of difference in the service of homogeneity and 'ultimately fails to understand the complexities of space and identity formation in the contemporary city' (p. 731). In his opinion, 'progressive politics can stimulate urban change in a world where urban planning has been used too often as a spatial technology of domination under the banner of betterment, order or progress' (p. 737), only by considering the nomadic nature of spaces and identities. 'Nomadism,' he explains, embraces change and multiplicity as it occurs 'in an ambivalent position between strangeness and familiarity' (p. 737), where identity is shaped. These ambivalent spaces allow us to read the city 'in terms of the presence of uncertain, uncontrolled identities in contested spaces that are in the process of transformation' as they are 'full of traces of past identities and memories' (p. 737). In this way, the city as nomadic space can be thought of as a "palimpsest" of historical layers' (p. 734), each of which leaves a trace that in turn narrates it.

The palimpsestic nature of urban space was explored before Cupers by cultural historian and literary critic Andreas Huyssen, as he studied the links between space and memory in *Present Pasts: Urban Palimpsests and the Politics of Memory* (2003). Huyssen chooses to return to de Certeau's notion of the city as text in order to focus on temporality and intertextuality, reading the city historically as palimpsest:

> My focus on reading palimpsests [...] is the conviction that literary techniques of reading historically, intertextually, constructively, and deconstructively at the same time can be woven into our understanding of urban spaces as lived

---

[18] Cupers, 'Towards a Nomadic Geography', p. 730, italics in the original.

spaces that shape collective imaginaries [...] to understand the fundamental temporality of even those human endeavours that pretend to transcend time through their material reality and relative durability.[19]

As Huyssen hastens to point out, this way of reading cities does not necessarily imply a denial of the materiality of its existing buildings, as it focuses not solely on the representation of an imagined past, but on its role as harbinger of the future, without neglecting the fundamental tension between past and present. Huyssen's approach is helpful, particularly, for the analysis of empty locations in Buenos Aires which have been constructed as Borgesian spaces, representations of memory where past and present coalesce.

The next section considers the evolution of the city of Buenos Aires during the twentieth century. This will allow an examination of the tension between the will of political forces that design and implement strategies in an attempt to homogenize the city, and the actual, social nature of lived, collective space.

Buenos Aires siglo XX: From Homogenizing Project to Fractured Reality

The modernizing process of urbanization which saw the city of Buenos Aires transformed from 'gran aldea' to modern city in the transition from the nineteenth to the twentieth centuries was a vertiginous one, at the core of which was a sort of symbolic void representing its lack of a history.[20] It was this void which Borges's 'Fundación mítica de Buenos Aires' sought to fill, as mentioned before. The evolution of the city runs parallel to Borges's life at the same time as it serves as setting for his early poetry.

The urban development of the city was based on the imposition of a grid design on the flatness of the 'pampas', which was modelled on that of Paris.[21] This modernization was launched during the so-called rule of the oligarchy, represented by ten presidencies of the conservative P.A.N. (Partido Autonomista Nacional, 1880–1916). It was this party who imposed the 'modelo agroexportador' on the Argentine economy (based mainly on the export of beef and grain to Europe), privileging the great cattle-rearing landowners of the country.[22] The mandate of these liberal right-wing presidents was also characterized by a clear Eurocentrism, a position which gave rise to the various

---

[19] Andreas Huyssen, *Present Pasts: Urban Palimpsests and the Politics of Memory* (California: Stanford University Press, 2003), p. 7.
[20] Beatriz Sarlo, 'Buenos Aires, el exilio de Europa', *Escritos sobre literatura argentina* (Buenos Aires: Siglo XXI, 2007), pp. 30–45 (p. 32).
[21] See Flora Pescador Monagas, 'De la ciudad de Buenos Aires de Borges a la calle sin esperanza de Le Corbusier', in *Variaciones Borges*, 8 (1999), 121–32 (pp. 121–2).
[22] See, for example, Rock, *Argentina 1516–1982*, pp. 167–72. Also Torcuato S. Di Tella, *History of Political Parties in Twentieth-Century Latin America*, pp. 12–13.

plans for the transformation of Buenos Aires into the 'Paris of South America'.[23] The process of modernization began with the laying of the grid system in 1898. This was followed-up by the design of avenues and boulevards in the Parisian Haussmanian style by French architect Joseph Bouvard in 1907.[24] This design populated the urban space with parks and avenues in an effort to escape 'el hermetismo del espacio libre ciudadano heredado de la forma española de construir la ciudad.'[25] It was complemented, notably, by the work of the French landscape designer Charles Thays (named 'director de Parques y Paseos' in 1891) and French urban design consultant Jean Claude Nicolas Forestier (employed by the city's 'Comisión de Estética Edilicia' as consultant in 1923).[26]

Alongside its beautification, the population of Buenos Aires was also transformed. The predominance of 'criollo' inhabitants gave way to an explosion of multiculturality brought by large waves of immigration from European countries (mainly Spain and Italy) as well as farther afield, such as Japan and Lebanon.[27] This did not exactly match the expectations of the ruling elite, whose plans for the city were based on the formula '*proyecto urbano* más *inmigración*,' as it did not fit the 'perfil del inmigrante ideal fantaseado por las elites (que buscaban artesanos y campesinos nórdicos que, a su vez, sensatamente, preferían inmigrar a Estados Unidos).'[28] Faced with a city predominantly inhabited by foreigners, the ruling 'criollo' elite responded with homogenizing projects of nationalization. Thus, in 1910, 'mientras se festeja la independencia de España y se cumplen todos los ritos de reafirmación de la nacionalidad, por las calles de Buenos Aires se escuchan esas lenguas exóticas o el castellano con acento peninsular' (p. 38). In the 1920s and 1930s, the cultural homogenizing of this kaleidoscopic mass was extended to first-generation Argentines, who received compulsory state education which, repressing all cultural diversity, 'a la fuerza [...] enseñaba a ser argentino' (p. 39). However, as Cupers underlines, 'space and identity cannot be fused unproblematically,'[29] and therefore, this imposed identity-building process resulted in policies of exclusion. Interestingly, the life stories of contemporaries Borges and Arlt (who were at opposite ends of the

---

[23] The myth of Buenos Aires as 'la París de Sudamérica' is mentioned, for example, in Andrew Graham-Yooll's *Buenos Aires, otoño de 1982: la guerra de Malvinas según las crónicas de un corresponsal inglés* (Buenos Aires: Marea, 2007), p. 80.
[24] See Rock, *Argentina*, p. 144.
[25] Pescador Monagas, 'De la ciudad de Buenos Aires', p. 122.
[26] The city's archives at the 'Centro documental de información y archivo legislativo' has documents that illustrate the work of both Thays and Forestier, available online at www.cedom.gov.ar/es/ciudad/paseos/capitulo4_c.html [last accessed 27 September 2013].
[27] Gorelik discusses this in detail in *La grilla y el parque: espacio público y cultura urbana en Buenos Aires, 1887–1936* (Bernal: Editorial de la Universidad Nacional de Quilmes, 1998).
[28] Sarlo, 'Buenos Aires', p. 38. Italics in the original.
[29] Cupers, 'Towards a Nomadic Geography', p. 733.

socio-political spectrum) are marked by their failure to thrive in the Argentine school system. The cultural and linguistic diversity of the period is evident, particularly, in Arlt's work.

By the mid-1940s, the masses which were originally constituted by immigrants blended with internal migrants from the provinces searching for work, and developed into the so-called 'Peronist hordes'. The negative connotations of the collective termed 'the masses' ('esa sustancia amorfa, ingobernable y no sujeta a las regulaciones ni de la razón ni de la moral'[30]) as a threat to the plans for a cosmopolitan modern city, appeared to justify the will to construct a 'national identity' based on a totalising erasure of difference. Consequently, by the middle of the twentieth century, the outcome of such demographic transformations was, as Sarlo points out, a predominantly white city 'rodeada de suburbios prósperos, de barrios obreros y de villas miseria' (p. 43). Policies of exclusion were taken to the extreme during the last period of military dictatorship in Argentina (1976–1983), with what Sarlo refers to as a 'política tecnocrática de modernización autoritaria'(p. 44). This consisted in the forced displacement of migrants and the poor away from the centre of the city, thus perpetuating the division of the urban landscape in terms of material wealth. Towards the end of the 1990s Buenos Aires's urban cycle closed with the city becoming the space of powerful businesses, as the modernizing thrust of the old state-centred elite was replaced by that of market forces (Sarlo). In the same way as the earlier process of modernization had attempted the defence of an imagined and desired national cultural homogeneity for the city, current capitalist interests focused not on the city itself, but on the businesses that operated in it (Sarlo). Thus, with the exodus of the economic elites and a portion of the middle class towards the suburbs and the banishing of the poorer sectors to the edges, the city reached the end of the twentieth century with a changed configuration, based on exclusion.[31]

In the first years of the twenty-first century, the once proud city which combined a variety of European models in its eclecticism showed signs of obvious decline and appeared fractured. Borges's rather romanticized outlying 'sur' area, as Sarlo points out, constituted 'la otra cara del Buenos Aires que conocen los turistas o les muestran a los visitantes extranjeros.'[32] As the city was ushered into the new century, the centre was gradually transformed into spaces of tourist interest and 'zonas museificadas' (p. 44). As powerful multinationals appropriated

---

[30] Sarlo, 'Buenos Aires', p. 43.
[31] Such attempts at ironing out difference (particularly though not exclusively, of ethnic origin, class and history), is portrayed in Argentine novelist Claudia Piñeiro's *Las viudas de los jueves* (2005), which is set in a gated community, a relatively recent suburban phenomenon in Buenos Aires which responds to the particular needs of former urban dwellers who continue to commute to the city for work.
[32] Sarlo, 'Buenos Aires', p. 44.

the cityscape, 'el exilio europeo ha concluido,' and the foreigners roaming Buenos Aires 'se dividen entre los latinoamericanos pobres, y los turistas que deambulan por el norte de la ciudad con una guía que les informa que Buenos Aires es la ciudad más europea de América' (p. 44). The result of a complex history of diversity and exclusion, this is the twenty-first-century context in which Borgesian spaces have been constructed for the benefit, largely, of foreign tourists.

This focus on cultural tourism in the context of Argentina's problematic attempt at globalization, is taken up by Argentine writer Tomás Eloy Martínez in his novel *El cantor de tango* (2004). Set in Buenos Aires, it revolves around the parallel quests of a certain elusive tango singer and the equally elusive Borgesian Aleph, as the places shown in it are 'los del turismo y los del desarrollo económico argentino, mostrados a partir de sus recorridos de "turismo cultural". Todo (lo poco) que Argentina tiene ahora para vender y vende es lo que nos muestra.'[33] The next section explores the development of this type of cultural tourism in Buenos Aires. It particularly focuses on how the current administration has capitalized on the figure of Borges as one of its most valuable and easily marketable cultural assets.

Buenos Aires Today

Since the constitutional reform of 1994, the city of Buenos Aires has had autonomous jurisdiction (a status equivalent to that of the 23 provinces that make up the Argentine Republic). Before the reform, the city's mayor used to be appointed by the President of the Republic, whereas now the 'chief of government' is elected directly by the city's constituents. The 'PRO' party — currently in power, with Mauricio Macri as 'Jefe de gobierno' of the city — is a centre-right coalition which was formed to run for the mayoralty in 2005. Their economic position is largely liberal and its policies have caused the party to become known as technocratic. In terms of local politics, the 'branding' of the city as the hub of cultural activity can be interpreted as a move on the part of the Macri administration to establish a strong contrast with the populism of the 'Kirchnerist' Peronism of the federal government, which could be said to lean towards the centre-left.[34] Buenos Aires shows signs of reinvigorated interest in

---

[33] Ariel Schettini, 'Un turista nada accidental', *Página/12*, 8 May 2004, online at www.pagina12.com.ar/diario/suplementos/libros/10-1042-2004-05-08.html [last accessed 27 September 2013]. Interestingly, Eloy Martínez had written about the objectification and veneration of Eva Perón in *Santa Evita* (1996).

[34] Argentine historian and academic Ernesto Laclau discusses this opposition in an interview published in *Rio Negro Online*, online at www1.rionegro.com.ar/diario/tools/imprimir.php?id=7075 [last accessed 27 September 2013]. Néstor Kirchner was president of Argentina between 2003 and 2007 and he was succeeded by his wife, Cristina Fernández de Kirchner, who was reelected in 2011 and is currently in power (September 2013).

education and the arts and, in particular, an emphasis on its beautification and marketing as a tourist destination, with an accent on its renewed Europeanized identity as 'la París del Plata.'[35] This may be generally interpreted as a nod to the elitist traditions of city design of a century ago while, at the same time, it sends a clear, if rather simplistic, anti-populist (and therefore anti-Peronist) message. Broadly speaking, it is one of the myths of Peronism that manual work has priority over culture, as expressed in the 1945 Peronist slogan 'Alpargatas sí, libros no' (literally 'yes to working shoes, no to books', a heavily charged phrase which opposes the most basic welfare, symbolized by shoes, to the 'indulgence' of learning).[36]

The city as a space in dispute between mass-serving Peronism and the intelligentsia is illustrated in Borges and Bioy Casares's story of mob brutality 'La fiesta del monstruo' (1947).[37] Here, a Jewish student is spontaneously executed by a large group of working-class Peronist supporters ('la merza')[38] on their way to a public appearance of their leader, referred to as 'el Monstruo' and clearly implying Perón: 'No pensaba más que en el Monstruo y que al otro día lo vería sonreírse y hablar como el gran laburante argentino que es.'[39] The narration follows the slow and eventful approach of the mob from the barrio to the heart of the city, Plaza de Mayo, where the rally is to be held. It describes how this gradual movement results in Buenos Aires appearing as a 'ciudad ocupada', as Rodríguez Monegal referred to Borges's impression of Peronist Buenos Aires.[40]

The association of the city with the figure of Borges, one of the country's best known anti-Peronists, is consistent with the semantic appropriation of space represented by the renaming of Serrano street as 'Jorge Luis Borges' by the UCR (Unión Cívica Radical) administration of the city in 1996. And it is especially in-keeping with the image of the cultural capital that the Macri administration appears keen to promote, as we shall see next.

---

[35] Pescador Monagas, 'De la ciudad de Buenos Aires', p. 122.
[36] Noé Jitrik offers a conciliatory revision of this opposition in his 2007 article 'Exquisitos y justos', in *Página/12*, 3 April 2007, online at www.pagina12.com.ar/imprimir/diario/contratapa/13-82698-2007-04-03.html [last accessed 27 September 2013].
[37] For a discussion of populism and its perception as ideologically simple and empty which normally leads to elitist dismissal, see Ernesto Laclau, *On Populist Reason* (London and New York: Verso, 2005).
[38] Jorge Luis Borges and Adolfo Bioy Casares, 'La fiesta del monstruo', *Nuevos Cuentos de Bustos Domecq*, OCEC, p. 400. 'Merza' is lunfardo for 'rabble'. 'Merza. v. Mersa: conjunto de personas de baja condición.', José Gobello, *Nuevo diccionario lunfardo* (Buenos Aires, Corregidor, 1998), p. 170.
[39] Borges and Bioy Casares, 'La fiesta del monstruo', p. 393.
[40] Emir Rodríguez Monegal, 'Viviendo en una ciudad ocupada', *Borges: Una biografía literaria*, pp. 354–62 (p. 356).

Buenos Aires 'marca literaria': Recorrido Jorge Luis Borges

The initiatives for the promotion of cultural tourism by the government of the city of Buenos Aires in recent years have been characterized by a strong emphasis on image. This section examines the creation of Borgesian spaces as instances of 'aesthetic spaces for cultural consumption.'[41]

In September 2008, the city's Minister for Culture and Tourism, former entrepreneur Hernán Lombardi explained his plans to turn Buenos Aires into a 'literary brand': 'Vamos a revalorizar el patrimonio literario, a través de las bibliotecas y los sitios de interés [...] y ampliaremos las acciones relacionadas con escritores. Además, vamos a desarrollar circuitos literarios, por autores y por barrios.'[42] The fact that, as Lombardi explains, part of the project included a European tour of photographs and objects relating to writers Borges, Puig and Mujica Lainez suggests a strong interest in publicizing the city abroad as a 'literary brand'. Lombardi refers, particularly, to the case of the photographic exhibition 'El Atlas de Borges', which was in Paris at the time and would also be shown in Salamanca and Berlin. 'Buenos Aires,' he said, 'merece ser literaria por los escenarios de obras plasmados en la ciudad, por sus monumentos y sitios de interés literario, por sus escritores' (para. 7).

In 2009, Lombardi explained that initiatives such as open top tourist buses are a way of developing 'nuestros productos turísticos que son básicamente culturales,' in the same way as the great cities of the world do.[43] A few months later, Buenos Aires was designated World Book Capital City for 2011 by UNESCO,[44] which brings this literary association to the international public eye and paves the way for potential economic benefits:

> Durante un año, toda la producción literaria y de publicaciones porteña se desplegará ante el mundo, se multiplicarán aquí las actividades vinculadas con los libros y la lectura, y se estrecharán vínculos con editoriales de distintos países, que abrirán la puerta a nuevos negocios.[45]

---

[41] Andreas Huyssen, 'The voids of Berlin', *Present Pasts: Urban Palimpsests and the Politics of Memory* (California: Stanford University Press, 2003), pp. 49–71 (p. 50).
[42] 'Lombardi proyecta convertir a Buenos Aires en una marca literaria', *La Nación*, 26 September 2008, online at www.lanacion.com.ar/nota.asp?nota_id=1053835 [last accessed 27 September 2013] (para. 8 of 12).
[43] 'Conmauricio', 8 April 2009, online at www.youtube.com/watch?v=dGu73QX5b2g& feature=video_response [last accessed 27 September 2013].
[44] 'World Book Capital City. Buenos Aires World Book Capital 2011', *United Nations Educational, Scientific and Cultural Organization*, online at https://en.unesco.org/world-book-capital-city [last accessed 27 September 2013].
[45] 'Buenos Aires fue elegida capital mundial del libro 2011', *La Nación*, 14 June 2009, online at www.lanacion.com.ar/nota.asp?nota_id=1139109 [last accessed 27 September 2013].

Efforts of this kind are meant to show that Buenos Aires is in line with the great cities of the world in terms of what it can offer to cultural tourism (Lombardi had referred to Edinburgh as an example of a successful 'literary city'). They also bring to mind Huyssen's reflection on the efforts of a changing city 'to better attract international attention: not the city as multiply coded text to be filled with life by its dwellers and its readers, but the city as image and design.'[46]

Amongst the monuments and places of literary interest mentioned by Lombardi in 2008 were the landmarks included in the city's official tourism website.[47] Launched in 2004 by the government of the city, it contained a variety of clearly laid out and user-friendly ways of exploring the city. Using up to date technology, it offered interactive maps and printable guides in foreign languages. There was even a space where users were invited to create their own profiles and in turn, participate in the configuration of a new space: 'Armá tu propio mapa de la ciudad. Subí tus fotos, ranqueá los sitios y formá parte de la comunidad virtual de amantes de Buenos Aires.'[48] The site is available in Spanish, English and Portuguese, providing ease of access to both local and foreign visitors. Through use of alluring graphics and friendly language, the site invites and guides the user through a carefully mapped out urban experience. The layered complexity of Buenos Aires is expressed in the montage of maps, old photographs, drawings of historical buildings and advertising logos. The site appears as a comprehensive service, offering easy access to information online or by telephone. Accessibility to the city — actual or virtual — is assisted by virtual photo-galleries, information about transport links and a variety of maps and itineraries. This is still the case today.

Among the ways in which 'bue.gov.ar'[49] proposed visitors should experience Buenos Aires there were a number of tours based on prominent figures from the city's history and culture. One of these figures was Borges, who appeared in three different 'circuitos': an audio guide which could be downloaded to mobile phones and MP3 players which was a recording of Borges's voice referring to the area of Palermo Viejo; a literary tour which showed sites of biographical interest and literary settings pinpointed on an interactive map of the city; and a biographical tour, which is the focus of this chapter.[50] A combination of media made this an attractive sensorial experience: the visitor would be able to take a walk around

---

[46] Huyssen, 'The voids', p. 63.
[47] Online at www.bue.gov.ar/home/ [last accessed 12 January 2010]. The website is described as it was up until 2010.
[48] 'Mi Buenos Aires querible', online at www.bue.gov.ar/home/ [last accessed 6 May 2010].
[49] The city's website is currently www.buenosaires.gov.ar, with its tourism portal at http://www.turismo.buenosaires.gob.ar/es [last accessed 27 September 2013].
[50] Formerly online at www.bue.gov.ar/audioguia/?info=recorrido&idrecorrido=37; www.bue.gov.ar/literario/?inc= recorrido&ncRecorrido=204 and www.bue.gov.ar/recorridos/index.php?menu_id=13&info=borges [all last accessed 19 January 2010].

the areas where Borges used to walk and, while doing so, listen to an audio file containing a recording of Borges's voice. To complete the package, each of the stops signposted on the printable map was marked by a brass plaque on the pavement. In addition to Borges's, two other biographical tours were available: those of Carlos Gardel and Eva Perón.[51] Interestingly, of the three, Borges's included the greatest number of landmarks. References to this tour can be found in foreign media, such as *The New York Times* (May 2006), and prestigious travel guides like *Frommers*.[52]

Following de Certeau, this strategy of mapping out the city 'assumes a place that can be circumscribed' and thus appropriated as a packageable, consumable whole.[53] As discussed before, the design and publication of 'bue.gov.ar' is part of a 'political [and] economic [...] rationality' that 'has been constructed on this strategic model' (p. xix). Superimposing the figure of Borges onto the cityscape, the city can be said to 'become' Borges, thus attracting visitors with the promise of access to a certain cultural pedigree or authenticity which is, in actual fact, elusive, as Henri Lefebvre points out:

> Maps that show [...] historical sites and monuments to the accompaniment of an appropriate rhetoric, aim to mystify in fairly obvious ways. This kind of map designates places where a ravenous consumption picks over the last remnants [...] of the past in search of [...] the *signs* of anything historical or original. If the maps and guides are to be believed, a veritable feast of authenticity awaits the tourist. The conventional signs used on these documents constitute a code even more deceptive than the things themselves.[54]

In this way, the creation of Borgesian spaces as a commercial strategy appears as an instance of the marketing strategy of 'retrograde innovation,' which taps into the need for consumption of the past.[55] As Chapter 2 has shown, the attempt by Argentine publishers to 're-package' Borges as a young man in the late 1990s, achieved instead a perpetuation of his image as an old man, as it emphasized a

---

[51] Formerly online at www.bue.gov.ar/recorridos/?menu_id=12&info=biograficos#itemo_ Biográficos [last accessed 19 January 2010]. 'Actualmente ese contenido no está online porque está siendo reeditado', Mónica Camps, web de turismo, Gobierno de la Ciudad de Buenos Aires, e-mail conversation, 27 September 2013.

[52] Larry Rother, 'Borges's Buenos Aires. A City Populated by a Native Son's Imagination', *The New York Times*, 14 May 2006, online at travel.nytimes.com/2006/05/14/travel/14foot.html?pagewanted=2; www.frommers.com/destinations/buenosaires/2299010008.html [both last accessed 27 September 2013].

[53] de Certeau, *The Practice of Everyday Life*, p. xix.

[54] Lefebvre, *The Production of Space*, p. 84.

[55] 'Retrograde innovation' is Nick Perry's phrase in 'Post-Pictures and Ec(h)o effects' in *Hyperreality and Global Culture* (London and New York: Routledge, 1998), pp. 38–39. As discussed in Chapter 2, it is a case of relying on the meanings already associated with the name to construct, in this case, a new (virtual) space by means of new technology.

sense of age and tradition through the medium of old photographs. In a similar way, the city council's effort to create new Borgesian spaces produces the effect of reviving the historical reality of places — especially of missing buildings, as we shall see, and consequently, of Borges as a historical figure. Adrián Gorelik refers to this essential signifying tension between old and new as 'operación mistificadora'.[56] Gorelik uses the term in the context of the process of construction of the identity of the 'barrio' within the city of Buenos Aires in the early part of the twentieth century. However, it may be applied to the analysis of present-day 'Borgesian spaces' insofar as they are expected to 'dar cuerpo a la identidad' (p. 46). In this case, a Borgesian identity contributed to the process of delineation of the city's own identity, condensing the image of Borges as an old sage with a strong aura of tradition for the city as cultural hub of the nation. This process also tapped into a dual perception of Buenos Aires's eminent cosmopolitanism and strong porteño sense. Borges, who constructs himself in terms of this dualism within his work, mirrors the city's mixed heritage and is himself constructed as a product of Buenos Aires.

Buenos Aires's Borgesian spaces create the author in different ways, but they have been established in real places that bear some relationship with his life. The next section examines Borges's chosen way of personally relating to these spaces and to the city in general, and the impact that this relationship had on his work.

Borges's Singular Mode of *Flânerie*

As discussed before, the image of Borges as a *flâneur* has been particularly brought to light in the critical bibliography of the last 20 years, which saw renewed interest in his earlier work and his relationship with the socio-political reality of Argentina. Up until then, there had been a strong focus on the 'universal' aspect of his work, which resulted in the perpetuation of the image of a writer detached from a context. In Adriana Bergero's words: 'La crítica tradicional ha tendido a leer la obra borgeana como una escritura capaz de sobrevolar y *trascender* los contextos materiales e históricos que la rodearon, empecinada en sortear toda referencia a realidades concretas.'[57] Carlos Alberto Zito summarizes the contemporary view which contradicts 'traditional' Borgesian criticism and that is echoed by contemporary critics: 'De todos los temas que abarcó su creación, pocos persisten a lo largo de toda su obra como la ciudad de Buenos Aires.'[58]

---

[56] Gorelik, 'El color del barrio', pp. 45–46.
[57] Adriana Bergero, 'Jorge Luis Borges/Buenos Aires: arrabales, fobias y dioramas de sublimación en la primera modernización de Buenos Aires', in *Delirios de grandeza; los mitos argentinos: memoria, identidad, cultura* ed. by Pons and Soria, pp. 309–31 (p. 309), italics in the original.
[58] Zito, 'El Buenos Aires de Borges', p. 108.

Borges's poetry has been interpreted as an attempt to create an apocryphal history for the city, particularly in his first published collections, *Fervor de Buenos Aires* (1923), *Luna de enfrente* (1925) and *Cuaderno de San Martín* (1929). These were followed by *Evaristo Carriego* (1930), a biography of sorts which at times reads as an excuse to delve deeper into the identity of his changing city by positioning himself on the edge of the 'arrabal'. The poems written on his return from Europe, where he had spent his teenage years, mourn the loss of the landscape that he had known as a child. Buenos Aires had become a bustling metropolis that would see its apogee of development and beautification in the first half of the twentieth century, a period which coincides with Borges's personal journey into adulthood and maturity.[59] His love for the city is well documented, in critical studies of his work, biographical accounts and interviews and documentaries.[60] Many of Borges's friends experienced the writer's incessant 'callejeo', part roaming, part conversation and part creation, a distinct habit that is also picked up by Jason Wilson in *Buenos Aires: A Cultural and Literary History* (1999).[61] Some of these accounts mention the crossing of bridges and railways, which mirrors Borges's well-known border-crossing as an aesthetic choice. María Esther Vázquez also underlines the extent of this life-long habit:

> Mantuvo el hábito de las caminatas nocturnas a lo largo de casi cuarenta años. [...] Tenía la costumbre de recorrer, entre el hollín y el humo, los puentes extendidos sobre las vías en la estación Constitución [...] Y luego volver por el Bajo hasta la calle 25 de Mayo [...] Desandábamos el camino hasta mi casa, y, ya del otro lado de la puerta, lo veía irse quizás hacia la Plaza San Martín. Y digo 'quizá' porque para este incansable caminador no se había agotado la noche.[62]

Borges's personal history defines his relationship with the city in varying ways. With the complete loss of his eyesight towards 1955, the city of the second half of the century ceases to be a visual experience. In his 1959 'Poema de los dones', for example, Borges condenses this particular way of feeling the city with his experience as the blind director of the Biblioteca Nacional. Here the idea of 'knowing himself' is combined with images of roaming through a space he knows

---

[59] In the poem 'La vuelta'(published in *Fervor de Buenos Aires* in 1923), Borges reflects on the process of re-familiarization that he must undergo on his return to the city, *OCI*, p. 36. Williamson examines Borges's avid roaming of the edges of Buenos Aires in this period in 'Buenos Aires', *Borges*, pp. 93–114.
[60] Studies published in the last two decades include Carlos A. Zito's *El Buenos Aires de Borges* (1998); the ten articles published in the dossier 'Borges y la ciudad' in *Variaciones Borges* 8, 1999 and León Tenenbaum's *Buenos Aires, tiempo de Borges* (2001). Many documentaries and televised interviews filmed in the 1970s also resort to the stroll around Buenos Aires as a preferred setting, thus emphasizing the ties between the writer and his environment. Consider, for example, *Los paseos con Borges* (Blakman, 1977).
[61] Jason Wilson, *Buenos Aires: A Cultural and Literary History* (Oxford: Signal, 1999), p. 47.
[62] Vázquez, *Borges*, pp. 73–74.

intimately but is unable to see: 'yo fatigo sin rumbo los confines / de esa alta y honda biblioteca ciega.'[63] The visual imagery of Borges's early poetry dominates the way in which the writer reacted against the sounds, smells and textures of a modernized city of highways and skyscrapers that he could not see. As Júlio Pimentel Pinto points out: 'A contramano de las celebraciones vanguardistas de la urbe como símbolo de furor modernizante, Borges hace de su memoria un recurso poderoso para exorcizar la nueva Buenos Aires.'[64] Thus in 'Elogio de la sombra' (1969), the city which 'antes se desgarraba en arrabales / hacia la llanura incesante,' has returned to 'las borrosas calles del Once / las precarias casas viejas / que aun llamamos el Sur.'[65] This poem, which appears to follow the perambulations of the elderly writer through the streets of Buenos Aires, equates the topographical identity of the city to that of his face (an idea that he had explored in the epilogue to *El Hacedor* in 1960[66]). Here, blindness and old age are praised as signs of a maturity which Borges believes will allow him to finally know himself: 'Pronto sabré quién soy.'[67] And, again, the city itself is seen as the fateful setting of his pathway to the discovery of his intimate centre: 'Del Sur, del Este, del Oeste, del Norte / convergen los caminos que me han traído / a mi secreto centro' (p. 395). It is this superimposition of cityscape and personal identity that the porteño city council later exploited to accompany the rebranding of Borges as eminently porteño with that of Buenos Aires as profoundly Borgesian, that is, traditionally literary and cosmopolitan.

Argentine critic and academic Sylvia Molloy considers that 'la *flânerie* ávida ya signa la letra borgesiana como justificación ontológica y a la vez crítica.'[68] Borges found in walking his preferred way of relating to the everyday practices of his environment. However, Molloy argues that Borges's mode of *flânerie* differs from the modernist Baudelairian roaming, which consists of a moment of dispersion amongst the crowd followed by a gathering in and return to the unity of the self. Borges, on the other hand, remains forever as a dispersed subject, dispensing with 'el recogimiento, el refugio en la unicidad, el regreso al yo' (p. 18) and instead remaining in a state of suspension.[69] This particular positioning in the context of the city has echoes of Borges's definition of the aesthetic phenomenon as the imminence of a revelation that never occurs. Borges's choice

---

[63] Jorge Luis Borges, 'Poema de los dones', *El Hacedor*, *OCII*, p. 187.
[64] Júlio Pimentel Pinto, 'Borges lee Buenos Aires. Un ejercicio crítico frente a la modernización de la ciudad', *Variaciones Borges*, 8 (1999), 82–94 (p. 83).
[65] Jorge Luis Borges, 'Elogio de la sombra', *OCII*, p. 395.
[66] Jorge Luis Borges, 'Epílogo', *El Hacedor*, *OCII*, p. 232.
[67] Borges, 'Elogio de la sombra', p. 396.
[68] Sylvia Molloy, '*Flâneries* textuales: Borges, Benjamin y Baudelaire', *Variaciones Borges*, 8 (1999), 16–29 (p. 18).
[69] Cf. Cristián Cisternas Ampuero's focus on Borges as a unified subject in 'Jorge Luis Borges: El "otro flâneur"', *Revista Chilena de Literatura*, 62 (2003), pp. 79–104.

of the sunset as setting for much of his poetry bears this out (Molloy), as is the case of his poem 'Caminata',[70] in which the subject drifts along, as Molloy puts it, in an act of continuous perception. Thus, the meaning of the self in the Borgesian text 'no es centralizarse y fundamentarse en el espacio solipsista del *flâneur* sino ser anhelo o codicia *flotantes*, no aposentados en un sujeto'.[71] The layered nature of this aimless walking which produces meaningful spaces is crucial. Borges narrates the city, as do his fellow city dwellers and visitors, superimposing layers of meaning which constantly weave and unravel the text that is the city, in the manner described by de Certeau: 'consumers produce through their signifying practices [...] 'indirect' or 'errant' trajectories obeying their own logic,' and 'their trajectories form unforeseeable sentences.'[72] This is an ongoing process in perpetual change and evolution. Molloy argues that, in addition, Borges's roaming constitutes 'una maniobra de inserción en una tradición literaria precisamente argentina [...] gesto que recalca (que inventa) una filiación nacional.'[73] This intimate link between Borges's *flânerie* and the construction of a national identity plays out in a Buenos Aires that Borges invents in his poetry, largely drawing from a 'memoria colectiva y ceremonial pero a la vez recuerdo preciso tomado del bric-à-brac mnemónico' (p. 28). The mechanisms of the interaction of city dwellers and visitors with this particular Borgesian imprint on Buenos Aires, is what de Certeau would call 'making the text habitable.'[74]

Molloy's analysis highlights the complexity of the tension between the *flâneur* as a wandering subject who perceives the city and in so doing, perceives himself; and a modernizing city. This relationship, she claims, is a double-sided exercise in self-portrayal, in which both the city and the *flâneur* are evanescent: the city is at the same time, 'telón de fondo y substancia misma del yo' (p. 17). It is fundamental to bear in mind, therefore, that the shared characteristic of the writer and the city is a transient nature. The reciprocity within this relationship makes it possible to shift the focus from the roaming subject to the city as a space that, in Cupers's words, 'actively remembers' and 'bears active witness to human action,' considering the city as self-defining subject in its relationship with the *flâneur*.[75] Thus, Buenos Aires's Borgesian spaces, where the author's life story and writing, the motivations behind their creation and the expectations of visitors converge, construct both the writer and the city. They condense the Borges that emanates from the poems in *Fervor de Buenos Aires*, and the Borges that the city council constructs as a product for international consumption.

---

[70] J.L. Borges, 'Caminata', *Fervor de Buenos Aires, OCI*, p. 43.
[71] Molloy, 'Flâneries textuales', p. 19.
[72] de Certeau, *The Practice of Everyday Life*, p. xviii.
[73] Molloy, 'Flâneries textuales', p. 27.
[74] de Certeau, *The Practice of Everyday Life*, p. xxi.
[75] Cupers, 'Towards a Nomadic Geography', p. 731.

Crossing Borders: 'La inútil discusión de Boedo y Florida'

This section explores Borges's view of urban space as 'spatial complexity'[76] in relation to the 'barrio' which by the 1920s had become the locus for urban, cultural and political polemic (Gorelik).[77] During the first decades of the twentieth century, Buenos Aires saw itself divided into two literary sides, each given the name of a street: the avant-garde, experimental Florida and the *engagé* Boedo. Roberto Segre explains:

> De la antítesis entre riqueza y pobreza surgió el contraste entre la modernidad de los edificios altos del centro y las estructuras tradicionales de los barrios suburbanos [...] Es la contraposición entre [...] las divergencias culturales entre el este de la élite de Florida y los artistas populares de Boedo al oeste.[78]

This distinction was not taken seriously when it first arose, but it gradually acquired significance in terms of the way in which these writers were thought of. This is particularly true of the 1960s and 1970s when Borges's perception as a foreign-loving writer had strong political connotations, as discussed in Chapter 3.

Borges's traditional association with the Florida group fuelled the construction of the writer's image as elitist and in opposition to Boedo writers such as Roberto Arlt, for example. However, Borges is known to have been unhappy with such labels, and as early as 1928, he felt it necessary to clarify the contrived nature of what he regarded as 'La inútil discusión de Boedo y Florida'.[79] In this article, which in parts anticipates the debate later revisited in 'El escritor argentino y la tradición' (1955), he rightly warns his readers that 'la ascendencia o justificación de los símbolos es lo de menos: lo importante es su aceptación.'[80] Borges demonstrates the futility of such polarization of Argentine literature by first referring to the areas of the city which they supposedly represented. His argument centres around the complex social and cultural topology of Boedo and Florida streets, from which he deduces the absurdity of such an apparently clear-cut distinction. This article, which is testimony to Borges's intimate knowledge of the city and the multifaceted meanings attached to places within it, conveys an image of a writer who protests his impartiality regarding the pigeonholing of cultural activity. This is far removed from that of the elitist, ivory-tower author examined

---

[76] Cupers, 'Towards a Nomadic Geography', p. 731.
[77] Gorelik, 'El color del barrio', p. 36.
[78] Roberto Segre, 'Buenos Aires en sus treinta. Los profetas de la modernidad porteña: Gardel y Le Corbusier', in *Delirios de grandeza*, ed. by Pons and Soria, pp. 289–307 (p. 292).
[79] Jorge Luis Borges, 'La inútil discusión de Boedo y Florida', *La Prensa*, Buenos Aires, 30 September 1928. After its first publication in the generally conservative Buenos Aires daily *La Prensa*, this article remained in obscurity for almost seven decades until it was included in Jorge Luis Borges, *Textos Recobrados. 1919–1929*, ed. by Sara Luisa del Carril (Buenos Aires: Emecé, 1997), pp. 365–68.
[80] Jorge Luis Borges, 'El escritor argentino y la tradición', *Sur*, 232 (1955), 1–8.

in previous chapters of this study. The image is especially clear in his analysis of what Borges refers to as contradictory fallacies at the heart of the Boedo-Florida opposition, one of which is 'la connotación erudita de la palabra "arte", superstición que nos invita a conceder categoría de arte a un soneto malo, pero a negársela a una bien versificada milonga.'[81] The arbitrary nature of the definition of a literary style and identity in relation to a geographical area is revisited by Borges in 1937 in 'Los escritores argentinos y Buenos Aires', where he reinforces his belief that there is much more to urban spaces than simplified labels.[82]

Many decades later, Borges writes that he would have preferred to be part of the 'grupo de Boedo, considerando que escribía sobre el viejo Barrio Norte y los conventillos, sobre la tristeza y el ocaso,' and rather mockingly regrets that 'uno de los dos conjurados [...] me informó que yo era un guerrero de Florida y ya no quedaba tiempo para cambiar de bando,' insisting that 'todo aquello estuvo amañado.'[83] Borges was aware that, as Cupers points out, 'the problem with dualist readings of the city is that they tend to run parallel with a kind of political theory that privileges binaries, and thus constructs boundaries between inside and outside.'[84] Borges's view of the city was one of a space of multiplicity whose boundaries are fluid rather than excluding.

As his opinion regarding the Boedo-Florida distinction illustrates, Borges preferred to embrace the complexity of what others perceived as a contradiction or dichotomy. In contrast with the mobile and nomadic city of Borges's work, the policies of the local council 'flatten' the relationship between the writer and the city in order to create a simplified space which can be easily packaged and commercialised. This is evident in the Biblioteca Miguel Cané, a space that the city council has made 'politically useful' (Lefebvre) by constructing both a deeply porteño and Anglophile Borges. Here, once conflicting images of Borges are juxtaposed to create a product for cultural tourism in order to advertise the city as 'literary', as we shall see. Situated in the 'barrio porteño'of Boedo and founded in 1927, this local public library is part of a long tradition of 'bibliotecas populares' first promoted by President Sarmiento in 1870. It has been an integral part of the cultural patrimony of the area ever since, and it is where Borges worked until his resignation after his notorious transfer to the 'inspectorship of poultry' by the Peronist government in 1946.[85] Borges had sad memories of his time at the library, in particular due to his difficulty in relating to the peculiar work habits

---

[81] Borges, 'La inútil discusión', p. 366.
[82] Jorge Luis Borges, 'Los escritores argentinos y Buenos Aires', *Textos cautivos, OC IV*, 254 (First published in *El Hogar*, 12 February, 1937), p. 254.
[83] Jorge Luis Borges, *Autobiografía*, pp. 90–91.
[84] Cupers, 'Towards a nomadic geography', p. 733.
[85] Borges, *Autobiografía*, p. 112. This incident has been retold numerous times by biographers and critics to illustrate the dichotomies Borges/Perón and intellectualism/populism, although Williamson offers a rather more conciliatory account in *Borges*, pp. 292–93.

of his colleagues, who both resented his hard work and ignored him as a writer. However, he valued those nine years as a period of close experience of the barrio, travelling through its landscape in the tram and enjoying the view of the traditional low rooftops which formed the backdrop to Borges's reading sessions on the terrace of the library.

The Miguel Cané library was included in the 'Recorrido Biográfico Jorge Luis Borges' (Stop 3), which British writer Julian Barnes took in February 2008, as he went in search of the traces of Borges, one of his favourite writers. This had clear echoes of the lust for relics explored in his own novel *Flaubert's Parrot* (1984), where the narrator wonders: 'Why does the writing make us chase the writer? Why can't we leave well alone? Why aren't the books enough?'[86] The visit was impeccably organized by the British Council in Buenos Aires in collaboration with the government of the city. In particular, Barnes's presence at the library was organised around a rather specific literary joke, which involved the creation of a space called 'El patio de los loros de Flaubert' within the library, to coincide with his visit. This was a reference to the aforementioned novel, which follows the search for the authentic stuffed parrot believed to have sat on Gustave Flaubert's desk.[87] Here, the British writer was invited to certify the 'likely authenticity of Flaubert's parrot' (para. 8), which he wrote himself, in English (para. 8), on a plaque underneath the wooden figure of a parrot.

The events surrounding the visit of the British writer provided valuable publicity for the city, tapping into and perpetuating the image of Borges as an Anglophile. The commemorative plaque (which was placed to match, symmetrically, Borges's on the other side of the front door of the library), which reads 'el escritor británico', attests to this.[88] The fact that the naming of the patio might only be understood by a chosen few (that is, only those who have knowledge of Barnes's novel), contributes to the construction of Borges as an elite writer, associated with a type of literature that is only available to an intellectual minority. This reinforces the opposition between the populism of the periphery (Boedo) and the elitism of the intellectuals linked with the centre of the city (Florida). There is no plaque commemorating the visit of Peruvian writer Mario Vargas Llosa — a fellow Latin American who writes in Spanish and therefore, arguably, more widely read in Argentina — to the Miguel Cané library the following month, even though he was declared 'huésped de honor de la Ciudad

---

[86] Julian Barnes, *Flaubert's Parrot* (London: Picador, 1984), pp. 2–3.

[87] Susana Reinoso, 'Julian Barnes: la *road movie* de su paso por Buenos Aires', *La Nación*, 7 February 2008, online at www.lanacion.com.ar/nota.asp?nota_id=985099 [last accessed 27 September 2013].

[88] The visit had coverage in the leading national papers: www.lanacion.com.ar/nota.asp?nota_id=985099; www.pagina12.com.ar/diario/suplementos/espectaculos/4-9138-2008-02-07.html [both last accessed 27 September 2013].

de Buenos Aires' in a ceremony held there.[89] Nor is there a plaque for the Chilean Jorge Edwards or any of the other Spanish language writers that subsequently visited the library. This points to a series of decisions, on the part of the city council, to superimpose the constructions of Borges as elitist and Anglophile, which are, in themselves, simplifications, on a landscape that Borges himself had constructed as mobile.

At the same time, the users and staff of Boedo's local library found themselves struggling against the efforts of the city's government to appropriate it as a 'Borgesian' tourist attraction. This exemplifies the tension between the powerful imposition of political strategies and the local tactics to retain a sense of community identity that both Lefebvre and de Certeau talk about. In this context, the figure of Borges becomes a clear exponent of a commodity whose exchange value resides in its power to 'sell' the city as a destination for cultural tourism. This appeared as an artificial imposition, particularly on the employees of the library, whose job is to promote reading in their barrio and not to market the city. It also created a certain antagonism at the local level, thus emphasizing the perception of Borges as removed from the actual needs of the community and perpetuating his image as an elitist, Florida writer.

After visiting the Miguel Cané library, Julian Barnes was treated to a drink at the traditional café Margot on Avenida Boedo which, according to the city's oficial website, constituted 'un cierre bien porteño para una tradición que recién comienza.'[90] Cafés are, undeniably, Buenos Aires's meeting place *par excellence*: they are also, traditionally, spaces for political and intellectual debate. This is another profoundly porteño trait that the city council exploits as tourist attraction, by naming 59 cafés as 'bares notables' of Buenos Aires.[91] The Margot is one of these, and by organizing a visit to it to immediately follow any official visits to the Miguel Cané, the council establishes a link between Borges and café culture. The next section examines how cafés such as the Margot condense meanings associated with porteño culture and have, as such,

---

[89] 'Un emocionado Vargas Llosa lanza elogios sobre Buenos Aires', online at http://edant.clarin.com/diario/2008/03/26/sociedad/s-03401.htm [last accessed 27 September 2013].
[90] 'Bibiblioteca municipal Miguel Cané', *Espacios*, Subsecretaría de Patrimonio Cultural, Gobierno de la Ciudad de Buenos Aires, online at www.buenosaires.gob.ar/areas/cultura/patrimonio_historico_cultural/ biblioteca_cane.php [last accessed 27 September 2013]. Spanish writer Juan Cruz Ruiz tells a similar story of his visit to Biblioteca Miguel Cané and subsequently to various nearby cafes: 'Luego llegó Josefina Delgado, la directora de todas las bibliotecas de Buenos Aires, y nos llevó a los viejos cafés que parecen rescatar del fondo de la historia aquellos cafés españoles o italianos de los que se hizo el alma de los cafés de Buenos Aires,' in *Egos Revueltos. Una memoria personal de la vida literaria* (Barcelona: Tusquets, 2010), p. 200.
[91] Online at http://www.youtube.com/watch?v=OFySf23HbGc [last accessed 27 September 2013].

been appropriated as Borgesian spaces. This is particularly in the context of one of the local government's initiatives to promote the city as 'Capital Mundial del Libro 2011.'

'Yo leo en el bar': 'Cafés porteños' as Borgesian Spaces

In February 2010, Buenos Aires's minister for Culture, Hernán Lombardi launched an initiative to promote reading in unconventional places such as merry-go-rounds and cafés. 'Yo leo en el bar' consists in 'la instalación de bibliotecas con la colección completa de Borges en quince bares notables de la capital argentina.'[92] Lombardi was eager to reinforce Buenos Aires's literary identity by stating that libraries and cafés are 'dos de los mejores aspectos de la porteñidad y dos características de una ciudad que se define como cultura y sobre todo literaria.'[93] This political strategy has the double effect of associating Borges with the eminently social space of the café, and therefore emphasizing his deeply porteño identity, whilst publicizing an attempt to bringing his work closer to the common man and woman.[94]

Amongst the initial 15 notable cafés where the government of the city placed copies of Borges's work (donated by publishing house *Planeta*) is the traditional Café Tortoni, whose iconic 'porteñidad' has been linked to the figure of the writer. Founded in 1858, it is a living testament, not only to the significance of café culture in the city, but also, together with Avenida de Mayo, where it is located, to its multifaceted cultural origins. These, in turn, echo the city's own cultural configuration, as Beatriz Sarlo explains:

> Como en la cultura argentina, la originalidad está en los elementos que entran en la mezcla, atrapados, transformados y deformados por un gigantesco sistema de traducción. Buenos Aires es una traducción de Europa, de muchas lenguas y de textos urbanos en conflicto, refractada por el hecho inevitable de su ubicación en América. Hay tanta imitación como *bricolaje* y reciclaje.[95]

Strongly Haussmaniann in design, Avenida de Mayo (built between 1883 and 1894) is said to have been 'pensada por argentinos que querían imitar a los

---

[92] Online at www.buenosaires.gov.ar/areas/cultura/al_dia/lectura_bar_10.php?menu_id=20277 [last accessed 27 September 2013].

[93] 'La obra de Borges, disponible desde hoy en bares porteños', 'Revista Ñ', *Clarín*, 25 February 2010, online at www.revistaenie.clarin.com/notas/2010/02/25/_-02147652.htm [last accessed 27 September 2013].

[94] This was reported at the time in the BBC News website: Candace Piette, 'Argentina aims to rediscover a love of books', 23 April 2010, online at news.bbc.co.uk/1/hi/world/americas/8635289.stm [last accessed 27 September 2013].

[95] Beatriz Sarlo, 'Buenos Aires', p. 32.

franceses, construida por italianos y habitada por españoles.'[96] Considered the civic axis of the city, it joins the historic Plaza de Mayo and its Casa Rosada (the seat of the national executive) with Plaza del Congreso and its legislative palace. This distinctly Parisian feature of the porteño landscape is a strong vestige of the years of the oligarchic presidencies mentioned before, during which much of the modern urbanization of the city took place.

Café Tortoni, in turn, takes its name from a nineteenth-century Parisian café located on Boulevard des Italiens. Traditionally a space for literary, artistic and political debate, it has become one of the tourist destinations of the city of Buenos Aires.[97] The café is situated in a beautiful Art Nouveau building and it boasts interiors of great architectural interest, as they retain their original character. But its main attraction lies in its illustrious regulars, as early twentieth-century owner Celestino Curutchet is known to have said: 'los artistas gastan poco pero le dan lustre y fama al café.'[98] The café cleverly exploits this by displaying photographs and other memorabilia to document it. Museum-style display cabinets flank the front door, showing images of the most select visitors and habitués, amongst whom is Jorge Luis Borges. However, Borges did not visit the café particularly regularly according to León Tenenbaum, who underlines Borges's preference for roaming: 'No fue Borges un concurrente regular, asiduo, empedernido del sedentario café barrial. Sin dudas sus inclinaciones [...] eran peripatéticas. La charla andando.'[99] Café Tortoni, he suggests, is among those cafés which Borges sporadically frequented but which left no individual mark on him.

Borges is also one of the three life-size figures around one of the café tables that make up a rather amateurish sculpture placed towards the back of the long room of the Tortoni (Fig. 31). The sculpture brings together the writer, tango singer Carlos Gardel and poet Alfonsina Storni, a scene only possible in fiction, as, interestingly, an elderly Borges leaning on his walking-stick is portrayed next to a young Gardel. The iconic singer died in the 1930s, when Borges was still a young man, which means that the sculpture does not show the historical figures

---

[96] This is a piece of local wisdom which is repeated by various local and international tourist websites and blogs, such as http://visitasurbanas.blogspot.co.uk/2011/11/avenida-de-mayo.html; www.almargen.com.ar/sitio/seccion/turismo/baires4/index.html; www.novelhotel.com.ar/Ingl/A_Histo.htm [all last accessed 27 September 2013]. It is an accurate summary of the avenue's politico-historical origins and its multicultural social profile: planned and started during the Europeanizing conservative government of Julio Argentino Roca, it is likely that the workforce hired to do the building works was mainly of Italian origin, as it coincides with the first wave of Italian immigration in Argentina. Spanish immigrants are known to have settled around the avenue, hence its nickname.
[97] As publicized on the café's homepage: www.cafetortoni.com.ar/html/tortoni.html [last accessed 27 September 2013].
[98] Online at www.cafetortoni.com.ar/html/historia.html [last accessed 27 September 2013].
[99] León Tenenbaum, *Buenos Aires tiempo de Borges* (Buenos Aires: Ediciones Turísticas, 2001), p. 278.

FIGURE 31. A contemporary sculpture brings together Jorge Luis Borges, Carlos Gardel and Alfonsina Storni at Café Tortoni, Buenos Aires, May 2008.

but, rather, the myths: Gardel as perpetually young and Borges as perpetually old. Tourists queue up to take the empty chair left just by it, to become part of this simulacrum by having their photograph taken with the great Argentine icons. The sculpture was funded by Paris-based 'Art Saint Michel' to promote 'la integración y el conocimiento de la cultura y el patrimonio franco-argentino.'[100] It is further testimony to the French cultural connection, which in turn taps into the legend of Gardel's French origins and the apogee of export tango in Paris in the 1920s and 1930s. At the back of the café, a room which used to function as a barber's shop has become a museum containing books, stamps and photographs related to Borges and other famous figures of porteño culture. This space was partially reproduced for the Café's stand at the 2008 Feria del Libro, which adds a further dimension to the efforts of the Tortoni's owners to fix a cultural identity

---

[100] Online at www.cafetortoni.com.ar/html/visitantes2.html [last accessed 27 September 2013].

to the café. The centrality of the figure of Borges both in the café and in its display at the book fair, speaks of the great benefits of these Borgesian spaces in terms of publicity for the café, and ultimately, for the city. The profound influence of Parisian culture in the history of the city's modernization and in the development of both its high and popular culture coalesce under one roof, constituting an attractive cultural tourist package. The city's 'Yo leo en el bar' initiative further reinforces Café Tortoni's construction as a Borgesian space and it constitutes an example of the combination of public and private initiatives that are associated with the management style of the Macri administration.

The next section explores the role of memory and history in the creation of 'empty' Borgesian spaces in areas of the city of Buenos Aires.

'Ghostly' Borgesian Spaces

Andreas Huyssen notes that even those spaces that seem 'among the most stable and fixed: cities, monuments, architecture, and sculpture' have become infused with 'memory and temporality,' in such a way that 'we have come to read cities and buildings as palimpsests of space, monuments as transformable and transitory.'[101] In the case of some of the stops in the 'Recorrido Jorge Luis Borges', this transformability of historical spaces has been taken full circle, as they no longer 'exist' physically, or their function or ownership has changed, therefore losing any physical trace of Borges. In this sense, they can be referred to as 'ghost' spaces, since, as Huyssen argues, they are both replete with historical meanings and open to current resignifications. In this sense, understanding the city as a 'fundamental multiplicity of spatialities where old and new ideologies' coexist (Cupers),[102] these spaces, which contain a strong ghostly presence of Borges, can be read as palimpsests in constant construction. The government of the city has thus created a virtual space, whose visual representation on the web has its referent in history. Its palimpsestic multiplicity emerges through the interaction between these meanings and the experiences and expectations that each visitor brings along.

Two of these 'ghostly' spaces have been demolished: Borges's birthplace, house number 842 of calle Tucumán; and his calle Serrano home. The two original buildings have disappeared from the landscape, leaving no material trace, which means that the roaming Borges enthusiast may have been surprised to see that the map from the city's official website has taken him/her to an apparent dead end. Those enthusiasts who have also read his work may be amused by such a Borgesian twist and may imagine, for example, that the house itself exists in a parallel universe of a Buenos Aires of forking paths, or in a creator's dream. This

---

[101] Huyssen, *Present Pasts*, p. 7.
[102] Cupers, 'Towards a Nomadic Geography', p. 734.

space may be thought of as constituting 'the site of the ruins of previous orders in which diverse histories, languages, memories and traces continually entwine and recombine in the construction of new horizons.'[103] Zito disentangles a few of the layers of historical signification of Borges's birthplace, or 'solar natal:'[104]

> La propia casa natal de Borges desaparecerá en ese terremoto edilicio que sacudió al centro de la ciudad en los primeros años del siglo. En ese lugar, ahora con la numeración 838, hay un local comercial. Sin embargo, la placa recordatoria del sitio natal de Borges se colocó en el edificio contiguo (Tucumán 842 al 846). Se trata de una casa de dos plantas, de fachada italianizante, construida en 1929 para sede del Club Oriental. Actualmente funciona allí la Asociación Cristiana Femenina.[105]

The house on calle Serrano (Fig. 32) is also absent. But the mention of the name 'Serrano' itself evokes the poem 'Fundación mítica de Buenos Aires', which situates this space within the so-called 'manzana mítica': 'La manzana pareja que persiste en mi barrio: / Guatemala, Serrano, Paraguay, Gurruchaga.'[106] It also brings to mind the fact that the name of a section of this street has been changed into 'Jorge Luis Borges' (Fig. 33), something which was ironically prefigured by the writer in life: 'Sería horrible pensar que algún día habrá una calle que se llame Jorge Luis Borges, yo no quiero ser una calle.'[107] Sandra Pien reminds us that Borges would have disapproved: 'rebautizaron con su nombre un tramo de la palermitana calle Serrano, destruyendo la idealizada manzana de su poema Fundación mítica de Buenos Aires.'[108]

In this way, the city administration succeeded in emphasizing the presence of the writer in a specific urban space and Borges ended up 'being a street.' As calle Jorge Luis Borges extends and makes visible the 'manzana mítica' to link up with the metropolitan Zoo nearby, this generated a tangible Borgesian area which was later incorporated into the 'Recorrido' by the following administration (Fig. 30, stops 10 and 11). This is yet another instance of the construction of the image of the writer as mythical as the characters he created and also, as the urban landscape that he narrated. In 1996, the then mayor of Buenos Aires Fernando de la Rúa[109]

---

[103] Iain Chambers, *Border Dialogues. Journeys in postmodernity*. (London: Routledge, 1990), p. 112, cited in Cupers, 'Towards a Nomadic Geography', p. 734.
[104] The use of 'solar' in this phrase, which is used in tourism discourse to refer to the birthplace of a historical figure, is appropriately vague, as it refers to a non-defined space (that is, not a house or building in particular).
[105] Carlos Alberto Zito, *El Buenos Aires de Borges* (Buenos Aires: Aguilar, 1999), p. 64.
[106] Borges, 'Fundación mítica de Buenos Aires', p. 81.
[107] Jorge Luis Borges in *Borges para millones* (Buenos Aires: Corregidor, 1997), cited by Zito in *El Buenos Aires de Borges*, p. 246.
[108] Sandra Pien, 'Ciudad de mitos', *La Nación*, 28 January 2007, online at http://www.lanacion.com.ar/877662-ciudad-de-mitos [last accessed 27 September 2013].
[109] U.C.R. (Unión Cívica Radical) Fernando de la Rúa was 'Jefe de gobierno' of the city of Buenos Aires between 1996 and 1999.

Serrano 2135/47. Casa de la familia Borges en Palermo. Ocupada entre los años 1901 y 1914. Con una muy breve estada en 1923.

FIGURE 32. House on calle Serrano 2147 where Borges spent much of his childhood. The house itself has been demolished. León Tenenbaum, *Buenos Aires. Tiempo de Borges* (Buenos Aires: Ediciones Turísticas, 2001), p. 194. Reproduced with permission of the copyright holder.

FIGURE 33. Calle Jorge Luis Borges (formerly Serrano), Barrio de Palermo, Buenos Aires, April 2008.

declared this section of calle Serrano officially renamed 'Jorge Luis Borges'. His words on that occasion contributed to the perpetuation of the image of the writer as the city's mythical elderly *flâneur*:

> 'Borges amó a Buenos Aires y la recorrió incansablemente', expresó De la Rúa. 'Su figura, la de un anciano apoyándose en un bastón alcanza hoy, como la de los personajes que creó, la estatura de mito. No lo olvidarán ni la calle Serrano, ni Palermo; pero tampoco la calle Brasil, el área de Constitución o Villa Crespo. Los hombres de un suburbio que nos devolvió, transformados en belleza.'[110]

The 'Ex sede de la Biblioteca Nacional', where Borges served as director from 1955 until his resignation in 1973, constitutes another 'ghost' space. In this case, this is due to its change of function: no longer a library, the links to Borges's life only exist in historical documents and memory. Opened in 1901, the building in calle México housed the National Library until it was moved to a purpose-built modern venue in calle Agüero in 1992; the old building now houses the 'Dirección Nacional de Música y Danza'. Designed by Italian architect Carlos Morra, the imposing Beaux-Arts building comprises three levels which combine an italianate layout with classical decorative elements. At its core, what used to be the central reading room, directly underneath a cathedral-style dome, has had lines painted on the floor, turning the extensive space into a court to double up as sports facility and rehearsal area.

Looking up at the empty shelves of the former library draws the eye to the source of light of the stained glass dome, causing the impression of an empty ancient site of worship, containing the vestiges of a previous order. As Huyssen explains:

> An urban imaginary in its temporal reach may well put different things in one place: memories of what there was before, imagined alternatives of what there is. The strong marks of present space merge in the imaginary with traces of the past, erasures, losses, and heterotopias.[111]

In the case of the former Biblioteca Nacional, the sense of the space as palimpsest is great. The physical presence of books has been erased and the silence of the reading room has been lost. However, the age and architectural style of the building speaks of the grand plans of the early twentieth-century ruling conservative elite for a powerful metropolis that, modelled on Paris, emulated the great capitals of Europe. In particular, this architectural grandeur associated Buenos Aires with European art, thus expressing the city's great cultural and intellectual ambitions. In addition, the particular historical context of Borges's

---

[110] Jorge Rouillon, 'En Palermo Viejo, Borges tiene calle', *La Nación*, 24 August 1996, online at www.lanacion.com.ar/nota.asp?nota_id=171789 [last accessed 27 September 2013].
[111] Huyssen, *Present Pasts*, p. 7.

time at the Biblioteca Nacional is imbued with significant political connotations. His appointment as director (by the military government of the Revolución Libertadora) and, later, his resignation (on Perón's return to power) place him in clear opposition to Peronism and causes him to be perceived as being in favour of military regimes in general.[112] It is an almost legendary fact that Borges was one of the three blind directors of the library (famously picked up in the character of the blind librarian in Umberto Eco's 1980 novel *Il nomme della rosa*). The conjunction of blindness and the seeming infinity of the empty shelves find literary expression in 'Poema de los dones', where even the library is referred to as 'blind'.[113] Here, the use of the word 'ciega' — which also means 'bottomless' or 'infinite' — brings Borges's experience of himself and of the library together. These are some of the most prominent traces of layers, although by no means the only ones, of this palimpsest.

Two other sites in Buenos Aires are worth mentioning in this context. The next section concentrates on the juxtaposition of public and private enterprise in another Borgesian space. After that, the last site to be considered here is a 'void' which represents the reclamation of the body of Borges.

From 'correcta interpretación' to Posthumous Possession

Headed by Borges's widow María Kodama, the 'Fundación Jorge Luis Borges' (Stop 14 of the 'Recorrido', Fig. 30) is located at number 1660 of Buenos Aires's calle Anchorena, directly next door to one of many of Borges's places of residence (number 1672). This proximity constitutes the Fundación's most immediately observable claim to Borgesian authenticity. A private residence, the neighbouring house, in turn, asserts its own Borgesian identity by boasting a plaque with a quotation from the story 'Las ruinas circulares', which Borges is said to have written whilst living there. The Fundación, whose mission statement is to 'difundir la obra de Jorge Luis Borges contribuyendo a su conocimiento y propiciando su correcta interpretación,' is a resource centre, with archives containing the writer's personal library, manuscripts and a variety of personal objects.[114] The organization of its events is both related to the life and work of the writer, including specialist conferences and other activities (bizarrely, a birthday party is organized here in his honour every 24th of August, cake and candles included). It also contributes to the cultural life of the city, through the

---

[112] Williamson examines the political aspect of Borges's directorship in 'Borges Against Perón', 'La Revolución Libertadora' and 'Between Sunset and Dawn', in *Borges*, pp. 311–41 and 403–15.

[113] Borges, 'Poema de los dones', p. 187. José Mármol and Paul Groussac were the other two illustrious blind men of letters who were directors of the Biblioteca Nacional before Borges.

[114] Online at www.fundacionborges.com [last accessed 27 September 2013].

arranging of literary contests in local schools, for example, and the provision of a variety of courses. In 2008, visiting times were restricted and access to the collections was by appointment only, so that the spontaneous visitor following the Recorrido would normally have been unable to enter or have any direct access to everything the Fundación had to offer.

Interestingly, the Fundación also boasts the bedroom Borges occupied in his last address in the city, Maipú 994, which it recreated in its premises. Thus, in spite of the efforts to legitimize certain places in the city as Borgesian spaces, it is impossible to reclaim all of the physical places which once provided a setting for the writer's life. This demonstrates that the creation of Borgesian spaces involves a complexity of meanings which do not necessarily have a real, physical embodiment in the form of bricks and mortar. Rather, Borgesian spaces are a weave of experiences, memories and expectations which are in constant construction and development and which can be superimposed onto other spaces for the sake of cultural capital. With this in mind, the proposed repatriation of Borges's remains represents a desire to possess the writer physically, filling the void left by his perceived absence. This is in spite of Borges's repeated assertion that his work and his history would always be in Buenos Aires: 'Mi cuerpo físico puede estar en Lucerna, en Colorado o en El Cairo, pero al despertarme cada mañana, al retomar el hábito de ser Borges, emerjo invariablemente de un sueño que ocurre en Buenos Aires.'[115]

The controversy surrounding the place and manner of Borges's death is where the notorious feud between Borges's family and his widow, María Kodama, most visibly plays out, although it has reverberations in the wider national context. In *Borges a Contraluz*, Estela Canto considers that Borges's decision to die in Geneva constituted 'su gran gesto de liberación,' although she admits that it was felt as a betrayal in Argentina.[116] The writer's final decision was generally perceived by some as consistent with his image of an artist in an ivory tower, with no link to his homeland. The fact that Borges wished to die privately, rather than in the public eye, was seen as a shunning of the people, who were not allowed access to his final hours. Further, María Kodama, whom Borges married just days before he died, has since been vilified in the public eye, as she was perceived to be an opportunist who took Borges away from the 'patria' for her own personal benefit. Public opinion has been divided ever since, between a majority who see Borges as cultural patrimony of Argentina, and therefore, having a duty to his country to remain in it; and those who perceive him as a private individual with the freedom to decide where his mortal remains rest. This polemic was by no means over after the writer's death in 1986, as is evident in readers' comments about a

---

[115] In Darío L. Luciano, *Borges en San Fernando. Jorge Luis Borges en el Ateneo Popular Esteban Echeverría* (Victoria, Pcia. Bs. As.: Ediciones Ocruxaves, 1996), p. 86.
[116] Canto, *Borges*, p. 15.

possible repatriation in national newspapers. In February 2009, a reader of *La Nación*, for example, says: 'fue un error llevarlo a morir a Suiza. Debería estar junto a su madre en Recoleta. Fue un argentino indiscutible, aquí vivió siempre, aquí veneró a sus antepasados, aquí caminó hasta el agotamiento Buenos Aires;' while another reader responds to the same article by saying: 'por más que haya sido un escritor fantástico, a los muertos hay que dejarlos descansar en paz, y en este caso seguir leyendo sus obras.'[117]

In the context of this dispute, the city of Buenos Aires also has claims over the remains of Borges, effecting the ultimate objectification of the writer. Borges is thus constructed as a tangible national treasure, a son of Buenos Aires, whose physical reality, the city claims, belongs in its bosom. The writer's 'betrayal' will be overlooked as long as he is prepared to do his duty and go back where he belongs. Juan Gasparini, author of *Borges: La posesión póstuma* (2000), cites a series of conversations in which Borges talks about his remains being buried in Recoleta as a matter of course. In one of them, Borges says: 'yo seré enterrado aquí, pero eso no tiene mucha importancia pues [...] yo no soy mi cuerpo, yo no creo ser solamente mi cuerpo.'[118] Gasparini states that 'no se conoce ningún testimonio legal que haya sido rubricado por su firma donde se trasluciera su deseo de ser enterrado en algún lugar en concreto' (p. 114). However, in 1988, Borges's nephew, Miguel de Torre, attempted the repatriation of the writer's remains from Geneva to Buenos Aires. This was unsuccessful, as María Kodama managed to block the proceedings, beginning a long battle between the parties in the Swiss courts. According to Argentine historian Raúl Efrom, cited by Gasparini, the solution lay in the passing of a law in the Argentine parliament, based on the precedent cases of other historical figures such as San Martín, Sarmiento or Rosas, all of whom died abroad and whose remains were subsequently successfully repatriated to Argentina.

This task was taken up by Peronist 'diputada' for the city of Buenos Aires, María Beatriz Lenz, who in February 2009 presented a bill to this effect.[119] This time, the person behind the repatriation of the author's remains was collector, biographer and president of S.A.D.E. (Sociedad Argentina de Escritoires), Alejandro Vaccaro. Vaccaro is famously opposed to María Kodama, as the following declarations to the Argentine media show: 'Sólo se podría oponer María Kodama. ¿Por qué? [...] si Borges viene a la Argentina, ella lo pierde ya que va a

---

[117] Readers' comments to 'Nace un proyecto para repatriar los restos de Borges', *La Nación*, 10 February 2009, online at www.lanacion.com.ar/nota.asp?nota_id=1098437. A similar discussion can be seen in Mendoza's *Los Andes* newspaper, online at www.losandes.com.ar/notas/2009/2/20/un-409241.asp [both last accessed 27 September 2013].
[118] Juan Gasparini, *La posesión póstuma* (Madrid: Foca, 2000), p. 171.
[119] 'Nace un proyecto para repatriar los restos de Borges', *La Nación*, 10 February 2009, online at www.lanacion.com.ar/nota.asp?nota_id=1098437 [last accessed 27 September 2013].

la bóveda de los sobrinos de Borges.'[120] Gasparini aptly refers to this complex debate, where Borges's widow sees herself involved in all manners of legal proceedings concerning the figure of Borges, as 'the battle for posthumous possession.' As the case of Borges's final resting place stands at the moment, Kodama has a 'concesión gratuita por 99 años otorgada por la municipalidad de Ginebra [...] para que en el cementerio de Plainpalais duerman de por muerte los restos de "su esposo".'[121] Even though her proposal had been given support in parliament, Lenz finally desisted after a meeting with Kodama, who expressed her disapproval and stated its legal weight.[122]

In the meantime, a phenomenon similar to the veneration of Eva Perón's grave at Recoleta cemetery has been taking place at Plainpalais. Here, the writer's grave has become a site of pilgrimage where people have taken to leaving letters to the writer, as *La Nación*'s Susana Reinoso observes: 'la tumba de Jorge Luis Borges en el cementerio de los reyes de Plainpalais, en Ginebra, convertida en una meca de lectores de todo el mundo, es testigo mudo de la admiración y el cariño.'[123] The empty space that his family claims is ready to welcome his mortal remains has thus become a void saturated with desire. It would be natural to expect the technocrats of the city to regret the loss of potential revenue that Borges's 'physical' absence in the city may cause. After all, as the local tour guides of the Recoleta cemetery can always be heard saying, as they stand before the Borges family vault: 'El gran ausente de la Recoleta es Jorge Luis Borges.' However, Lenz's proposal is better interpreted as a populist move: a grandiloquent gesture that resembles the capturing of the body of the enemy more than it does the veneration of the sage. A form of revenge, it may be argued, for 'La fiesta del monstruo', where the 'merza' were disappointed that they were not able to carry out a 'remate de anteojos y vestuario'[124] belonging to their victim, the intellectual who had failed to venerate the 'estandarte y foto del Monstruo' (p. 400).

Yet again, the battle for the 'possession' of Borges is played out at various, interconnected, levels: that of the private circle of his close family and friends, that of politicians whose appropriation of the body of the writer serves to make various points, and that of Borges 'experts' whose interest in the writer has crossed over to the public arena and serves their own self-publicity. Each constructs a

---

[120] 'Borges, de Ginebra a la Recoleta', *Diario Perfil*, 8 February 2009, online at http://www.perfil.com/contenidos/2009/02/07/noticia_0045.html [last accessed 27 September 2013].
[121] Gasparini, *La posesión póstuma*, p. 128.
[122] 'Un refugio contra el asedio', *Página/12*, 28 February 2009, online at http://www.pagina12.com.ar/diario/suplementos/espectaculos/4-13004-2009-02-28.html [last accessed 27 September 2013].
[123] 'Lectores de diversos países dejan mensajes en la tumba de Borges', *La Nación*, 9 February 2009, online at www.lanacion.com.ar/nota.asp?nota_id=1098156 [last accessed 27 September 2013].
[124] Borges and Bioy Casares, 'La fiesta del monstruo', p. 402.

different Borges, according to their motivations and agendas. Perhaps most relevant, however, is the role of Argentine public opinion, the sounding board for these interconnected debates. Everybody seems to want a piece of Borges, as pilgrims of the Middle Ages treasured their relics, and this constructs the author as an objectified figure of veneration.

Conclusion

It was the purpose of this closing chapter to examine the creation of Borgesian spaces in the city of Buenos Aires as an economic and political strategy. This strategy aimed to create an identity for the city as eminently cultural (literary in particular) for the promotion of cultural tourism. This in turn feeds into the delineation of the anti-populist and anti-Peronist stance of the Macri administration. The city has seen enormous change since the beginning of its modern urbanization, a particular view of which permeates the life and work of Borges, especially his poetry. Thus, in writing the city's mythology, Borges wrote himself into the fabric of the urban landscape. Buenos Aires, on its part, has recognized that its history and idiosyncrasy are inextricably linked to the writer. Borges is therefore constructed as intimately porteño and eminently cosmopolitan at the same time. This complexity is in turn associated with the city as the backdrop to his work and *flaneries* but also, crucially, as 'essence of the Borges self' (Molloy). At a deeper level, while cultural policies rest on a 'new', more local Borges, the political implications of this double construction of the author and the city tap into Borges's undeniable anti-Peronism. They also exploit and perpetuate his construction as an elite writer to serve the clear anti-populist stance of the Macri administration. The writer as creator of an 'apocryphal past' for the city treats Buenos Aires as his muse. The city, in turn, creates the author's image. Borges and Buenos Aires are undoubtedly inextricably linked: this chapter unveiled some of the complex ways in which, paraphrasing the writer, 'Borges estaba y estará en Buenos Aires.'[125]

---

[125] Jorge Luis Borges, 'Arrabal', *OCI*, p. 32.

CONCLUSION

~

> Lo único que existe es el camino. No se llega nunca a ninguna parte. Nada termina, Perramus.[1]

In the context of Argentina's bicentenary celebrations, which propitiated the consideration of the concept of 'Argentineness', the figure of Borges emerged as a constant in a variety of discourses. These discourses pertain, in turn, to the construction of a sense of national cultural identity. This study has explored this link and it has come to the conclusion that the anxieties and expectations projected onto the iconic figure of Borges are those which have contributed to defining Argentina's sense of cultural identity. These rest largely on the oscillation between being 'local' and being 'foreign', an opposition which is intimately linked with another set of binaries at the heart of Argentina's historical development: civilization versus barbarism. These oscillations manifested themselves in Argentine literary production, as Piglia argued, since its inception and throughout much of the twentieth century. Therefore, this study concludes that the unique coincidence and intertwining of Argentine historical circumstances with those pertaining to Borges's own life-span — in terms of his personal and his public life, and also, in terms of his literary yield — have resulted in his construction as a national cultural icon.

Chapter 1 argued that the construction of Borges as an Anglophile, which Rodríguez Monegal in particular construes in relation to the anti-Argentine prejudice, which di Tella refers to as 'Borges nightmare', responds to this conflicting relationship between being Argentine and being foreign.[2] The scenario described in Borges's 'El sur', for example, where all manner of boundaries — geographical, cultural and narrative — are crossed, is a reflection of this type of conflict, and it attests to Borges's choice to position himself in between, that is, astride these oppositions. The tension between imitation and rejection of the foreign, in turn, has played out in the reception of Borges in Argentina, in the shape of both his condemnation as anti-Argentine on the part of the left-wing intelligentsia and the celebration of his greatness as corroborated by his consecration in Europe and the United States. This acknowledges the legitimising

---

[1] These words are spoken by the character 'Borges' in Alberto Breccia and Juan Sasturain, *Perramus: Diente por diente* (Buenos Aires: Ediciones de la Flor, 2006), p. 169.
[2] Torcuato S. di Tella, *History of Political Parties in Twentieth-Century Latin America* (New Brunswick and London: Transaction, 2004), p. 34, as quoted in the Introduction.

power of the foreign. In his narratives, Borges does not tackle these tensions by choosing sides. Instead, he develops a sense of 'Argentineness' which embraces what would otherwise be perceived as irreconcilable differences. This is his most valuable contribution to the process of construction of Argentine identity.

The figure of Borges has been approached here as a set of narratives about him and which also narrate elements of Argentine history and idiosyncrasy (foreign constructions achieve this by contrast). This link has been explored by examining the discourses that went into the construction of Borges as a cultural icon in Argentina in the course of the twentieth century and the transition into the twenty-first century. The cultural artefacts and urban spaces examined, through which Borges's visual image, his biographical details and his work have been appropriated, were shown to have contributed, and to continue to contribute, to the unending configuration of a mosaic which will never be completed, but which we refer to as 'Borges'.

The present work focused on the concepts of de-centring and in-betweenness and challenged the notion of identity as homogeneous end-result, embracing, instead, a fragmented, fluid, kaleidoscopic view of the process of construction of what it is to be Borges, and through this, of what it is to be Argentine. It has been able to regard the construction of identity as a perpetual process. This is also consistent with Borges's narrative technique, and with his idea of the aesthetic phenomenon as a journey rather than a destination, as Chapter 1 in particular explored in relation to the futile quest for the Borges essence by the 'genre' of literary biography.

Chapter 1 exposed the illusory nature of the notion of an essence of Borges by examining the narrative devices that construct the author as biographical subject, and which, in turn, construct a biographer's own identity. The examination of literary biographies here established the methodology that the other three chapters followed. By focusing on the narrative nature of the genre of biography and exposing the mechanisms which narrate the life and work of Borges, it drew attention to the significance of these mechanisms. In this way, the material that was subsequently analysed was approached with this in mind, that is, as mentioned in the Introduction, with a permanent suspicion which would allow the discovery, not of things beneath discourses, but of discourses beneath things.[3] The chapter also argued for the paramount importance of how cultural products such as biographies and photographs were packaged and marketed as mediations between the readers and the Borgesian oeuvre. The comparison of the five biographies in relation with the particular contexts in which each was written has allowed me to assess the historical evolution of certain constructions of Borges and to demonstrate that these responded to certain issues pertaining to Argentine

---

[3] Umberto Eco, *La estrategia de la ilusión*, pp. 9-10.

identity. The contrast between biographies by Argentine writers and one by a non-Argentine served to emphasize these conclusions.

Chapter 2 concentrated on the visual aspect of the construction of Borges as an icon. To do this, it addressed the question of Borges's portrayal as elderly, and came to the conclusion that this responds to the need to erect him as cultural monument, a figure of cultural authority that could provide a sense of cultural history, condensing a desire for a lasting and cohesive sense of national identity. Chapter 2 argued that by constructing Borges as a cohesive force, following his international acclaim, this showed a certain national sense of inferiority, given the anti-Argentine prejudice mentioned by di Tella. This took the shape of a need for foreign legitimisation, from Europe and the United States in particular.

In the particularly turbulent years of the 1960s and 1970s, expectations regarding cultural cohesion in Argentina were expressed in relation to political engagement: on the left meant siding with the people — and therefore, with a 'national' culture; on the right, with the foreign-loving oligarchy. Chapter 3 demonstrated that this tension was played out in the construction of Borges as a traitor by the Argentine left-wing intelligentsia and the attempt, on the part of the military regime, to appropriate him. The constructions of Borges as an Anglophile, foreign-loving writer, who was detached from the reality of his country were emphasized in the first biographies and were then perpetuated by the intellectuals of the left. These constructions pivot around the political implications of the definition of Argentine culture as peripheral which dominated the mainly national-populist critical scene of the time. In this sense, what was demanded of Borges by the left in the 1960s and 1970s related to a need for political definition: Borges should assume a clear 'Argentine' position that was in touch with its people, or be condemned as an enemy. Either way, Borges was seen as a way of legitimising a particular version of Argentine identity.

By analysing the appropriation of the writer by comic strip artists in the 1980s, Chapter 3 argued that the transition to democracy, after 1983, ushered in a new way of confronting political and cultural activity in relation to Borges and a need to reassess the ways in which national identity was constructed. This occurred as a consequence of a sense of defeat, which forced a repositioning of the left-wing intelligentsia. The chapter showed that this, in turn, favoured a revision of the construction of Borges as political enemy. Consequently, it brought about a renewed perception of a more diverse Borges who could be a cultural father-figure, embracing — rather than attempting to erase — what had been perceived as contradictions. This was established by an examination of the depiction of a subversive Borges in the comic strip *Perramus* in particular.

The first decade of the twentieth century found the city of Buenos Aires being marketed as a product for international cultural tourism, with Borges as integral part of that package. An analysis of the city's Borgesian spaces has shown how the various constructions of Borges considered in the first three chapters converge in them. It also revealed how, in spite of the efforts of the city council to homogenize them, these are social spaces in constant construction. Argentina's complex relationship with foreignness also comes into play here: these spaces also bring to mind a Borges who inhabits the in-between, who is eminently local and cosmopolitan at the same time, whose ultimate definition is as elusive as that of an Argentine identity.

As suggested in the Introduction, common epithets chosen to refer to Borges, such as 'vende patria' and 'maestro' have coexisted in Argentina over the last sixty years. Although they are at opposite ends of the spectrum, both terms are equally valid, equally true of how Argentines have related to Borges over the years: each of these names is imbued with meanings originating in a variety of discourses that construct a multiplicity of Borgeses and stem from Argentina's need to fix a cultural identity for itself.

BIBLIOGRAPHY

~

Abadi, Marcelo, 'Siete noches y un error' *Variaciones Borges*, 8 (1999), 134–37
Aizenberg, Edna, *Borges and his Successors: the Borgesian Impact on Literature and the Arts* (Columbia: University of Missouri Press, 1990)
Alazraki, Jaime, 'Recepción de Borges en los EE.UU.', in *El siglo de Borges: vol. I: Retrospectiva-Presente-Futuro*, ed. by Alfonso de Toro and Fernando de Toro (Madrid: Iberoamericana; Frankfurt am Main: Vervuert, 1999) pp. 337–56
Alemán, Alvaro, 'Paraliterary Immersion and the Puzzleform: An Essay in Social Restitution', *ImageTexT: Interdisciplinary Comics Studies*, 2.1 (2005) <www.english.ufl.edu/imagetext/archives/v2_1/aleman/> [last accessed 27 September 2013]
Alifano, Roberto, *Borges: biografía verbal* (Barcelona: Plaza y Janés, 1988)
Almeida, Iván, 'Jorge Luis Borges, autor del poema 'Instantes'', *Variaciones Borges*, 10 (2000), 227–46
Amaro Castro, Lorena, *Autobiografía y nombre propio en los textos de Jorge Luis Borges* (unpublished doctoral thesis, Universidad Complutense de Madrid, 2003)
—— 'La imposible autobiografía de Jorge Luis Borges', *Variaciones Borges*, 17 (2004), 229–52
Anderson, Linda, *Autobiography* (London & New York: Routledge, 2001)
Arana, Juan, 'Las primeras inquietudes filosóficas de Borges', *Variaciones Borges*, 7 (1999), 6–27
Arbus, Doone, and Marvin Israel, *Diane Arbus: Magazine Work* (New York: Aperture, 2004)
Asociación Borgesiana de Buenos Aires, *Borges: 1001 Imágenes* (Buenos Aires: Fundación Banco Ciudad, 2003)
Balderston, Daniel, ''Beatriz Viterbo c'est moi': Angular Vision in Estela Canto's *Borges a contraluz*', *Variaciones Borges*, 1 (1996), 133–39
—— *Borges: realidades y simulacros* (Buenos Aires: Biblos, 2000)
—— *El deseo, enorme cicatriz luminosa: ensayos sobre homosexualidades latinoamericanas* (Beatriz Viterbo Editora, 2004)
Barnes, Julian, *Flaubert's Parrot* (London: Picador, 1984)
Barrenechea, Ana María, *La expresión de la irrealidad en la obra de Jorge Luis Borges* (Buenos Aires: Paidós, 1967)
Barthes, Roland, *Image Music Text*, trans. by Stephen Heath (London: Fontana, 1977)
—— *Mythologies*, sel. and trans. by Annette Lavers (London: Vintage, 1993)
—— *Camera Lucida: Reflections on Photography*, trans. by Richard Howard (London: Vintage, 2000)
Bastos, María Luisa, *Borges ante la crítica argentina: 1923–1960* (Buenos Aires: Hispamérica, 1974)

Baudrillard, Jean, *Symbolic Exchange and Death*, trans. by Iain Hamilton Grant (London: Sage, 1993)
—— *Simulacra and Simulation*, trans. by Sheila Faria Glaser (Michigan: The University of Michigan Press, 1994)
Benjamin, Walter, 'A Small History of Photography', in *One-Way Street and Other Writings*, trans. by Edmund Jephcott and Kingsly Shorter (London: Verso, 1978)
Benton, Michael, 'Literary Biography: The Cinderella of Literary Studies', *The Journal of Aesthetic Education*, vol. 39, No. 3 (2005), 44–57
—— *Literary Biography: An Introduction* (Oxford: Wiley-Blackwell, 2009)
Bergero, Adriana, 'Jorge Luis Borges/Buenos Aires: arrabales, fobias y dioramas de sublimación en la primera modernización de Buenos Aires', in *Delirios de grandeza; los mitos argentinos: memoria, identidad, cultura*, ed. by María Cristina Pons and Claudia Soria (Rosario: Beatriz Viterbo, 2005), pp. 309–31
Bioy Casares, Adolfo, *Borges*, ed. by Daniel Martino (Barcelona: Destino, 2006)
Blaustein, Eduardo, and Martín Zubieta, *Decíamos ayer: La prensa argentina bajo el Proceso* (Buenos Aires: Colihue, 1998)
Borges, Jorge Luis, 'El escritor argentino y la tradición', *Sur*, 232 (1955a), 1–8
—— 'L'Illusion Comique', *Sur*, 237, 9–10 (1955b)
—— *Obras completas*, 3rd edn, vol. 1 (Barcelona: Emecé, 1996a)
—— *Obras completas*, vol. 4 (Barcelona: Emecé, 1996b)
—— *Obras completas*, vol. 3 (Barcelona: Emecé, 1997a)
—— *Obras completas en colaboración*, 5th edn (Buenos Aires: Emecé, 1997b)
—— *Autobiografía: 1899–1970*, trans. by Marcial Souto and Norman Thomas Di Giovanni (Buenos Aires: El Ateneo, 1999a)
—— *Obras completas*, 2nd edn, vol. 2 (Barcelona: Emecé, 1999b)
—— *Borges en El Hogar: 1935–1958* (Buenos Aires: Emecé, 2000)
Borges, Jorge Luis, and Osvaldo Ferrari, *Borges en diálogo* (Buenos Aires: Sudamericana, 1985)
Bosworth, Patricia, *Diane Arbus: A Biography* (New York: Norton, 1984)
Bourdieu, Pierre, *Photography: A Middle Brow Art*, trans. by Shaun Whiteside (Stanford: Stanford University Press, 1990)
Bravo, Pilar and Mario Paoletti, *Borges Verbal* (Buenos Aires: Emecé, 1999)
Breccia, Alberto, and Juan Sasturain, 'El fin', in *Alberto Breccia, Obras Completas*, vol.1 (Buenos Aires: Doedytores, 1994)
—— *Perramus: Diente por diente* (Buenos Aires: Ediciones de la Flor, 2006)
Brilliant, Richard, *Portraiture* (London: Reaktion Books, 1991)
Burke, Seán, *Authorship: From Plato to the Postmodern. A Reader* (Edinburgh: Edinburgh University Press, 1995)
—— *The Death and Return of the Author: Criticism and Subjectivity in Barthes, Foucault and Derrida* (Edinburgh: Edinburgh University Press, 2004)
Burzaco, Raúl Horacio, 'Tiempo de Borges', *ATC*, 28 June 1985, *Audiovideoteca de Buenos Aires*, Centro Cultural Recoleta, Gobierno de la Ciudad de Buenos Aires
Canaparo, Claudio, 'De Bibliographica Ratio: Un comentario acerca de 'lo Borgiano' como narración historiográfica. Las *Ficciones* de Josefina Ludmer', in *Jorge Luis Borges: Intervenciones sobre pensamiento y literatura*, ed. by William Rowe, Claudio Canaparo and Annick Louis (Buenos Aires: Paidós, 2000), pp. 199–247
Canto, Estela, *Borges a contraluz* (Madrid: Espasa Calpe, 1989)

—— *Borges à Contraluz*, trans. by Carmem Garcez (São Paulo: Illuminuras, 1991)
Carrizo, Antonio, *Borges el memorioso: Conversaciones de Jorge Luis Borges con Antonio Carrizo* (Mexico and Buenos Aires: Fondo de Cultura Económica, 1982)
Ceñedo, Jeffrey, 'Un nuevo Borges: Literatura y globalización en América Latina', *Iberoamericana. América Latina-España-Portugal*, vol. VI, No. 24 (2006), 43–61
Cisternas Ampuero, Cristián, 'Jorge Luis Borges: El "otro flâneur"', *Revista Chilena de Literatura*, 62 (2003), 79–104
Clarke, Graham (ed.), *The Portrait in Photography* (London: Reaktion Books, 1992)
Cruz Ruiz, Juan, *Egos Revueltos. Una memoria personal de la vida literaria* (Barcelona: Tusquets, 2010)
Cupers, Kenny, 'Towards a Nomadic Geography: Rethinking Space and Identity for the Potentials of Progressive Politics in the Contemporary City', *International Journal of Urban and Regional Research*, vol. 29, No. 4 (2005), 729–39
D'Allemand, Patricia, 'Hacia una crítica literaria latinoamericana: Nacionalismo y cultura en el discurso de Beatriz Sarlo', in *Mapas culturales para América Latina: culturas híbridas, no simultaneidad, modernidad periférica*, ed. by Sarah de Mojica (Bogotá: CEJA, 2001), pp. 189–200
de Certeau, Michel, *The Practice of Everyday Life*, trans. by Steven Rendall (Berkeley and Los Angeles: University of California Press, 1984)
del Carril, Sara Luisa (ed.), *Jorge Luis Borges: Textos recobrados 1919–1929* (Buenos Aires: Emecé, 1997)
del Carril, Sara Luisa and Mercedes Rubio de Socchi (eds.), *Borges En Sur 1931–1980* (Buenos Aires: Emecé, 1999)
—— *Jorge Luis Borges: Textos recobrados 1931–1955* (Buenos Aires: Emecé, 2007a)
—— *Jorge Luis Borges: Textos recobrados 1956–1986* (Buenos Aires: Emecé, 2007b)
Derrida, Jacques, *Of Grammatology*, trans. by Gayatri Chakravorty Spivak (Baltimore: John Hopkins University Press, 1976)
—— *Deconstruction in a Nutshell. A Converstaion with Jacques Derrida*, ed. by John D. Caputo (New York: Fordham University Press, 2004)
de Toro, Alfonso, 'Borges/Derrida/Foucault: *Pharmakeus*, heterotopia o más allá de la literatura ('hors-littérature'): escritura, fantasmas, simulacros, máscaras, carnaval y … Atlön/Tlön, Ykva/Uqbar, Hlaer/Jangr, Hrön (N)/Hrönir, Ur y otras cifras', in *Jorge Luis Borges: Pensamiento y saber en el siglo XX*, ed. by Fernando de Toro and Alfonso de Toro (Madrid: Iberoamericana, 1999) <www.uni-leipzig.de/~detoro/sonstiges/Pharmakeus_spanisch.pdf> [last accessed 27 September 2013]
de Torre Borges, Miguel (comp.), *Borges. Fotografías y manuscritos* (Buenos Aires: Ediciones Renglón, 1987)
Di Tella, Torcuato S., *History of Political Parties in Twentieth-Century Latin America* (New Brunswick and London: Transaction Publishers, 2004)
Duttlinger, Carolin, 'Imaginary Encounters: Walter Benjamin and the Aura of Photography', *Poetics Today*, 29:1 (Spring 2008), 79–101
Dyer, Geoff, *The Ongoing Moment* (New York: Pantheon, 2005)
Dyer, Richard, *Film Stars and Society* (London: Routledge, 2004)
Eco, Umberto, *La estrategia de la ilusión*, trans. by Edgardo Oviedo (Buenos Aires: Lumen, 1992)
—— 'Between La Mancha and Babel', *Variaciones Borges*, 4 (1997), 51–62

Ellis, David, 'Images of D.H. Lawrence: On the Use of Photographs in Biography', in Graham Clarke (ed.), *The Portrait in Photography* (London: Reaktion Books, 1992), 155-72
—— *Literary Lives: Biography and the Search for Understanding* (New York: Routledge, 2002)
Eloy Martínez, Tomás, *Santa Evita* (Buenos Aires: Planeta, 1995)
—— *El cantor de tango* (Buenos Aires: Planeta, 2004)
Facio, Sara, *Jorge Luis Borges en Buenos Aires* (Buenos Aires: La Azotea, 2005)
Ferrari, Osvaldo, *Jorge Luis Borges-Osvaldo Ferrari. Reencuentro: Diálogos Inéditos* (Buenos Aires: Sudamericana, 1999)
Fishburn, Evelyn, and Psiche Hughes, *A Dictionary of Borges* (London: Duckworth, 1990)
—— (ed.), *Borges and Europe Revisited* (London: Institute of Latin American Studies, 1998)
Flores, Alfredo, and Norberto Buscaglia, 'Historia del guerrero y de la cautiva', in *La Argentina en pedazos*, ed. by Ricardo Piglia (Buenos Aires: Ediciones de la Urraca, 1993), pp. 105-13
Foster, David William, *Buenos Aires: Perspectives on the City and Cultural Production* (Gainesville: University Press of Florida, 1998)
Foucault, Michel, 'What is an Author?', in *Modern Criticism and Theory: A Reader*, ed. by David Lodge and Nigel Wood, 2nd edn (New York: Pearson Education, 2000), pp. 174-87
Franco, Jean, 'Comic Stripping: Cortázar in the Age of Mechanical Reproduction', in *Critical Passions: Selected Essays*, ed. by Mary Louise Pratt and Kathleen Newman (Durham and London: Duke University Press, 1999), pp. 405-25
Gambini, Hugo, *Historia del peronismo: El poder total (1943-1951)* (Buenos Aires: Planeta, 1999)
García Morales, Alfonso, 'Jorge Luis Borges, autor del *Martín Fierro*', *Variaciones Borges*, 10 (2000), 29-64
Gasparini, Juan, *La posesión póstuma* (Madrid: Foca, 2000)
Gelman, Juan, 'Borges o El valor', *Página/12* (1993), in *Antiborges*, ed. by Martín Lafforgue (Buenos Aires: Vergara, 1999), pp. 333-35
Genette, Gerard, *Paratext: Thresholds of Interpretation*, trans. by Jane E. Lewin (Cambridge: Cambridge University Press, 1997)
Gledhill, Christine (ed.), *Stardom, Industry of Desire* (Abingdon: Routledge, 1991)
Gobello, José, *Nuevo diccionario lunfardo* (Buenos Aires: Corregidor, 1998)
Gociol, Judith, and Diego Rosemberg, *La historieta argentina: una historia* (Buenos Aires: Ediciones de la Flor, 2003)
Gorelik, Adrián, *La grilla y el parque: espacio público y cultura urbana en Buenos Aires, 1887-1936* (Bernal: Editorial de la Universidad Nacional de Quilmes, 1998)
—— 'El color del barrio', *Variaciones Borges*, 8 (1999), 36-68
Graham-Yooll, Andrew, *Buenos Aires, otoño de 1982: la guerra de Malvinas según las crónicas de un corresponsal inglés* (Buenos Aires: Marea, 2007)
Grosz, Elizabeth, *Space, Time and Perversion* (London and New York: Routledge, 1995)
Hamilton, Nigel, *Biography: A Brief History* (Cambridge: Harvard University Press, 2007)

Hariman, Robert and John Louis Lucaites, *No Caption Needed: Iconic Photographs, Public Culture, and Liberal Democracy* (Chicago and London: The University of Chicago Press, 2007)

Hart, Stephen and Richard Young (eds.), *Contemporary Latin American Cultural Studies* (London: Arnold, 2003)

Hernández Arregui, Juan José, 'La imagen colonizada de la Argentina: Borges y el *Martín Fierro*', *Imperialismo y cultura (La política de la inteligencia argentina)* (Buenos Aires: Editorial Amerindia, 1957), in *Antiborges*, ed. by Martín Lafforgue (Buenos Aires: Vergara, 1999), pp. 147–66

Hernández Martín, Jorge, 'Textual Polyphony and Skaz in *Seis problemas* by Bustos Domecq', *Variaciones Borges*, 6 (1998), 13–32

Huyssen, Andreas, *Present Pasts: Urban Palimpsests and the Politics of Memory* (California: Stanford University Press, 2003)

Insúa, Juan, 'Fundación mítica', in *Cosmópolis. Borges y Buenos Aires* (Barcelona: Centre de Cultura Contemporánia, 2002)

Jauretche, Arturo, 'Moraleja de Borges: su "guerrero y su cautiva"', *Marcha*, 1259 (1965) in *Antiborges*, ed. by Martín Lafforgue (Buenos Aires: Javier Vergara, 1999), pp. 169–78

Jurado, Alicia, *Genio y figura de Jorge Luis Borges*, 2nd edn. (Buenos Aires: EUDEBA, 1966)

King, John, 'Review: Literary Biography in Argentina', *Latin American Research Review*, vol. 18, No. 1 (1983), 246–53

Laclau, Ernesto, *On Populist Reason* (London and New York: Verso, 2005)

Lafforgue, Martín, *Antiborges* (Buenos Aires: Jarvier Vergara, 1999)

Lefebvre, Henri, *The Production of Space*, trans. by Donald Nicholson-Smith (Oxford: Blackwell, 1991)

Lister, Martin, 'Photography in the Age of Electronic Imaging', in *Photography: A Critical Introduction*, ed. by Liz Wells (London and New York: Routledge, 2005), pp. 297–336

Louis, Annick, 'Nota bibliográfica: María Esther Vázquez, *Borges: Esplendor y Derrota*', *Variaciones Borges*, 2 (1996), 223–28

— 'La biografía o las formas del yo', *Variaciones Borges*, 3 (1997), 207–13

Luciano, Darío L., *Borges en San Fernando: Jorge Luis Borges en el Ateneo Popular Esteban Echeverría* (Victoria, Pcia. Bs. As.: Ediciones Ocruxaves, 1996)

Ludmer, Josefina, '¿Cómo salir de Borges?', in *Jorge Luis Borges. Intervenciones sobre pensamiento y literatura*, ed. by William Rowe, Claudio Canaparo and Annick Louis (Buenos Aires: Paidós, 2000), pp. 289–300

Lynch, John, Roberto Cortés Conde, Juan Carlos Torre and Liliana de Riz, *Historia de la Argentina* (Barcelona: Crítica, 2001)

Lyon, Ted, 'Jorge Luis Borges and the Interview as Literary Genre', *Latin American Literary Review*, vol. 22, No. 44 (1994), 74–89

Machín, Horacio, 'Intérpretes culturales y democracia simbólica', in *Nuevas perspectivas desde/sobre América Latina: el desafío de los estudios culturales*, ed. by Mabel Moraña (Providencia, Santiago: Cuarto propio/Instituto Internacional de Literatura Iberoamericana, 2000), pp. 335–50

Marengo, María del Carmen, 'El autor ficticio en la obra de Jorge Luis Borges: Crítica y renovación de la literatura argentina', *Variaciones Borges*, 10 (2000), 167–83

Martín, Marina, 'Borges, perplejo defensor del idealismo', in 'Dossier: Borges: Perplejidades filosóficas', *Variaciones Borges*, 13 (2002), 7–21
Matamoro, Blas, 'Detrás de la penumbra está Inglaterra', *Borges o el juego trascendente* (Buenos Aires: Peña Lillo, 1971), in *Antiborges*, ed. by Martín Lafforgue (Buenos Aires: Vergara, 1999), pp. 193–250
Mateos, Zulma, *La filosofía en la obra de J.L. Borges* (Buenos Aires: Biblos, 1998)
McKinney, Mark, *History and Politics in French-Language Comics and Graphic Novels* (Jackson: University Press of Missisipi, 2008)
Mercer, Kobena, 'Monster Metaphors: Notes on Michael Jackson's *Thriller*', in *Reading Images*, ed. by Julia Thomas (New York: Palgrave, 2001)
Miller, Nicola, 'Contesting the Cleric: The Intellectual as Icon in Modern Spanish America', in *Contemporary Latin American Cultural Studies*, ed. by Stephen Hart and Richard Young (London: Arnold, 2003), pp. 62–75
Moliner, María, *Diccionario del uso del Español* (Madrid: Gredos, 2000)
Molloy, Sylvia, *Signs of Borges*, trans. by Oscar Montero (Durham: Duke University Press, 1994)
—— 'Lost in Translation: Borges, the Western Tradition and Fictions of Latin America', in *Borges and Europe Revisited*, ed. by Evelyn Fishburn (London: Institute of Latin American Studies, 1998), pp. 8–20
—— '*Flâneries* textuales: Borges, Benjamin y Baudelaire', *Variaciones Borges*, 8 (1999a), 16–29
—— *Las letras de Borges y otros ensayos* (Rosario: Beatriz Viterbo, 1999b)
Nouzeilles, Gabriela and Graciela Montaldo (eds.), *The Argentina Reader. History, Culture, Politics* (Durham and London: Duke University Press, 2002)
Orgambide, Pedro, 'Borges y su pensamiento político' (México: Comité de Solidaridad con el Pueblo Argentino, 1978), in *Antiborges*, ed. by Martín Lafforgue (Buenos Aires: Vergara, 1999), pp. 257–331
Parodi, Cristina, 'Alicia Jurado, *Genio y figura de Jorge Luis Borges*', *Variaciones Borges*, 4 (1997), 239–40
Pastormelo, Sergio, 'Borges crítico', *Variaciones Borges*, 3 (1997), 6–16
Pauls, Alan, *El factor Borges: Nueve ensayos ilustrados* (Buenos Aires: Fondo de Cultura Económica, 2000)
— 'La herencia Borges', *Variaciones Borges*, 29 (2010), 177–88
Pera, Cristóbal (ed.) *Jorge Luis Borges: Cartas del fervor. Correspondencia con Maurice Abramowicz y Jacobo Sureda (1919–1928)* (Barcelona: Emecé, 1999)
Perry, Nick, 'Post-Pictures and Ec(h)o effects', *Hyperreality and Global Culture* (London and New York: Routledge, 1998)
Pescador Monagas, Flora, 'De la ciudad de Buenos Aires de Borges a la calle sin esperanza de Le Corbusier', in *Variaciones Borges*, 8 (1999), 121–32
Petit de Murat, Ulyses, *Borges — Buenos Aires* (Buenos Aires: Municipalidad de Buenos Aires, 1980)
Pezzoni, Enrique, *Enrique Pezzoni, lector de Borges. Lecciones de literatura 1984–1988*, ed. by Annick Louis (Buenos Aires: Sudamericana, 1999)
Piglia, Ricardo, *La Argentina en pedazos* (Buenos Aires: Ediciones de la Urraca, 1993)
Pimentel Pinto, Júlio, 'Borges lee Buenos Aires. Un ejercicio crítico frente a la modernización de la ciudad', *Variaciones Borges*, 8 (1999), 82–94

Piñeiro, Claudia, *Las viudas de los jueves* (Buenos Aires: Alfaguara, 2005)
Pons, María Cristina and Claudia Soria (eds.), *Delirios de grandeza: Los mitos argentinos: memoria, identidad, cultura* (Rosario: Beatriz Viterbo, 2005)
Price, Derrick, and Liz Wells, 'Thinking about photography', in *Photography: A Critical Introduction*, ed. by Liz Wells (London and New York: Routledge, 2005), pp. 9–63
Prieto, Adolfo, *Borges y la nueva generación* (Buenos Aires: Letras Universitarias, 1954)
Rabinowitz, Paula, *They Must be Represented: The Politics of Documentary* (London: Verso, 1994)
Ramos, Jorge Abelardo, 'Borges, bibliotecario de Alejandría', in *Crisis y Resurreción de la literatura Argentina* (Buenos Aires: Coyoacán, 1954), in *Antiborges*, ed. by Martín Lafforgue (Buenos Aires: Vergara, 1999), pp. 127–40
Rock, David, *Argentina 1516-1982* (London: Tauris, 1986)
—— *Authoritarian Argentina. The Nationalist Movement, its History and its Impact* (Berkeley, Los Angeles and London: University of California Press, 1995)
Rodríguez Monegal, Emir, *El juicio de los parricidas: la nueva generación argentina y sus maestros* (Buenos Aires: Deucalión, 1956)
—— *Jorge Luis Borges. A Literary Biography* (New York: E.P. Dutton, 1978)
—— 'Borges y Derrida: Boticarios', *Maldoror. Revista de la ciudad de Montevideo*, 21 (1985), 125–32 <http://www.archivodeprensa.edu.uy/biblioteca/emir_rodriguez_monegal/bibliografia/criticas/crit_06.htm> [last accessed 27 September 2013]
—— *Borges: una biografía literaria*, trans. by Homero Alsina Thevenet (México: Fondo de Cultura Económica, 1993)
Rubenstein, Anne, *Language, Naked Ladies, & Other Threats to the Nation: A Political History of Comic Books in History* (Durham and London: Duke University Press, 1998)
Rufinelli, Jorge, 'La sonrisa de Gardel', in *Delirios de grandeza: Los mitos argentinos: memoria, identidad, cultura*, ed. by María Cristina Pons and Claudia Soria (Rosario: Beatriz Viterbo, 2005), pp. 73–100
Ruiz, Fernando, *Las palabras son acciones: Historia política y profesional de La Opinión de Jacobo Timerman (1971-1977)* (Buenos Aires: Perfil, 2001)
Sá, Lúcia, *Life in the Megalopolis. Mexico City and São Paulo* (London and New York: Routledge, 2007)
Sábat, Hermenegildo, *Georgie Dear* (Buenos Aires: Crisis, 1974)
—— *Georgie dear. Edición conmemorativa del centenario de Borges* (Buenos Aires: Nuevos Tiempos y Biblioteca Nacional, 1999)
Sabsay-Herrera, Fabiana, 'Para la prehistoria de H. Bustos Domecq', *Variaciones Borges*, 5 (1998), 106–22
Salas, Horacio, *Borges: una biografía* (Buenos Aires: Planeta, 1994)
Saraceni, Mario, *The Language of Comics* (London and New York: Routledge, 2003)
Sarlo, Beatriz, 'La izquierda ante la cultura: del dogmatismo al populismo', *Punto de vista*, 20 (1984), 22–25
—— 'Intellectuals: Scission or Mimesis?', in *The Latin American Cultural Studies Reader*, ed. by Ana del Sarto, Alicia Ríos and Abril Trigo (Durham and London: Duke University Press, 2004), pp. 250–61

—— *Tiempo pasado. Cultura de la memoria y primera persona* (Buenos Aires: Siglo XXI, 2005)
—— *Escritos sobre literatura argentina* (Buenos Aires: Siglo XXI, 2007a)
—— *Borges, un escritor en las orillas* (Madrid: Siglo XXI, 2007b)
Sasturain, Juan, *El domicilio de la aventura* (Buenos Aires: Colihue, 1995)
Schodt, Frederik, *Dreamland Japan: Writings on Modern Manga* (Berkeley: Stone Bridge Press, 1996)
Schwartz, Margaret, 'Dissimulations: Negation, the Proper Name, and the Corpse in Borges's "El simulacro"', *Variaciones Borges*, 24 (2007), 93–111
Scolari, Carlos, *Historietas para sobrevivientes: Comic y cultura de masas en los años 80* (Buenos Aires: Colihue, 1999)
Sebreli, Juan José, 'Borges: El nihilismo débil', *Escritos sobre escritos, ciudades bajo ciudades* (Buenos Aires: Sudamericana, 1997), in *Antiborges*, ed. by Martín Lafforgue (Buenos Aires: Vergara, 1999)
—— *Comediantes y Mártires: Ensayo contra los mitos* (Buenos Aires: Debate, 2008)
Secretaría de Derechos Humanos. Comisión Nacional sobre la Desaparición de Personas, *Nunca Más: Informe de la Comisión Nacional sobre la Desaparición de Personas* (Buenos Aires: EUDEBA, 2007)
Segre, Roberto, 'Buenos Aires en sus treinta. Los profetas de la modernidad porteña: Gardel y Le Corbusier', in *Delirios de grandeza: Los mitos argentinos: memoria, identidad, cultura*, ed. by María Cristina Pons and Claudia Soria (Rosario: Beatriz Viterbo, 2005)
Shanahan, Mary (ed.), *Richard Avedon: Evidence. 1944-1994* (New York: Random House, 1994)
Sontag, Susan, *On Photography* (New York: Farrar, Straus and Giroux, 1977)
Sosnowski, Saúl, 'Memorias de Borges (Artificios de la historia)', *Variaciones Borges*, 10 (2000), 79–95
Soussloff, Catherine M., *The Subject in Art: Portraiture and the Birth of the Modern* (Durham: Duke University Press, 2006)
Tenenbaum, León, *Buenos Aires, tiempo de Borges* (Buenos Aires: Ediciones turísticas, 2001)
Titelboim, Volodia, *Los dos Borges: vida, sueños, enigmas* (Buenos Aires: Sudamericana, 1996)
'Todo Borges', *Gente* (Buenos Aires: Atlántida, 1977)
Un amor de Borges, dir. by Javier Torre (Artistas Argentinos Asociados, 2000)
Uveda de Robledo, Epifanía and Alejandro Vaccaro, *El Señor Borges* (Buenos Aires: Edhasa, 2004)
Vaccaro, Alejandro, *Georgie, 1899-1930: Una vida de Jorge Luis Borges* (Buenos Aires: Editorial Proa/Alberto Casares, 1996)
—— *Una Biografía En Imágenes: Borges* (Buenos Aires: Ediciones B, 2005)
—— *Borges. Vida y Literatura* (Buenos Aires: Edhasa, 2006)
Vázquez, María Esther, *Borges: Esplendor y derrota* (Barcelona: Tusquets, 1996)
Wells, Liz (ed.), *Photography: A Critical Introduction* (London and New York: Routledge, 2005)
West, Shearer, *Portraiture* (Oxford: O.U.P., 2004)
Williamson, Edwin, *Borges: A Life* (London: Viking Penguin, 2004)

—— *The Penguin History of Latin America* (London: Penguin, 2009)
Wilson, Jason, *Buenos Aires: A Cultural and Literary History* (Oxford: Signal, 1999)
—— *Jorge Luis Borges* (London: Reaktion, 2006)
Woodall, James, *The Man in the Mirror of the Book: A Life of Jorge Luis Borges* (London: Hodder and Stoughton, 1996)
Yánover, Héctor, 'Crónica de relación con Dios/Borges', *Cuadernos Hispanoamericanos*, 505-07 (1992), 171-76
Zito, Carlos Alberto, 'El Buenos Aires de Borges', *Variaciones Borges*, 8 (1999a), 108-21
—— *El Buenos Aires de Borges* (Buenos Aires: Aguilar, 1999b)

Newspaper and Magazine Articles

Breccia, Alberto, and Juan Sasturain, 'Perramus: No saber y saber', *Fierro*, II, 18, February 1986
Burzaco, Raul Horacio, 'Tiempo de Borges', *Tiempo Argentino/Cultura*, 28 June 1985
Carbone, Alberto L., 'Fue prohibida la emisión de un sketch sobre Borges', *Clarín*, 4 July 1981
Ferro, Hellen, 'Una antología de frases borgeanas', 'Espectáculo', *Clarín*, 25 August 1979
—— 'La televisión y un Borges para todos', *Clarín*, 27 August 1980
García, Martín, 'Oesterheld releído: El eternauta, la zona de exclusión y la democracia', *Fierro*, I, 2, October 1984
Pereyra Iraola, Susana, 'Programa de la BBC sobre Borges', *La Nación*, 29 April 1979
Ranieri, Sergio, and Pablo Marchetti, 'Breccia y Borges', *La Maga* (1993) in *Archivos Negros*, 1 (2006), 2-9
Sasturain, Juan, 'Editorial', *Fierro*, I, 2, October, 1984
'Difundiose una entrevista a J.L. Borges en Italia', *La Nación*, 21 September 1971 (author unknown)
'Borges en la TV Italiana', *La Razón*, 22 September 1971 (author unknown)
'Borges, en la TV Francesa', *La Razón*, 28 March 1979 (author unknown)
'Si Borges lo dice', *Somos*, 10 September 1982 (author unknown)
'Editorieta', *Fierro*, II, 18, February, 1986 (author unknown)

Articles and Audiovisual Material Accessed Online

Avedon, Richard, 'Borrowed Dogs', *Richard Avedon Portraits* (2002) <www.richardavedon.com/data/web/richard_avedon_borrowed_dogs.pdf> [last accessed 27 September 2013]
Beccacece, Hugo, 'Un personaje de película', *La Nación*, 5 September 2000 <www.lanacion.com.ar/nota.asp?nota_id=31672> [last accessed 27 September 2013]
'Bibilioteca municipal Miguel Cané', 'Espacios', *Subsecretaría de Patrimonio Cultural, Gobierno de la Ciudad de Buenos Aires* <http://www.buenosaires.gob.ar/areas/cultura/patrimonio_historico_cultural/biblioteca_cane.php> [last accessed 27 September 2013] (author and date unknown)

Blejman, Mariano, 'Un testamento que deja dudas', *Página/12*, 9 October 2004 <www.pagina12.com.ar/diario/cultura/index-2004-10-09.html> [last accessed 27 September 2013]

'Books: Greatest in Spanish', *Time Magazine*, 22 June 1962 <www.time.com/time/magazine/article/0,9171,870003,00.html> [last accessed 27 September 2013] (author unknown)

Bordón, Juan Manuel, 'Reeditarán una obra de Borges con Vázquez: El texto es de 1966 y será publicado por Emecé, luego de una disputa judicial entre Vázquez y Kodama', *Clarín*, 10 September 2008 <http://edant.clarin.com/diario/2008/09/10/sociedad/s-01756834.htm> [last accessed 27 September 2013]

Bragg, Melvyn, 'In Our Time', *BBC Radio 4*, 4 January 2007 <http://www.bbc.co.uk/programmes/b0076182> [last accessed 27 September 2013]

'Conmauricio', 8 April 2009 <http://www.youtube.com/watch?v=dGu73QX5b2g&feature=video_response> [last accessed 27 September 2013]

de Santis, Pablo '*Perramus*, la mítica historieta con Borges y Gardel como personajes', *Clarín*, 3 June 2006, <www.clarin.com/diario/2006/06/03/sociedad/s-06401.htm> [last accessed 27 September 2013]

Donovan, Hedley, 'Time Essay: South America: Notes on a New Continent', *Time Magazine*, 1 December 1975 <www.time.com/time/magazine/article/0,9171,913779,00.html> [last accessed 27 September 2013]

Eloy Martínez, Tomás, 'Viaje a las tinieblas de Diane Arbus', *La Nación*, 28 May 2005 <www.lanacion.com.ar/nota.asp?nota_id=707933> [last accessed 27 September 2013]

Fernández, Hernán, '¿Quién lee cuál?', *Infobrand Digital*, 6 February 2007 <www.infobrand.com.ar/notas/8556-%BFQui%E9n-lee-cu%E1l%3F> [last accessed 27 September 2013]

'Fiction: The Decade's Most Notable Books', *Time Magazine*, 26 December 1969 <www.time.com/time/magazine/article/0,9171,941837,00.html> [last accessed 27 September 2013] (author unknown)

Fresán, Rodrigo, 'Una guía de las biografías de Borges escritas en la Argentina', *Página/12*, 16 January 2005 <www.pagina12.com.ar/diario/suplementos/radar/9-1953-2005-01-16.html> [last accessed 27 September 2013]

—— 'No-Ficciones', 'Radar', *Página/12*, 16 January 2005 <www.pagina12.com.ar/diario/suplementos/radar/9-1953-2005-01-16.html> [last accessed 27 September 2013]

—— 'Caro Diario: Adivina quién viene a comer', *Página/12*, 13 May 2007 <www.pagina12.com.ar/diario/suplementos/radar/9-3806-2007-05-13.html> [last accessed 27 September 2013]

Galván, Carlos, 'San Martín y Maradona, los que mejor representan al país', *Clarín*, 31 March 2005 <www.clarin.com/diario/2005/03/31/sociedad/s-03015.htm> [last accessed 27 September 2013]

'Interview with Ernesto Laclau', *Río Negro Online*, <www1.rionegro.com.ar/diario/tools/imprimir.php?id=7075> [last accessed 27 September 2013] (author and date unknown)

Jitrik, Noé, 'Apuntes sobre el manto borgeano', *Página/12*, 14 June 2006 <www.pagina12.com.ar/diario/suplementos/espectaculos/subnotas/2826-1022-2006-06-14.html> [last accessed 27 September 2013]

—— 'Exquisitos y justos', *Página/12*, 3 April 2007 < http://www.pagina12.com.ar/diario/contratapa/13-82698-2007-04-03.html> [last accessed 27 September 2013]

'Juan Sasturain: cronología', *Audiovideoteca de Buenos Aires. Literatura*, <www.buenosaires.gov.ar/areas/com_social/audiovideoteca/literatura/sasturain_bio2_es.php> [last accessed 27 October 2010] (author unknown)

Krebs, Edgardo, 'Borges', 'Cartas de lectores', *La Nación*, 19 October 2004 <www.lanacion.com.ar/nota.asp?nota_id=646152> [last accessed 27 September 2013]

—— 'Borges en inglés: problema de traducción', *La Nación*, 14 November 2004 <www.lanacion.com.ar/nota.asp?nota_id=653713> [last accessed 27 September 2013]

'La obra de Borges, disponible desde hoy en bares porteños', 'Revista Ñ', *Clarín*, 25 February 2010 <www.revistaenie.clarin.com/notas/2010/02/25/_-02147652.htm> [last accessed 27 September 2013] (author unknown)

Marinelli, Diego, 'El sueño del Eternauta: el proyecto inconcluso de Oesterheld', *Revista Ñ*, 21 November 2009 <www.revistaenie.clarin.com/notas/2009/11/21/_-02045193.htm> [last accessed 27 September 2013]

Montero, Hugo, 'Ernesto Sábato: mejor no hablar de ciertas cosas', *Revista Sudestada*, 27 (2004) <www.revistasudestada.com.ar/web06/article.php3?id_article=124> [last accessed 27 September 2013]

Montesoro, Julia, 'Jean Pierre Noher es Borges enamorado', *La Nación*, 5 September 2000 <www.lanacion.com.ar/nota.asp?nota_id=31673> [last accessed 27 September 2013]

Moreno, María, 'Era insoportable saber, pero sabíamos', 'Radar Libros', *Página/12*, 25 March 2001 <www.pagina12.com.ar/2001/suple/Libros/01-03/01-03-25/nota2.htm> [last accessed 27 September 2013]

Muleiro, Vicente, 'Listas negras y escritores desaparecidos', *Clarín*, 24 March 2006 <www.clarin.com/suplementos/especiales/2006/03/24/l-01164155.htm> [last accessed 27 September 2013]

'Nace un proyecto para repatriar los restos de Borges', *La Nación*, 10 February 2009 <www.lanacion.com.ar/nota.asp?nota_id=1098437> [last accessed 27 September 2013] (author unknown)

Pien, Sandra, 'Ciudad de mitos', *La Nación*, 28 January 2007 <http://www.lanacion.com.ar/877662-ciudad-de-mitos> [last accessed 27 September 2013]

Piette, Candace, 'Argentina aims to rediscover a love of books', 23 April 2010 <news.bbc.co.uk/1/hi/world/americas/8635289.stm> [last accessed 27 September 2013]

'Por ahora, los restos de Borges no volverán al país', *Los Andes Online*, 20 February 2009 <www.losandes.com.ar/notas/2009/2/20/un-409241.asp> [last accessed 27 September 2013] (author unknown)

Prieto, Ana, 'La viuda, la elegida, la guardiana', *Clarín*, 07 October 2006 <www.clarin.com/suplementos/cultura/2006/10/07/u-01285316.htm> [last accessed 27 September 2013]

Reato, Ceferino, 'Quieren repatriar los restos de Jorge Luis Borges', *Perfil.com*, 8 February 2009 <www.perfil.com/contenidos/2009/02/08/noticia_0012.html?commentsPageNumber=3#comentario1> [last accessed 27 September 2013]

—— 'Borges, de Ginebra a la Recoleta', *Diario Perfil*, 8 February 2009 <http://www.perfil.com/contenidos/2009/02/07/noticia_0045.html> [last accessed 27 September 2013]

Reinoso, Susana, 'Julian Barnes: la *road movie* de su paso por Buenos Aires', *La Nación*, 07 February 2008 <www.lanacion.com.ar/nota.asp?nota_id=985099> [last accessed 27 September 2013]

—— 'Lombardi proyecta convertir a Buenos Aires en una marca literaria', *La Nación*, 26 September 2008 <www.lanacion.com.ar/nota.asp?nota_id=1053835> [last accessed 27 September 2013]

—— 'Lectores de diversos países dejan mensajes en la tumba de Borges', *La Nación*, 9 February 2009 <www.lanacion.com.ar/nota.asp?nota_id=1098156> [last accessed 27 September 2013]

Repar, Matías, 'A Borges le incomodaba su reputación de escritor frígido', *Clarín*, 13 May 2006 <www.Clarin.com/diario/2006/05/13/sociedad/s-06201.htm> [last accessed 27 September 2013]

Rother, Larry, 'Borges's Buenos Aires. A City Populated by a Native Son's Imagination', *The New York Times*, 14 May 2006 <travel.nytimes.com/2006/05/14/travel/14foot.html?pagewanted=2> [last accessed 27 September 2013]

Rouillon, Jorge, 'En Palermo Viejo, Borges tiene calle', *La Nación*, 24 August 1996 <www.lanacion.com.ar/nota.asp?nota_id=171789> [last accessed 27 September 2013]

San Martín, Raquel, 'Buenos Aires fue elegida capital mundial del libro 2011', *La Nación*, 14 June 2009 <www.lanacion.com.ar/nota.asp?nota_id=1139109> [last accessed 27 September 2013]

Sasturain, Juan, 'Los modos de J.L.B.', *Página/12*, 14 June 2006 <www.pagina12.com.ar/diario/suplementos/espectaculos/subnotas/2826-1021-2006-06-14.html> [last accessed 27 September 2013]

Schettini, Ariel, 'Un turista nada accidental', *Página/12*, 8 May 2004 <www.pagina12.com.ar/diario/suplementos/libros/10-1042-2004-05-08.html> [last accessed 27 September 2013]

Seitz, Maximiliano, 'Por qué Borges nunca obtuvo el premio Nobel', *La Nación*, 21 August 1999 <www.lanacion.com.ar/nota.asp?nota_id=150373> [last accessed 27 September 2013]

Singer Kovacs, Katherine, 'Borges on the Right', *Boston Review* (Fall 1977) <http://bostonreview.net/kovacs-borges-on-the-right> [last accessed 27 September 2013]

Soler Serrano, Joaquín, 'A fondo', *Televisión Española* (1980) <www.youtube.com/watch?v=2sYkW3TmT6E&feature=PlayList&p=219795CD64423371&index=0> [last last accessed 27 September 2013]

'Un refugio contra el asedio', *Página/12*, 28 Febraury 2009 <www.pagina12.com.ar/diario/suplementos/espectaculos/4-13004-2009-02-28.html> [last accessed 27 September 2013] (author unknown)

Vaccaro, Alejandro, 'Un trabajo bochornoso', *Clarín*, 13 May 2006 <www.clarin.com/diario/2006/05/13/sociedad/s-06201.htm> [last accessed 27 September 2013]

'Vargas Llosa fue declarado Huésped de Honor', *Sitio oficial del Gobierno de la Ciudad de Buenos Aires* <www.buenosaires.gov.ar/noticias/?modulo=ver&item_id=3&contenido_id=21729&idioma=es> [last accessed 11 May 2010] (author and date unknown)

Vázquez, María Esther, 'Los amores de Borges', 'Cartas de lectores', *La Nación*, 16 October 2004 <www.lanacion.com.ar/nota.asp?nota_id=645355> [last accessed 27 September 2013]

Williamson, Edwin, 'Los amores de Borges', 'Cartas de lectores', *La Nación*, 31 October 2004 <www.lanacion.com.ar/nota.asp?nota_id=649821> [last accessed 27 September 2013]

'World Book Capital City. Buenos Aires World Book Capital 2011', *United Nations Educational, Scientific and Cultural Organization* <portal.unesco.org/culture/en/ev.php-URL_ID=39258&URL_DO=DO_TOPIC&URL_SECTION=201.html> [last accessed 27 September 2013]

Yánover, Héctor (dir.), *Jorge Luis Borges por él mismo: sus poemas y su voz* (Buenos Aires: AMB Discográfica, 1967) <http://rarebooks.library.nd.edu/collections/latin_american/south_american/southern_cone_lit/borges-audio.shtml> [last accessed 27 September 2013]

Zaccagnini, Guillermo, 'Cuentos borgeanos: Nada de "rock literario"', *Clarín*, 3 January 2008 <www.clarin.com/diario/2008/01/03/espectaculos/c-1576361.htm> [last accessed 27 September 2013]

Miscellaneous Websites

Borges in YouTube: <www.youtube.com/watch?v=aBVpq6oolLw> <www.youtube.com/watch?v=rnYUULJDoBo&feature=related> <www.youtube.com/watch?v=coc3Wtqn6I8> <www.youtube.com/watch?v=jV515nEaJUc&feature= related> [all last accessed 27 September 2013]

<www.youtube.com/watch?v=coc3Wtqn6I8> [last accessed 27 September 2013]

'Bares notables de Buenos Aires': <www.bue.gov.ar/actividades/index.php?buscar=1&info=bares&menu_id=74> [last accessed 18 May 2010]

Buenos Aires World Book Capital 2010: <www.buenosaires.gov.ar/areas/cultura/al_dia/lectura_bar_10.php?menu_id=20277> [last accessed 27 September 2013]

'Centro documental de información y archivo legislativo de la Ciudad de Buenos Aires' <www.cedom.gov.ar/es/ciudad/paseos/capitulo4_c.html> [last accessed 17 May 2010]

'Ley 18.248 del nombre de las personas naturales': <www.gob.gba.gov.ar/portal/documentos/ley18248.pdf> [last accessed 9 September 2009]

'Recorrido 'Jorge Luis Borges', Sitio oficial de Turismo de la Ciudad de Buenos Aires: <www.bue.gov.ar/recorridos/?menu_id=13&info=borges> [last accessed 25 January 2010]

'Red de contenidos digitales del patrimonio cultural, Ministerio de Cultura, Ciudad Autónoma de Buenos Aires': <www.acceder.gov.ar>

'Sitio oficial de Turismo de la Ciudad de Buenos Aires': <www.bue.gov.ar/home> [last accessed 2010]; <http://www.turismo.buenosaires.gob.ar/es> [last accessed 27 September 2013]

'Sistema de Consumos Culturales (Secretaría de Medios de Comunicación, Presidencia de la Nación)': <http://industriasdecontenido.files.wordpress.com/2010/08/ic-arg-sistema-nacional-de-consumos-culturales-3-20061.pdf> [last accessed 27 September 2013]

INDEX

Abadi, Marcelo 8
Acevedo, Leonor 48
Aesthetic experience (Borges's view of) 6, 33, 155, 170, 189
Alazraki, Jaime 95 nn. 78 & 80, 106–07, 111
Almeida, Iván 17
Arbus, Diane 107–09
Argentina:
 Bicentennial 8, 10, 153, 188
 cultural identity 1–4, 6, 9, 10, 12, 17, 21, 33, 62, 65, 70, 72, 107, 112, 146, 151, 155, 188, 191
 dictatorship (1976–1983) 13, 20, 21, 77 n. 53, 98, 107, 122, 126, 127, 130–35, 141, 150, 162
 immigration 10–11, 13, 37, 41, 62, 77, 157, 161–62, 177 n. 96
 post-dictatorship 21, 125, 126
 relationship with Europe 9, 13, 14, 37, 77–78, 95, 160, 161, 163, 177 n. 96, 164, 182, 188, 190
 Revolución Libertadora 13, 53, 73, 183
 Revolución Argentina 141
 Triple A 141
 UCR 10, 12, 164, 180
 See also history *and* politics
Argentina al día 97
Argentineness 9, 10, 15, 37, 42, 72, 102, 104, 188–89
Arlt, Roberto 138, 161–62, 172
autobiographical impulse 50, 51, 84
Avedon, Richard 97, 105, 107–10

Balderston, Daniel 17, 35 n. 41, 46, 50 n. 77, 51
Barker, Martin 113–14
Barnes, Julian 174–75
Barrenechea, Ana María 38

Barthes, Roland 5, 25–26, 66–68
Baudrillard, Jean 67, 80
Benton, Michael 27–30
Berkeley, George 75
Biblioteca Nacional 39 n. 56, 53, 82, 85 n. 69, 95, 96, 105, 123, 125, 169, 182–83
Bioy Casares, Adolfo 24, 32, 87, 89, 142 n. 89, 164
 'La fiesta del monstruo' (with Borges) 164
Boedo and Florida 172–75
Borges, Jorge Luis:
 life 1–3
 works:
  El Aleph 138
  Autobiografía 86, 95
  Cuaderno de San Martín 152, 169
  Elogio de la sombra 74
  Evaristo Carriego 33 n. 34, 34–35, 44, 169
  Fervor de Buenos Aires 169, 171
  Ficciones 52, 80–82, 106, 123, 149 n. 110
  El hacedor 112, 170
  Historia universal de la infamia 34
  El libro de seres imaginarios 124
  Luna de enfrente 169
 short stories:
  'El Aleph' 32, 34, 48, 50, 52, 71–73, 79, 124, 142
  'La Biblioteca de Babel' 34, 41
  'Biografías sintéticas' 34
  'Borges y yo' 25, 31, 32
  'La escritura del dios' 50
  'Examen de la obra de Herbert Quain' 32
  'La fiesta del monstruo' (with Bioy Casares) 164, 186

'El Fin' 34 n. 39, 149, 150
'Funes, el memorioso' 32, 33, 50–51
'Historia del guerrero y de la cautiva' 40, 138, 139
'L'Illusion Comique' 71, 73, 75
'La intrusa' 50
'La memoria de Shakespeare' 34
'La muerte y la brújula' 124
'Pierre Menard, autor del Quijote' 32
'Ragnarök' 31
'Las ruinas circulares' 183
'El simulacro' 71, 73–74, 76
'El sur' 15 n. 51, 32, 34, 41, 188
'There Are More Things' 34
'Utopía de un hombre que está cansado' 71, 75
'El zahir' 50
poems:
  'Arrabal' 152
  'Cambridge' 63, 71, 74
  'Caminata' 171
  'Elogio de la sombra' 170
  'Fundación mítica de Buenos Aires' 31, 152, 157 n. 13, 160, 180
  'Isidoro Acevedo' 44–45
  'El otro' 25, 32
  'Poema de los dones' 105, 169–70, 183
  'La vuelta' 169 n. 59
essays:
  'Autobiographical Essay' 42, 86
  'El escritor argentino y la tradición' 172
  'Los escritores argentinos y Buenos Aires' 173
  'La esfera de Pascal' 6
  'La inútil discusión de Boedo y Florida' 172–73
  'La muralla y los libros' 6, 33, 155 n. 7
  'El truco' 124
and popular magazines 123–24
as Anglophile 2, 9, 38–41, 47, 62, 173–75, 188, 190
as cultural role model 3, 18, 21
as icon 4, 5, 7–9, 12, 18, 21, 23, 26, 35, 60, 62, 64, 65, 68–70, 76, 78–80, 96, 102, 107, 108, 110, 120, 151, 133, 136, 138, 151, 153, 156, 178, 188, 189, 190
as an old man 3, 20, 21, 36, 48, 53, 57, 62–65, 70, 74–76, 80, 82, 83, 86, 87, 94, 96, 98, 102, 105, 110, 140, 142, 167, 168, 170, 177, 178, 182, 190
as detached from Argentine reality 2, 3, 44, 52, 64, 94, 111, 129, 140, 168, 190
as 'maestro' 2, 3, 128, 144, 191
as 'vende patria' 2, 3, 191
street 156, 164, 180–82
death of 2, 13, 55, 62, 131, 133, 184–87
blindness 3, 20, 42, 48, 57, 64, 65, 75, 76, 80, 82, 84, 94, 98, 102, 105, 107, 108–10, 133, 151, 169, 170, 183
centenary 65, 87
in an ivory tower 2, 3, 13, 42, 60, 96, 124, 172, 184
denied Nobel Prize 127, 130, 143, 38 n. 55
Fundación 183–84
International Publisher's Prize 2, 80, 95
media exposure of 2, 16–17, 20, 26, 30, 35, 55, 62, 65, 75, 80, 94–98, 101–06, 115–17, 123, 130–33, 185
Premio Nacional de Literatura 72
Borges, Norah 55
Borgesian spaces 22, 151, 153, 156, 160, 163, 165, 167–68, 171, 176, 179, 183, 184, 187, 190
Bosworth, Patricia 107
Bourdieu, Pierre 67–68, 70
Bouvard, Joseph 161
Bragg, Melvyn 61
Breccia, Alberto 21, 115, 122, 136, 138, 141, 143–50
with Sasturain:
  Perramus 21, 122, 136, 141–48, 150, 188, 190
  'El Fin' 21, 122, 149, 150

Brilliant, Richard 66 nn. 9 & 10, 75
Buenos Aires 2, 13, 14, 17, 22, 34, 35, 39, 41, 44, 48, 52, 73, 77, 82, 84, 86, 90, 94, 95, 97, 104, 109, 115, 141, 143, 151–53, 156, 157, 159–66, 168–85, 187, 190
   Café Tortoni 156, 176–79
   cultural tourism 151, 158, 163, 165, 166, 173, 175, 187, 190
   history 22, 160, 162 n. 31, 163, 166, 169, 179, 187
   literary 153, 165, 176, 187
   Recorrido Jorge Luis Borges 153, 154–55, 156, 165–67, 174, 179, 180, 183, 184
   World Book Capital 166, 176
   See also politics
Burke, Séan 5 n. 16, 31, 32 n. 30
Buscaglia, Norberto 21, 122, 138–40
   'Historia del guerrero y de la cautiva' (with Flores) 21, 122, 138–40
Burzaco, Raúl 96 n. 86, 101, 105

Canaparo, Claudio 80, 82
Canto, Estela 19, 24, 45–52, 56, 61–62, 81–82, 84, 184
Carrizo, Antonio 24 n.1, 63
Castillo, Abelardo 130
censorship 20, 131, 141
chora 68, 69
civilization and barbarism 10, 11, 40, 56, 139, 188
Clarín xii, 17, 57, 98 n. 93, 99–101, 102, 103, 104, 116 n. 13, 127, 131
Clark, Graham 67
Comesaña, Eduardo 82 n. 64
commodity 25, 113, 137, 138, 175
Conti, Haroldo 132
Contorno magazine 14, 128
Cortázar, Julio 84–85
Crítica 123
Cupers, Kenny 156, 159, 161, 171–72, 173, 179

de Certeau, Michel 23, 156, 158–59, 167, 171, 175
de la Rúa, Fernando 180, 182

de Man, Paul 29
Derrida, Jacques 4–6
de Santis, Pablo 143, 151
de Toro, Alfonso 6, 95
de Torre Borges, Miguel 21, 185
di Tella, Torcuato S. 10, 11, 13 n. 39, 78 n. 54, 160 n. 22, 188, 190
Duncan, Randy 113, 114
Dyer, Geoff 109, 110 n. 121
Dyer, Richard 68

Echeverría, Esteban 11
Eco, Umberto 5, 46 n. 67, 67, 79, 183, 189
Edwards, Jorge 175
Efrom, Raúl 185
Ellis, David 27, 28 n. 17, 65 n. 3
Eloy Martínez, Tomás 73 n. 40, 108, 163
EPA 97
'Estrategia Marca País' 8, 22

Facio, Sara 21, 82, 84, 85, 153, 157 n. 11
Fernández, Elbio 102, 104 n. 96
Feria del Libro 178–79
Ferro, Hellén 102, 104 n. 99
Fierro 21, 122, 134–38, 141, 143, 145
Fishburn, Evelyn 46, 61 n. 106, 82 n. 64
flâneur 90, 96, 156, 168, 171, 182
Flores, Alfredo 21, 122, 138–40
   'Historia del guerrero y de la cautiva' (with Buscaglia) 21, 122, 138–40
Forestier, Jean Claude Nicolas 161
Foucault, Michel 5–6, 24–25, 33
Franco, Jean 122, 124, 137, 138
Fresán, Rodrigo 35 n. 44, 53, 59, 87

García, Martín 135
García Morales, Alfonso 46 n. 67, 149
Gardel, Carlos 1, 133 n. 62, 142 n. 88, 144–47, 167, 172 n. 78, 177–78
Gasparini, Juan 55, 185–86
gaze 69–70, 71, 72, 140, 159
Gelman, Juan 133
Genette, Gerard 19–20, 26, 30, 62
Gledhill, Christine 68

Gociol, Judith 115 n. 9, 142, 144, 150
Gorelik, Adrián 156, 157–58, 161 n. 27, 168, 172
Groussac, Paul 105, 183 n. 113

Hamilton, Nigel 27
Hariman, Robert 66, 70, 111
Haslam, Fanny 40–41
Heker, Liliana 130
Hernández, José:
  Martín Fierro 11, 32, 34 n. 39, 149, 150
historieta 114, 115, 134, 136–37, 144
history 1, 6, 8, 28 n. 19, 29, 70, 75, 84, 96, 111, 112, 115, 136, 141, 143–44, 156
  Borges's personal 12, 40, 169, 184
  of Argentina 12, 13, 60, 61, 73, 110, 116, 125, 127, 130, 132, 135, 139, 144, 189, 190
  of Argentine comics 115
  of biography 27
  of portraiture 66, 67, 69
  See also Argentina *and* Buenos Aires
Huyssen, Andreas 23, 156, 159, 160, 165 n. 41, 166, 179, 182

Ibarra, Néstor 128
icon 65, 66, 68, 69, 74, 76, 78
  Carlos Gardel 144, 146, 177–78
  El eternauta 135, 141
  Eva Perón 73, 76, 133 n. 62
  intellectuals 7
  Julio Cortázar 84–85
  See also Borges, Jorge Luis
indexicality 67, 79, 104 n. 97

Jauretche, Arturo 38, 139–40
Jitrik, Noé 4, 12 n. 34, 128, 164 n. 36
Jurado, Alicia 16, 19, 24, 36–40, 47, 51, 53, 54, 61–62, 82, 83, 87 n. 72, 102

King, John 47
Kodama, María 40 n. 58, 54–56, 57, 62, 142, 183, 184–86
Krebs, Edgardo 60

Laclau, Ernbesto 12, 163 n. 34, 164 n. 37
Lafforgue, Martín:
  Antiborges 4, 16, 38 n. 52, 73 n. 38, 86–88, 122, 124 n. 24, 127–31, 133 n. 63, 134 n. 65–66, 139 n. 80–81
Latin America 2, 7, 13, 14, 77, 78, 116, 129
Lefebvre, Henri 23, 153, 155–56, 158–59, 167, 173, 175
Lenz, María Beatriz 185–86
Lombardi, Hernán 165–66, 176
Louis, Annick 34, 53, 56
Lucaites, John 66, 70, 111
Ludmer, Josefina 4, 82, 87, 90
lunfardo 157, 164 n. 38
Lyons, Ted 96

Macri, Mauricio 153, 163–64, 179, 187
Madres de Plaza de Mayo 98, 131
Malvinas War 77 n. 53, 134
Mármol, José 105, 183 n. 113
Matamoro, Blas 2, 3, 129–30
memory 1, 34, 44, 111, 136, 139, 142, 141, 143, 144, 159, 160, 179, 182
Mercer, Kobena 68
Miguel Cané Library 38, 39, 123, 173–75
Miller, Nicola 7–8
Molloy, Sylvia 15, 33, 35, 170–71, 187
Montaldo, Graciela 1 n. 2, 90
Morra, Carlos 182
Mujica Lainez, Manuel 165
myth 26, 34, 38, 39, 40, 41, 44, 51, 57, 60, 62, 66, 72, 76, 78, 86, 95, 98, 130, 136, 144, 146, 161 n. 23, 164, 178, 182

Nación, La xii, 17, 38, 51, 53, 60, 131, 149, 185, 186
National Library *see* Biblioteca Nacional
Neruda, Pablo 130
Nunca más 132, 134

Oesterheld, H.G. 115, 135, 141, 142
  El Eternauta 135–36, 141, 142

Operación Ja Ja 20, 131
Opinión, La 115–16, 133, 141, 98 n. 92
Orgambide, Pedro 131

Página/12 17, 59, 133, 134
Palacio, Lino 115, 124
palimpsest 156, 159, 179, 182, 183
paratext 20, 26, 30, 42, 44, 62, 65 n. 4, 84
Parodi, Cristina 38
parricidas 3, 125, 128
Pauls, Alan 1, 3 n. 8, 21, 53 n. 89, 79, 94, 95, 123–24
Perón, Eva 1, 73–74, 76, 133 n. 62, 140 n. 85, 163 n. 33, 167, 186
Peronism 12, 13, 37, 38, 47, 62, 129, 133, 162–64, 173, 183, 185
Perry, Nick 90, 94, 167 n. 55
Petit de Murat, Ulyses 22
Pezzoni, Enrique 126, 143
Piglia, Ricardo 11, 122, 138–41, 188
    La Argentina en pedazos 122, 138
politics 1, 4, 5, 14, 37, 113–15, 116, 126, 137, 150, 157, 158, 159, 173
    Argentine 8, 10–14, 17, 18, 37, 62, 66, 73, 75–78, 98, 110, 113, 115, 116, 118, 121, 122, 126–29, 133, 141, 144, 168, 190
    Borges and 2, 3, 7, 9, 20, 21, 23, 29, 31 n. 26, 36–7, 57, 60–62, 75, 87, 90, 111, 116, 118, 122, 125, 130, 132–33, 139, 144, 150–51, 156, 162, 168, 183 n. 112, 187, 190
    Buenos Aires 22, 90, 151, 153, 160, 162–63, 167, 172–73, 175, 176, 177, 183, 187
Pons, María Cristina 1 n. 3, 70, 72, 76, 78, 95, 98, 146, 168 n. 57, 172 n. 78
Popular culture 5, 9, 13, 14, 22, 62, 66, 113, 122–25, 137–38, 150, 179
Popular media 18, 19–21, 82 n. 64, 102, 123–24, 130 n. 50, 131, 138
Price, Derrick and Liz Wells 69 n. 28, 70, 79 n. 58

Prieto, Adolfo 16, 128
progresista xii, 13, 17, 21, 113, 122, 142, 144, 150
projection 6, 17, 25, 26, 29, 36, 68–70, 74, 75, 78, 79, 102, 107, 146, 188
Propp, Vladimir 114
Puig, Manuel 138, 165

Quiroga, Horacio 138

Rabinowitz, Paula 78
radio (Borges on) 24 n. 1, 63, 97, 100, 106
Rama, Ángel 14, 116
Ramos, Jorge Abelardo 129
Raota, Pedro Luis 82 n. 64, 147 n. 108
retrograde innovation 87, 90, 167
Rock, David 12, 13 nn. 38 & 40, 77, 78, 160 n. 22, 161 n. 24
Rodríguez Monegal, Emir 3 n. 9, 6, 19, 24, 37–47, 51, 57, 61, 62, 87 n. 72, 95–96, 116, 123, 125, 128, 164, 188
Rosemberg, Diego 115 n. 9, 142, 144, 150
Roux, Raúl 115, 134
Rozitchner, León 128
Rubenstein, Anne 113, 114, 115

Sábat, Hermenegildo xii, 21, 116–21
    Georgie Dear 116, 118–21
Sábato, Ernesto 132
S.A.D.E. 124, 185
Sarlo, Beatriz 13–16, 33, 35, 126–27, 137, 149 n. 112, 156–58, 160–62, 176
Sarmiento, Domingo Faustino 11, 173, 185
Sasturain, Juan 3, 21, 122, 136, 137 n. 72, 138 n. 78, 141, 142 n. 90, 143 n. 92, 144–50, 188 n. 1
    with Breccia:
        Perramus 21, 122, 136, 141–48, 150, 188, 190
        'El Fin' 21, 122, 149, 150

Satragno, Lidia 105
Scolari, Carlos 137, 143–44
Schwartz, Margaret 73
Sebreli, Juan José 66 n. 7, 77, 96, 128, 134
Segre, Roberto 172
Shakespear, Ronald 86
Singer Kovacs, Katherine 106–07, 131
Smith, Matthew 113, 114
Sontag, Susan 67, 108–09
Sosnowski, Saúl 112, 133, 136
Sousloff, Catherine 66, 68, 69
Stern, Grete 82–83
Storni, Alfonsina 177–78
Sur xiii, 73, 82, 138

television (Borges on) xii, 17, 20, 87, 96, 97, 99, 101–06, 131
Tenenbaum, León 52, 169 n. 60, 177
Thays, Charles 161
Theroux, Paul 97
Timerman, Jacobo 116
'Todo Borges' 21, 102, 104
Torre, Javier 52

Vaccaro, Alejandro 16 n. 53, 38 n. 51, 46, 53 n. 89, 59, 84, 94, 185
Vargas Llosa, Mario 57, 174–75
Variaciones Borges 17, 46, 61, 157 n. 10, 169 n. 60
Vázquez, María Esther 19, 22 n. 63, 24, 38, 40 n. 58, 45–47, 53–56, 60–62, 169
Videla, Jorge Rafael 130–32
Viñas, David 128, 138
Viñetas Serias 115

Wells, Liz 69, 78 n. 55
West, Shearer 66
Williamson, Edwin xii, 11, 15, 16 n. 53, 19, 24, 31 n. 26, 36–38, 41, 45, 47, 50–52, 55–62, 80 n. 62, 81, 94, 96, 130 n. 48, 132 n. 57, 133 n. 64, 169 nn. 59 & 85, 183 n. 112
Wilson, Jason 16 n. 53, 169

Yánover, Héctor 125

Zito, Carlos Alberto 152, 168, 169 n. 60, 180

Lightning Source UK Ltd.
Milton Keynes UK
UKOW04f1658200514

231993UK00001B/29/P